LESBIAN C

LESBIAN GOTHIC

TRANSGRESSIVE FICTIONS

Paulina Palmer

CASSELL
London and New York

Cassell
Wellington House, 125 Strand, London WC2R 0BB
370 Lexington Avenue, New York, NY 10017–6550

First published 1999

British Library Cataloguing-in-Publication Data
A catalogue record for this book is available from the British Library.

ISBN 0-304-70153-X (hardback)
       0-304-70154-8 (paperback)

Library of Congress Cataloging-in-Publication Data
Palmer, Paulina, 1937–
       Lesbian Gothic: transgressive fictions/Paulina Palmer.
              p.   cm.
       Includes bibliographical references and index.
       ISBN 0-304-70153-X. — 0-304-70154-8 (pbk.)
       1. Horror tales, English—History and criticism. 2. English
fiction—20th century—History and criticism. 3. American fiction—
Women authors—History and criticism. 4. American fiction—20th
century—History and criticism. 5. English fiction—Women authors—
History and criticism. 6. Lesbians' writings, American—History
and criticism. 7. Lesbians' writings, English—History and
criticism. 8. Gothic revival (Literature)—Great Britain.
9. Gothic revival (Literature)—United States. 10. Lesbians in
literature. I. Title.
PR888. T3P35   1999
823'.08729099206643—dc21   99–12385
                                                              CIP

The subjects of the photograph on the front cover are a transsexual and a person of
the third gender. The picture was taken for a Gender project, not for this book.

Typeset by Bookens Ltd, Royston, Herts.
Printed and bound in Great Britain by Biddles Ltd, Guildford and King's Lynn

Contents

To Cambridge Lesbian Line

Preface

This book develops the interest in contemporary lesbian fiction, in particular the manipulation and transformation of popular genres, which has motivated the previous critical studies I have produced. While reading novels and stories and teaching seminars in lesbian writing at the University of Warwick, I have become intrigued by the attraction that different forms of Gothic, such as the vampire narrative, the Gothic thriller and works of fiction recasting the image of the witch, hold for writers and readers today. Their popularity is reflected in the numerous publications in the category of lesbian Gothic on the shelves of feminist/lesbian bookshops, such as Silver Moon and Gay's the Word in London and OUT! in Brighton. Novels and stories by Jewelle Gomez, Pat Califia, Sarah Schulman, Emma Donoghue, Jeanette Winterson and other writers discussed in this study exemplify this trend. Fiction of this kind has received, up to now, little attention from critics. This study represents, in fact, the first substantial discussion it has received. It will, I hope, prove useful to teachers and students in Literature and Women's Studies departments in colleges and universities, as well as attracting readers with a general interest in lesbian writing and its cultural significance.

While working on the study, I've been fortunate to have access to an exceptionally supportive and intellectually stimulating environment. Teaching an MA course in Feminist Literary Theory at Warwick and attending meetings of the Cambridge University Queer Studies Group have been particularly useful in this respect, providing a forum for a lively exchange of ideas. Working in the Cambridge Lesbian Line collective has increased my awareness of the complexities of lesbian existence and kept me up to date with current issues and ideas. I've also received assistance from colleagues and friends. I'm grateful to Gina Wisker for reading the typescript of the book and making perceptive suggestions and to Grant Chambers for giving a detailed critique. Discussions I've held with Grant on the topic of fantasy and concepts of the family and 'origins' have proved immensely enjoyable and valuable. I'm indebted to Emma Donoghue for taking an interest in the project, lending me fiction from her library and allowing me a pre-publication reading of her collection of stories *Kissing the Witch*. I'm also grateful to Veronica Groocock, Julia Long, Ashley Tellis and Linda West for encouragement, comments and assistance with the chore of proofreading.

Here it is necessary to explain the procedural methods I employ regarding the dating and editions of the works of fiction to which I refer. Some of these have been published in different editions by different publishing houses. On first mentioning a particular novel or story in the text, I cite in brackets the initial date of publication. In quoting from it, however, I frequently use a later edition (generally a British one, if it is available) and give details of it in a note. Details of both editions are to be found in the Bibliography.

CHAPTER 1

Introduction: Gothic and lesbian narrative

'I wondered what a twentieth-century gothic for queers would present as fear and terror'[1]

GENRE, TEXTUALITY, TRANSFORMATIONS

An episode in Jody Scott's *I, Vampire* (1984), an example of lesbian Gothic discussed in this study, portrays the narrator Sterling O'Blivion taking stock of her past life and reviewing her experiences as a member of the living dead. Scott emphasizes the shifts of identity and lifestyle which Sterling has undergone since her birth in the Middle Ages. Having been thrown out of her family home in Eastern Europe for sucking the blood of the local priest and reviled as a limb of Satan by the local community, she passes the following centuries performing the classic vampire role, 'keeping bats in a tower, carrying blazing candelabra up and down winding staircases' and dressing in 'yards of black lace'.[2] With the advent of the twentieth century, however, vampire culture undergoes a change of location and, having outlived fifty-two lovers, she crosses the Atlantic to take up residence in North America. In 1970s New York she finds herself having to accommodate to an urban lifestyle, an entertainment diet of TV sitcoms – and encountering lurid images of herself in popular fiction and film. She feels even more disoriented when her lover Benaroya, a visitor from an alien planet and a student of poststructuralism, proceeds to demolish her identity by arguing that she has no essential self but is merely a projection created by 'the people of Transylvania out of boredom and frustration' (p. 201)!

Reference to Scott's novel makes an appropriate introduction to this study since, like the other writers discussed below, she exploits the connections between 'Gothic' and 'lesbian', utilizing a genre that is notable for its marginality and stylistic eccentricities to portray an eccentric, disruptive subject who exists in marginal relation to mainstream society. The transformations that her protagonist Sterling undergoes over the centuries signal yet another link between the two terms, since both reveal shifts of emphasis and interpretation which are similarly pronounced. Gothic, critics agree, is a genre which, on account of its multifaceted character, resists a single definition and displays a number of different shades of meaning. It has been variously described as a specific historical movement, a system of fantasy and a cultural tendency or mode.[3] Some critics, such as Chris Baldick, define it in terms of the themes it conventionally treats. Prominent among these, Baldick maintains, are 'a fearful sense of inheritance in time with a claustrophobic sense of enclosure in space', the two combining to produce 'an impression of sickening descent into disintegration'.[4]

Gothic is also notable for its mobility and another characteristic it displays − and one that helps to explain its powers of survival − is its ability to reconstitute itself anew in the light of changing social and cultural circumstances. Since its advent in the eighteenth century, it has assumed a variety of different manifestations and forms, adapting and developing in response to transitions in literary and intellectual fashion. Originating in the 1780s as an offshoot of the romance in the novels of Matthew Lewis and Ann Radcliffe (popular with readers for their archaic settings, representation of supernatural events and evocation of terror) the genre moved into the nineteenth century where, influenced by Romanticism, it generated a new set of themes and motifs. In the fiction of John Polidori, Mary Shelley and Charles Maturin the roles of naive heroine and wicked villain, inherited from the previous century, were supplemented by the figures of the vampire, the searcher after illicit knowledge and the wanderer. In the novels of James Hogg and Robert Louis Stevenson the motif of the double acquired prominence. The fragmentation and diversification that increasingly characterized the genre gave rise, as the interests of the reading public altered, to new categories and subdivisions. These include the ghost story centering on uncanny experiences and events, exemplified by the texts of Henry James, H. P. Lovecraft and Walter de la Mare; the tale of terror focusing on psychological disturbance and obsessive states of mind, represented by the stories of Edgar Allan Poe; and the Gothic thriller, foregrounding melodrama and strategies of suspense, associated with the fiction of Sheridan Le Fanu and Wilkie Collins. In addition, certain literary and cultural forms have emerged which, although they cannot strictly be defined as Gothic, are nonetheless related to it. Important in this respect are stories involving the grotesque, such as E.T.A. Hoffmann's 'The Sand-Man' (1816–17) and Poe's 'Hop-Frog' (1849), and narratives focusing on horror and the occult exemplified by the novels of Stephen King and Dennis Wheatley. In the twentieth century the cinema has furnished a vehicle for some of these. It has made them accessible to a wider audience, giving rise to films as diverse in subject matter and style as Terence Fisher's populist *Brides of Dracula* (1960), David Cronenberg's psychoanalytic study of the double, *Dead Ringers* (1988), and David Lynch's postmodern experiment in horror, *Lost Highway* (1997).

The versatility of Gothic is also reflected in the parodic versions it has inspired, which treat its conventions humorously or satirically.[5] Jane Austen's *Northanger Abbey* (1818) and Margaret Atwood's *Lady Oracle* (1976) playfully critique the Gothic heroine and her trajectory, while, in the field of film, *Love at First Bite* (1979) and *The Lost Boys* (1987)[6] exploit the comic potential of the vampire narrative. Developments of this kind, while extending the scope of the genre and increasing its range of theme and mood, raise questions about its boundaries. They problematize traditional definitions of Gothic and challenge assumptions about the texts it comprises, provoking argument about which merit the designation and which not.

Gothic is controversial in other ways as well. Debate centres on its literary value and on the contradictions of radicalism/conservatism that the texts exemplifying it encode. As Anne Cranny-Francis[7] and Rosemary Jackson[8] illustrate, Gothic narratives are potentially subversive in that they challenge realist perspectives and investigate dimensions of experience that realist fiction tends to ignore or repress. In addition, they frequently focus on acts of sexual or social transgression. However, many works of Gothic fiction and film, particularly those in the popular subsection of horror, reproduce the values of the dominant culture. As a result, they contain or neutralize the subversive perceptions and points of view that the genre inscribes, if handled in a politically challenging way. Gothic, while inspiring literary and cinematic texts that are ideologically radical, such as Angela Carter's *The Bloody Chamber* (1979) and Carl Dreyer's *Day of Wrath* (1943), has also produced ones notorious for their misogyny (William Friedkin's *The Exorcist* (1973)),[9] lesbophobia (Alasdair Gray's *Something Leather* (1990))[10] or racism (Lovecraft's *The Lurker at the Threshold* (1945)).[11] The attempts to tease out and evaluate these contradictions have provoked animated debate. Critical approaches to Gothic and the textual interpretations they have generated are, in fact, as varied as the subsections and categories which the genre comprises. Studies adopting a historical or a social point of view coexist with ones focusing on motif and narrative structure. Whereas some critics, influenced by Freud's essay on 'The "Uncanny"' and the theory of 'the return of the repressed'[12] which it articulates, adopt a psychoanalytic approach to the genre,[13] others interpret it in terms of nationality or gender. Donald A. Ringe[14] and David Punter[15] concentrate attention on 'American Gothic', citing as its distinctive features a preoccupation with guilt and obsessive states of mind and the depiction of Europe as evil and decadent. Kate Ferguson Ellis explores the tradition of women's fiction popularly known as 'Female Gothic'. She contrasts the representation of female entrapment and imprisonment in the interior setting of a castle or mansion in the novels of Radcliffe, Charlotte Brontë and Daphne du Maurier with the narratives of persecution and wandering in an external location created by Maturin and Hogg.[16] Yet another branch of Gothic fiction centres on female sexual orientation and its cultural and political ramifications. This is *lesbian* Gothic, the subject of this study.

In contrast to the other subdivisions of the genre cited above, which are well established and have generated an amount of commentary, lesbian Gothic fiction, particularly novels and stories published recently, has received little attention. In this, it differs from film. Films in the category of Gothic and horror dealing with lesbian themes have prompted several studies.[17] Fiction, meanwhile, has been relegated to the critical margins – and only now, in the 1990s, is it starting to arouse the interest of critics. Terry Castle in *The Apparitional Lesbian* (1993) explores the contradictory implications of the utilization of spectral imagery in works of fiction published in the first half of this century. In a lively essay Mary Wings discusses the writing of her Gothic thriller *Divine Victim* (1992), a text reviewed in Chapter 5 of this study, exploring its parodic relation to du Maurier's *Rebecca* (1938). She also debates the strengths and problematic aspects of the lesbian appropriation of Gothic structures and motifs and surmises what would constitute 'fear and terror'[18] in a work of this kind. Sue-Ellen Case also acknowledges the existence of queer Gothic. However, her study of the vampire as a signifier of queer politics takes the usual course of prioritizing film and makes only a cursory reference to the fictional treatment of the creature.[19]

The tendency of critics to ignore or marginalize lesbian Gothic fiction and the neglect that the texts exemplifying it have suffered in consequence, reflects several different factors. Lesbian critical studies are, of course, a relatively new discipline. They have evolved comparatively recently and, as a result, many aspects of lesbian writing that merit attention are only now starting to be addressed. Moreover, although, as is illustrated by Djuna Barnes's *Nightwood* (1936) and by stories in 'Isak' Dinesen's *Last Tales* (1957),[20] the utilization of Gothic motifs and imagery as a vehicle for lesbian representation is by no means new, only since the 1970s, in the wake of the lesbian feminist movement and the tide of publications which it generated, has lesbian Gothic found a context favourable to its production and novels creating full-scale Gothic narratives have started to appear in print. Examples include Barbara Hanrahan's reworking of the motif of the witch in *The Albatross Muff* (1978), Rebecca Brown's tale of spectral visitation *The Haunted House* (1986) and Jewelle Gomez' vampire narrative *The Gilda Stories* (1991). These novels, rather than utilizing Gothic motifs and conventions to decorporealize lesbian desire or to depict lesbian relations in a prejudiced light which, as Castle illustrates,[21] has often been the case in hetero-patriarchal versions of the genre, seek, on the contrary, to reclaim them. They employ them to explore, from a lesbian viewpoint, erotic female relations and their transgressive dimension. It is, in fact, the popularity that lesbian Gothic fiction is currently enjoying and the wealth of texts exemplifying the mode available for analysis which has prompted me to concentrate on discussing works of fiction published in the past thirty years. Novels and stories produced in this period make interesting reading since, while differing markedly in style and ideological perspective, they share a common cultural context. In fictional form they rework and contribute to the debates about sexuality and politics that have informed the lesbian movement since its advent in the 1970s.

In addition to giving an insight into the shifting kaleidoscope of contemporary lesbian culture, my decision to focus on texts produced within this timespan furnishes an opportunity to explore the connections and discontinuities between works of fiction produced today and those published in the initial stages of the lesbian movement, in the 1970s and the early 1980s. The latter, on account of the current interest in postmodern trends in fiction as exemplified by the novels of Emma Donoghue and Jeanette Winterson, have suffered neglect – and this study gives an occasion to address and re-evaluate them. It also provides an opportunity to compare certain well-known texts which have met with critical acclaim, such as Jeanette Winterson's *Sexing the Cherry* (1989) and Sarah Schulman's *After Delores* (1988), with ones which are less well-known. While I plan to focus primarily on works of fiction published during the period from 1972 to 1997, in discussing the lesbian reworking of traditional themes and motifs I shall refer, when appropriate, to works published earlier.

The success which, to judge from the titles on display in alternative bookstores, novels and stories with Gothic affiliations are enjoying at the moment can be explained in different ways. Like other categories of lesbian fiction, such as science fiction and the thriller, publications of this kind form part of the lesbian/feminist appropriation and transformation of popular genres which occupies a prominent position on the contemporary literary agenda.[22] In addition to being influenced by the current vogue for the appropriation and transformation of popular genres, the proliferation of lesbian Gothic texts also reflects a move away from the focus on realist modes of writing to an emphasis on fantasy and the inscription of desire which typifies lesbian critical studies and discussions of lesbian narrative in the 1990s. Lesbian narrative, as critics acknowledge, is by no means an easy term to define. As Marilyn R. Farwell comments, in discussing the different forms that 'writing lesbian'[23] can take, 'Instead of a recognisable literary genre, lesbian narrative is, in reality, a disputed form, dependent upon various interpretative strategies.'[24] In the 1970s and the early 1980s it was assumed to treat, as Zimmerman explains, 'a central, not marginal, lesbian character, one who understands herself to be a lesbian' and to focus firmly on 'love between women, including sexual passion'.[25] It also depended on the presence of the lesbian writer, a figure brought into prominence by the lesbian feminist movement, who addresses the texts she produces to the lesbian community.[26] Today, however, with the concept of a lesbian identity open to question and the writer no longer regarded as unequivocally in charge of the text, these definitions appear less valid. They are being supplanted by poststructuralist approaches which, foregrounding textuality, investigate the way in which the narrative constructs a lesbian subject position, inscribes lesbian desire or subverts and transforms heterosexual structures and conventions. Just as in poststructuralist and queer theory the lesbian is regarded as an 'eccentric' disruptive subject[27] who transgresses sexual and social convention, so the narratives that portray her and inscribe her sexuality are expected to disrupt traditional patterns and structures.[28] The interweaving of alternative storylines, the introduction of fantasy episodes and the subversive rescripting of fairy-tales and episodes from history are strategies that writers employ to achieve this.[29] Texts of a realist kind treating 'coming out', which were popular in the 1970s, are no longer the focus of critical attention. Instead discussion centres on fantasy narratives or on texts that interweave fantasy and realism. Julia Penelope Stanley, commenting on the representation of the lesbian as Other, associates her with 'a mythology of darkness' and a world of 'dreams and shadows'.[30] Farwell examines the way in which, in Marion Zimmer Bradley's fantasy romance *The Mists of Avalon* (1982), the introduction of an erotic female relationship has the effect of critiquing and destabilizing heterosexist values by problematizing a dualistic approach to gender.[31] Castle, in discussing Sylvia Townsend Warner's *Summer Will Show* (1936), argues that from an ideological point of view one of the main achievements of lesbian fiction is to deconstruct the triangular arrangement of male desire relegating woman to object of exchange or mediator between two men which, until recently, has dominated Western literature.[32] She illustrates that writers either substitute a female-male-female triangle, or, as often occurs in contemporary novels and stories, erase the male term altogether. These observations serve as a preface to her analysis of the way in which lesbian writers, in striving to transcend the sexual and social restrictions imposed on women in hetero-patriarchal society, frequently relinquish the territory of realism and move, during episodes of key importance, into the realm of the utopian and the fantastic.

The focus on fantasy and the inscription of desire, which, as illustrated above, are key features of lesbian critical studies today, are relevant to the growth of lesbian Gothic. They furnish a sympathetic context for its production and publication and shed light on the attraction that the genre holds for writers and readers. The comments voiced by Stanley and Castle are particularly significant in this respect. A preoccupation with 'darkness, dreams and shadows' and an oscillation between realist and fantastic modes of writing characterize many of the texts discussed in this study.

These changes in the approach to lesbian narrative have been accompanied by and reflect the influence of developments of a equal importance in the interpretation of the sign *lesbian* and the theorization of the lesbian subject. These are likewise pertinent to the growth of lesbian Gothic. The identification of lesbianism with woman-bonding and feminist camaraderie articulated by lesbian feminists such as Charlotte Bunch[33] and Adrienne Rich,[34] writing in the early years of the lesbian movement, has recently given way to a focus on its transgressive aspect, both sexual and social. Sexual radicals such as Pat Califia[35] and Joan Nestle,[36] in an attempt to reaffirm the erotic dimension of lesbianism which they believe has been marginalized and undervalued, discuss butch-femme roles, S&M partnerships and erotic fantasy. Meanwhile Monique Wittig[37] and Judith Butler[38] approach the sign from a poststructuralist viewpoint. They foreground the element of 'excess' that lesbian sexuality represents in a hetero-patriarchal economy and, in emphasizing its ability to destabilize the *status quo*, illustrate the way in which the lesbian, by means of her very existence, disrupts conventional cultural codes and gender dualisms. 'Lesbian' signifies, they demonstrate, the site of a gap or rupture in the political system of phallocentric signification.

Changes have also occurred in recent years in approaches to lesbian identity. The poststructuralist emphasis on the fluidity of desire and on the multiple sexualities and erotic fantasies to which the individual has access has resulted in the questioning of the concept of a unitary lesbian identity, as envisaged by lesbian feminists and gay liberationists in the 1970s. Developments in queer theory have hastened this deconstructive process. Eve Kosofsky Sedgwick, problematizing orthodox assumptions about sexuality – gay as well as straight – challenges the usual division between homosexual/heterosexual identifications. Emphasizing the different forms that sexual desire can take, she questions the commonly held view 'that each person's most characteristic erotic expression will necessarily be oriented toward another person and not autoerotic; that if it is alloerotic, it will be oriented toward a single partner or kind of partner at a time; that its orientation will not change over time'.[39] Butler identifies 'queer' with theatricalized forms of protest, such as the dramatic acting out by the gay community of the injuries it has suffered through being outlawed by mainstream society. She sees one of the aims of the queer movement as the resignification of the boundaries of the abject, the site of exclusion to which lesbians and gay men have traditionally been relegated.[40]

The works of fiction discussed in this study display a notably wide range of ideological approaches and perspectives. Jeannine Allard's *Légende*, published in the early 1980s and focusing on the figure of the witch, reproduces a lesbian feminist viewpoint. Associating lesbianism with feminist camaraderie and emotional involvements between women, Allard structures her narrative on the concept of lesbian continuum formulated by Rich. Texts published more recently, however, such as Paula Martinac's *Out of Time* (1990), which addresses the theme of spectral visitation, and Katherine V. Forrest's vampire story 'O Captain, My Captain' (1993), foreground lesbian sexuality. By introducing episodes of erotic fantasy and focusing on butch–femme role play, S&M sex and other experimental sexual practices, they highlight the diversity of lesbian sex and challenge lesbian feminist principles of political correctness. Gomez' *The Gilda Stories*, in keeping with the shifts of attitude that have occurred in the gay community, reproduces ideas relating to queer politics. Instead of restricting the scope of her novel to lesbian experience, Gomez explores a range of transgressive sexualities, including bisexuality and male homosexuality. In centring her narrative on characters who are African-American or American-Indian, she also concentrates attention on the politics of race.

However, although the novels and stories discussed below display a range of different approaches to lesbianism, it is the attitudes and priorities of the lesbian sexual radicals and the queer movement which they chiefly encode. Some, such as Hanrahan's *The Albatross Muff*, anticipate these attitudes, whereas others published more recently, such as Califia's 'The Vampire' (1988) and Sarah Schulman's *Rat Bohemia* (1995), reflect their influence. The prominence assumed by queer perspectives in these texts can be explained by the connections, admittedly very general, that exist between the interests of the lesbian sexual radicals and the queer movement and Gothic themes and motifs. Gothic and 'queer' share a common emphasis on transgressive acts and subjectivities. In addition both acknowledge the importance of fantasy, sexual as well as cultural, and represent subjectivity as fractured and fluid. Whereas Gothic narrative explores the disintegration of the self into double or multiple facets, queer theory foregrounds the multiple sexualities and roles that the subject produces and enacts.[41] The two are further linked by a focus on the concept of the abject,[42] the different manifestations that it can assume, and the anxieties and fears that it generates. Gothic fiction and film, in creating images of the monstrous and the uncanny, either reinforce and perpetuate existing definitions of the abject or, in the case of texts that are ideologically radical, problematize and challenge them. Queer theory and politics interrogate society's relegation of the homosexual to the realm of the abject and, by challenging expressions of homophobia and parodically re-enacting incidents of lesbian/gay oppression, attempt to renegotiate and resignify its boundaries.[43]

As these links and correspondences indicate, the influence exerted by the lesbian sexual radicals and the queer movement has created a cultural climate conducive to the production of lesbian Gothic fiction, facilitating its development and encouraging experimentation with Gothic structures and motifs. By foregrounding the importance of erotic fantasy and transgressive subjectivities and promoting an interest in the abject and the renegotiation of its borders, it has prompted writers to explore these topics in works of fiction. It has also promoted a readership and a market for the novels and stories they produce.

CONTRADICTIONS AND QUESTIONS

The utilization of Gothic as a vehicle for lesbian narrative, though in accord with current trends in lesbian critical studies and queer theory, can nonetheless confront the writer with difficulties, challenging her skills of revision and transformation. The recasting of fictional genres – whether 'popular' or 'classic' – from a lesbian/feminist point of view is by no means as easy to achieve as critics, such as Zimmerman, who question the value of the practice and treat it dismissively,[44] suggest. On the contrary, it requires the inventive manipulation of literary structures and ideological codes. The writer, while keeping within the parameters of the generic form that she adopts and respecting its conventions, seeks to interrogate the hetero-patriarchal ideology that it encodes. The path she treads in this respect is hazardous and beset by pitfalls. If she fails to transform the values of the genre in which she writes, she disappoints her lesbian/feminist readership. However, if she strays too far from its conventions or treats them in a crass manner, she risks erasing the genre's distinctive features – and likewise ends up alienating her readers. As Cranny-Francis remarks, readers 'may find a heavily transformed text unreadable, no longer recognisable as a member of the generic family to which it belongs'.[45]

In addition to confronting the writer with difficulties relating to the transformation of genre in general, Gothic also presents her with problems of a more specific kind. Gothic, as mentioned above, as well as being multifaceted and comprising a number of different strands and subsections, reveals an element of ideological ambiguity. While challenging conventions of realism and exposing the fragility of the *status quo* by focusing on dimensions of existence that transcend the everyday reality that realist texts tend to ignore, it is not necessarily politically subversive. Gothic fiction and film, particularly texts in the category of horror, often encode a reactionary value system that conflicts with or undermines the radical potential of the genre. As Jackson comments, texts of this kind 'serve rather than *subvert* the dominant ideology'.[46] As a result, Gothic confronts the writer with contradictions. While many of the features typifying it are well suited to lesbian representation, others, as we shall see, are problematic.

One of the chief attractions that Gothic holds for the writer of lesbian fiction is its tendency to question mainstream versions of 'reality' and to interrogate the values associated with them. A passage from Stephen King's *Bag of Bones* (1998) furnishes a pertinent illustration. Attempting to put into words the uncanny sensation he experiences on returning to his country home after his wife's death, the narrator remarks on his sudden recognition of the fact 'that reality was thin'. He continues, 'I think it *is* thin, you know, thin as lake ice after a thaw.... What comes in when the daylight leaves is a kind of certainty: that beneath the skin there is a secret, some mystery, both black and bright. You feel this mystery in every breath, you see it in every shadow.'[47] However, the interrogation of mainstream versions of reality that characterizes Gothic fiction is, in many cases, more than merely eerie in the effect it produces. By distancing the reader from orthodox assumptions of realism through a process of estrangement, Gothic texts prompt her/him to question conventional narrative structures and the normalizing images of reality that they create. These 'normalizing images' include, particularly in works of fiction by women, representations of sexuality and gender. Two themes that women prioritize are, as Cranny-Francis remarks, 'The way gender ideologies construct "reality" for the individual', and, related to this, the problems that arise when 'ideological reality' and 'experiential reality' conflict.[48] Conflicts between contrary versions of reality and value schemes are, of course, particularly intense in the case of the woman who identifies as lesbian or bisexual and lives in a society that refuses to recognize her sexual orientation, or condemns it as sinful or immoral. Gothic, as lesbian versions of the genre illustrate, furnishes an effective vehicle for exploring these conflicts and tensions.

Gothic also holds other attractions for the writer of lesbian fiction. In addition to questioning mainstream versions of reality and the ideological perspectives they encode, the genre has strongly female associations. As Richard Dyer observes, referring to the work of its two founding mothers Radcliffe and Mary Shelley, Gothic is 'a "female" genre first developed by women, centering on female protagonists and exhibiting a strong sense of being addressed to women'.[49] In employing it for lesbian representation, present-day writers have access to a rich tradition of fiction produced by their female predecessors. As well as appropriating ideas from Barnes, who in *Nightwood* utilizes Gothic imagery in a specifically lesbian context, they develop the perceptions of writers who employ the genre to treat topics relating to femininity in general. Radcliffe and her female peers introduce a number of motifs which, though not specifically lesbian, lend themselves to lesbian adaptation. Three of the most significant are woman's problematic relationship with her own body, the transgressive aspects of female sexuality and the psychological intricacies of female friendships and antagonisms.[50] Relations between mother and daughter[51] and the antithetical portrayal of woman as courageous hero/victim of persecution[52] are also important. The haunting of one woman by another, either literally or figuratively, is a key topic in Female Gothic. It is central to novels as different in period and style as Radcliffe's *The Mysteries of Udolpho* (1794), Charlotte Brontë's *Jane Eyre* (1847) and du Maurier's *Rebecca*. Critics interpret the spectral visitor in different ways, assigning to her the role of the heroine's mother,[53] *doppelgänger*,[54] rival,[55] or lover.[56] Whichever reading the motif receives, it is particularly well suited to lesbian recasting. It is popular, as we shall see, with writers of lesbian Gothic, achieving prominence in the novels of Hanrahan, Wings and Molleen Zanger.

Another facet of Gothic that attracts the writer of lesbian fiction is the frequency with which the texts exemplifying it – as critics who interpret the genre from a psychoanalytic point of view illustrate – treat themes relating to sexuality and repressed desire. Freud draws attention to this feature of the genre when, in discussing the concept of 'the uncanny' and the literature relating to it, he argues that the power that Gothic fantasy reveals to disturb and frighten the reader stems from its ability to articulate emotions and anxieties relating to 'the return of the repressed'.[57] The uncanny sensations that we experience in relation to certain objects or people stem, he argues, from the unconscious projection of our desires and anxieties on to the world around us. As Rosemary Jackson comments, paraphrasing Freud's theories, the uncanny 'uncovers what is hidden and, by so doing, effects a disturbing transformation of the familiar into the unfamiliar'.[58] Some theorists maintain, in fact, that the concept of the uncanny, as defined by Freud, carries predominantly female connotations. Linda Ruth Williams points out that, in locating the origins of uncanny in the subject's repressed yearning for 'the former *Heim* [home] of all human beings',[59] the female reproductive organs and the mother's body, Freud specifically relates it to female sexuality and to pre-oedipal mother/daughter relations. She argues that, as a result, the uncanny and the literature relating to it furnish women in particular with a fertile fantasy space where their imaginations can flourish.[60]

Freud's perception of the connections existing between the uncanny and repressed anxieties and desires provides the frame for numerous critical readings of Gothic narrative. Rosemary Jackson maintains that Gothic specializes in exploring repressed fears and desires, particularly those that are transgressive and socially taboo.[61] Sedgwick, another exponent of a psychoanalytic approach, discusses the way that certain early examples of the genre, such as Radcliffe's *The Italian* (1797) and Maturin's *Melmoth the Wanderer* (1820), investigate 'the position of the self massively blocked off from something to which it ought normally to have access'.[62] Clarifying this comment, she explains, 'Typically there is something going on inside the isolation ... and something intensely relevant going on impossibly out of reach.'[63] Repressed desires and emotions, of the kind to which Jackson and Sedgwick refer, are, of course, pertinent to the situation of the homosexual/ lesbian in hetero-patriarchal society – and it is understandable that certain classic Gothic texts, such as Bram Stoker's *Dracula* (1897)[64] and Stevenson's *The Strange Case of Dr Jekyll and Mr Hyde* (1886),[65] have been interpreted in a homosexual light. Critics increasingly recognize that Gothic makes an excellent vehicle for the coded representation of homosexuality. Commenting on the work of James Whale, the homosexual director who created the Hollywood version of *Frankenstein* and other well-known horror films, Jonathan Jones observes that films of this kind 'gave Whale the freedom to put his sexuality on screen'; they vividly express 'both the homosexual's fear of betrayal and society's most lurid fears of strangeness'.[66] The correspondence existing between the topics that Gothic conventionally treats and issues of importance to lesbians and gay men is further illustrated by Ken Plummer. Discussing the gay 'coming out' story, Plummer pinpoints four motifs on which it often centres: secrets, frustrated desire, shame and persecution. Though he does not mention the fact, all four are standard themes in Gothic fiction and film.[67]

A common location of secrets and persecution, as many lesbians and gay men discover to their cost, is the family unit. Here again the writer of lesbian fiction finds, in Gothic, reference to interests and experiences corresponding to her own. Gothic narrative generally depicts family relationships as oppressive and claustrophobic. In classic texts, such as the novels of Collins, Radcliffe and Charlotte Brontë, husbands are portrayed persecuting their wives, incarcerating them in locked rooms or mental asylums and, on occasion, even certifying them as dead, while parents or parental substitutes bully and torment their offspring. Present-day horror fiction represents family life as similarly malfunctional – if not more so! In King's *The Shining* (1977) the alcoholic Jack Torrance, influenced by the spectral scenes of murder and brutality which he witnesses at the Overlook Hotel, is transformed into a monster, terrorizing his wife and young son and subjecting them to acts of violence. Even if the family is not, in actual fact, a den of vice and violence, the protagonist of the horror novel frequently assumes it to be so. This is the case in James Herbert's *The Survivor* (1976), in which the assassin excuses the aircrash he instigates on the cynical grounds that its victims are no doubt as inhuman and heartless as his own kith and kin and thus merit the violent death they suffer. Writers of lesbian Gothic develop these scenes of familial persecution and entrapment, manipulating them to suit lesbian/queer circumstances. Brown's *The Haunted House* represents the family as the site of incestuous emotional ties between father and daughter, Zanger's *Gardenias Where There Are None* associates it with parental insensitivity and hypocrisy, while Schulman's *Rat Bohemia* (1995) describes it in terms of homophobia and parental neglect.

In addition to exploring the oppressive aspects of family life, writers of lesbian Gothic also utilize the fantasy dimension of the genre to create images of alternative familial structures which transform and subvert hetero-patriarchal forms. These, in folding together relationships which mainstream society regards as separate and incompatible, merit the adjective 'queer'.[68] The protagonist of Martinac's *Out of Time* experiences, in the attachment that she establishes with the spectral figures whom she encounters, a new, intense form of involvement in which the borders between the maternal and the sexual collapse and merge. Gomez' *The Gilda Stories*, in representing the eponymous protagonist's relationship with her fellow vampires, creates a queer version of family life which brings together roles generally regarded as incompatible. Here, as in Schulman's *After Delores*, alternative family formations, existing in parodic relation to the patriarchal family, compensate emotionally for the protagonist's lack of supportive biological ties.

One of the strongest encouragements to writers of lesbian fiction to experiment with the Gothic mode comes from contemporary theorists who utilize imagery relating to the genre to discuss and analyse lesbian and queer issues. Butler and Diana Fuss, though treating the concept differently, both describe lesbianism/homosexuality as signifying 'the repressed' at the heart of phallocentric culture. Butler, indicting heterosexual society for denying lesbians and gay men full humanity and subjecthood by relegating them to the realm of the abject, portrays these excluded subjectivities as 'haunting the boundaries [of the human] as the persistent possibility of their disruption and rearticulation'.[69] Fuss, discussing the relation between heterosexual and homosexual economies, describes 'each as haunted by the other', with 'the other' representing 'the very occurrence of ghostly visitation'.[70] Critics working in the field of film also foreground the links between Gothic and lesbianism. Patricia White, discussing the portrayal of the lesbian in the American horror film, argues that the transgressive effects of lesbian desire and the excess that it signifies in phallocentric culture are most effectively expressed by reference to the supernatural.[71] She makes the intriguing suggestion that the monster which conventionally appears in the horror film, which feminist critics interpret as a symbolic representation of woman, can be read in some cases as an image of the lesbian and the threat that she poses to hetero-patriarchal values and social structures. Case, in her theorization of the vampire, likewise interprets the monster in the horror film as a signifier of lesbian/queer desire. The queer subject, she argues, performs the role of the breaker of social and sexual taboos that is conventionally assigned to the monster.[72] The utilization of Gothic imagery and motifs as a vehicle for discussing lesbian/homosexual theoretical issues is, in fact, by now sufficiently commonplace to have aroused comment. Fuss, summing up the trend, observes that a distinctive feature of Lesbian Studies in the 1990s is 'a preoccupation with the figure of the homosexual as spectre and phantom, as spirit and revenant, as abject and undead'.[73]

However, it is not only theorists working in the field of lesbian and queer studies who appropriate Gothic motifs and imagery. Feminist theorists do too. Whereas Butler and Fuss utilize spectral imagery to explore the roles of the abject and the 'repressed' which mainstream society projects upon the lesbian, and the excess which lesbian desire signifies, Mary Daly and Luce Irigaray employ it to discuss a topic that is relevant to women in general – male oppression. Daly, commenting on the destructive effect that sexist attitudes have upon women, coins the phrase 'spooking from the locker room'[74] to describe the way in which men bombard the female sex with obscenities and verbal abuse. Irigaray, discussing the effects of *déréliction*, the state of exile and alienation in which she regards women currently existing as a result of the male suppression of a female genealogy, portrays them as reduced to the insubstantial condition of phantoms. She describes women as 'dissolved, absent, empty, abandoned', relegated to the status of 'a dream, a shade or even a ghost ...'.[75]

The attributes of Gothic cited above, such as its ability to interrogate mainstream versions of reality, its strongly female focus and homoerotic associations, and the radical manner in which lesbian and feminist theorists utilize its motifs and imagery, make it, in many ways, admirably suited to lesbian fiction. These attributes demonstrate the strengths of Gothic as a vehicle for lesbian representation, understandably attracting writers to experiment with the motifs and narrative structures the genre has produced. However, Gothic also reveals features of a less positive kind. Significant in this respect is the reactionary ideology that texts exemplifying it frequently encode and the misogynistic/homophobic attitudes they inscribe. Gothic narrative often includes in its cast of characters representatives of the monstrous and the abject, and it is woman – and particularly the woman who identifies as lesbian or forms primary relationships with members of her own sex – who tends to be assigned these roles. This is especially the case in popular fiction and film. Here, the lesbian is portrayed not merely as alien and Other but, to cite the term employed by Barbara Creed in her study of the horror film, as the epitome of 'the monstrous-feminine'. She is positioned, Creed illustrates, as the target of intense homophobic fear and loathing.[76]

The representation of the lesbian in fiction and film as monstrous and the relegation of her to the realm of the abject are so common as to require little illustration. In Shirley Jackson's *The Haunting of Hill House* (1959) the heroine's attachment to her mother and the lesbian orientation in which, according to the logic of narrative, it results doom her to emotional frustration and, as illustrated by the novel's grim conclusion, death. In Alasdair Gray's *Something Leather* (1990), a work of urban Gothic focusing on a group of women involved in an S&M sex ring, lesbianism is associated with female aggression and manipulation. Horror films, such as *Blood and Roses* (1960) and *Vampyres* (1974), stigmatize the lesbian as sexually voracious and depict the relationships she forms as narcissistic and violent.[77] That the cinematic representation of the lesbian as a bloodthirsty fury is by no means a thing of the past is demonstrated by *Basic Instinct* (1992), which portrays the psychotic murderess and her confederates as lesbian or bisexual. The connection that the film makes between lesbianism and the urge to annihilate men is made all the more disturbing by the fact that, as Creed points out, it is assigned no motive or explanation.[78] In assuming it to exist, films of this kind develop the tradition of the murderous, predatory lesbian established in nineteenth-century *fin-de-siècle* art. In paintings by Jean-Francois Auburtin, Fernand LeQuesne and John William Whiteley, which show witches and sirens luring the unsuspecting male voyager to his death, the seductress seldom works alone but is portrayed in a lesbian embrace or as a member of an erotic female coven.[79] The tendency of hetero-patriarchal culture to displace female violence on to lesbian identity is discussed by Lynda Hart in her study *Fatal Women: Lesbian Sexuality and the Mark of Aggression* (1994). Hart traces a series of characters in fiction, drama and film whose portrayal illustrates this process.

Confronted with the question, how best to interrogate and challenge the homophobic representation of the lesbian as a monstrous and abject figure exemplified by the fictional and cinematic texts cited above, writers adopt different strategies. Some, such as Elizabeth Riley[80] and Nancy Toder,[81] employ a feminist realist style and challenge it directly by normalizing her image. By focusing on the attributes that she shares with heterosexual women, they foreground her common femininity. Others, including many writers of lesbian Gothic, take the opposite line. They utilize strategies emphasizing lesbian specificity and 'difference'. Acknowledging the element of excess that lesbian sexuality signifies in phallocentric culture, they create, with subversive intent, parodic versions of the monstrous images that society projects upon the lesbian. The tactics they adopt in this respect reveal connections with poststructuralist theory. They agree with the recommendations for lesbian representation proposed by Teresa de Lauretis. Discussing the portrayal of the lesbian in works of fiction, de Lauretis describes the writer as waging a war with language 'to dislodge the erotic from the [phallocentric] discourse of gender, with its indissoluble knot of sexuality and reproduction'.[82] She argues that, in order to undomesticate the female image and subvert the conventional portrayal of woman as wife, mistress and mother, the writer has to reinscribe her image and construct it afresh in a new erotic economy. The writer, de Lauretis maintains, must reject normalizing images of womanhood and dare to reinscribe the lesbian 'in excess – as excess – in provocative counterimages sufficiently outrageous, passionate, verbally violent and formally complex to destroy the male discourse on love and redesign the universe' (pp. 149, 150). These images, de Lauretis emphasizes, rather than being conventionally attractive, may represent the lesbian as 'monstrous or grotesque' (p. 150). Writers of lesbian Gothic engage in a similar struggle with language and convention. Influenced by the parodically grotesque depictions of the lesbian created by earlier writers such as Barnes and Wittig, as well as by the queer movement's emphasis on the destabilizing effect that lesbian desire has on mainstream codes and conventions, they foreground the transgressive excess which her sexuality signifies. This 'excess', it is important to note, is not the supplementary *jouissance* referred to by Jacques Lacan which, since it is defined from a masculinist viewpoint and is ascribed to woman by male specularization, is, as Elizabeth Grosz argues, 'a phallic refusal to accept an otherness not modelled on [the economy of] the same'.[83] On the contrary, it has more in common with Irigaray's definition of *jouissance*. This acknowledges the autonomy and 'otherness' of female pleasure and thus serves to liberate woman from male specularization and control. In fact Irigaray describes it as a 'disruptive excess', since she sees it as capable of 'jamming the theoretical machinery of phallocentric culture'.[84]

The strategies of parodic reworking that writers of lesbian Gothic employ also reveal links with Irigaray's concept of mimesis and with Butler's theory of 'gender as performance', which develops Irigaray's ideas from a queer point of view. Both theories hinge on the concept of the subversive effect of the parodic re-enactment of oppressive images and roles. Irigaray proposes that the female subject, instead of attempting to reject outright the oppressive roles and scripts which masculinist culture assigns to her, a task that she regards as futile, should challenge them surreptitiously by re-enacting them in a parodic manner.[85] Butler argues that lesbian and gay roles, such as butch–femme and drag, rather than imitating heterosexual gender roles as is generally assumed to be the case, enact a transgressive commentary on them, thus exposing their inauthenticity.[86] She regards the abject (the realm to which society has traditionally relegated the homosexual) not as a position of impotence but as the site from which the gay community can challenge hetero-patriarchal power and the regulatory discourses that enforce it. She describes parodic mimicry as one of the strategies available to lesbians and gay men to resignify the boundaries of the abject. The parodic performance and re-enactment of the oppressive roles and images that society assigns to us have the effect, Butler argues, of 'reworking abjection into political agency, recasting it into defiance and legitimacy'.[87]

Writers of lesbian Gothic, in parodically reworking the homophobic and misogynistic images associated with the genre, similarly engage in an attempt to resignify the boundaries of the abject. The strategies they employ vary from text to text. They include revising conventional narrative patterns and character stereotypes, inscribing a lesbian/queer viewpoint with which the reader can identify, and introducing episodes of comic parody. Images of the monstrous feminine are interrogated and problematized and their oppressive effects exposed. The witch, the vampire and the spectral visitor, conventionally depicted in fiction and film as abject and alien, achieve subjectivity and agency. By being positioned as the narrator or focalizer of events, they realign the viewpoint of the text and the values which it encodes.

In interrogating these images and the homophobic perspectives they inscribe, writers take significant liberties with Gothic conventions, manipulating, stretching and, on occasion, even inverting them. Martinac and Zanger radically modify the representation of the Gothic heroine, transforming her from the conventionally naïve victim to a figure who is assertive and sexually experienced. This paves the way for further modifications. Whereas some novels, such as Hanrahan's *The Albatross Muff* and Brown's *The Haunted House*, portray the heroine following the conventional Gothic trajectory of psychological enthralment, fragmentation and annihilation,[88] others, such as Donoghue's *Hood* (1995) and Schulman's *After Delores*, take her to the brink of experiencing loss of self or death. However, by assigning to her attributes of strength and detachment appropriated, one suspects, from the protagonist of the lesbian/feminist thriller or sci-fi novel, they ensure that she survives to tell her tale.

The novels and stories discussed in this study, as well as varying in their treatment of the heroine, also differ in the response they elicit from the reader. While Hanrahan's *The Albatross Muff* and Brown's *The Haunted House* evoke the conventional response of disquiet and fear, Scott's *I, Vampire* and Anna Livia's *Minimax* (1991) provoke laughter – albeit of an uneasy kind. Scott and Livia develop, in fact, the tradition of comic Gothic established by Atwood's feminist *tour de force* of wit *Lady Oracle*. They utilize the device of humour to explore constructs of role and identity and to critique hetero-patriarchal codes and values.

Strategies of the kind described above play a key role in the fictional treatment of the four topics on which this study centres: the witch, spectral visitation, the vampire and the Gothic thriller. The topics vary as to the date at which they achieved prominence in novels and stories and exemplify, as a result, different moments of lesbian culture and politics. Their treatment ranges from the portrayal of the witch as a signifier of female resistance to male control in the novels of Hanrahan and Allard, published in the 1970s and the early 1980s, to the representation of the vampire as a vehicle for exploring the transgressive effects of lesbian desire and for addressing different aspects of lesbian sexual practice in the fiction of Forrest and Gomez published in the 1990s. Martinac, Zanger and Brown, writing in the late 1980s and the 1990s, utilize scenarios of spectral visitation to treat issues relating to 'the return of the repressed'. Influenced by the debates about sexuality[89] which have entered the lesbian agenda during this period, they concentrate on representing examples of erotic fantasy and examining the darker reaches of lesbian desire and subjectivity. Winterson likewise employs reference to ghostly presences and doubles to evoke the disruptive effect of lesbian sexuality on heterosexual conventions. Donoghue and Shulman, in two novels published in the mid-1990s, introduce spectral imagery to explore an important theme in the present era of AIDS: lesbian/ gay bereavement and mourning. The Gothic thriller is exemplified in this study by a selection of novels by Vicki McConnell, Rebecca O'Rourke, Wings and Schulman, their dates of publication ranging from the mid-1980s to the 1990s. They illustrate, in different ways, the destabilizing effect that the introduction of Gothic motifs and structures has on the format of the thriller. The interplay they achieve between the two genres, in addition to creating a protagonist who embodies contradictions, complicates the conventional trajectory of the crime investigation. The introduction of supernatural events or the focus placed on the irrational power of memory has the effect of undermining the processes of justice, rendering the outcome of the investigation ambiguous.

The novels and stories cited above differ in the perspective on lesbianism they adopt and in the aspects of Gothic which they develop and rework. However, they are linked in a number of cases by the introduction of certain common themes and ideas. Reference to the abject and the attempt to renegotiate its boundaries by employing strategies of parodic transformation furnish one such link. Related to this is a focus on the concept of 'excess'. The inscription of lesbian desire in terms of excess, and the importance which it assumes in lesbian representation in fiction and film, stems from the perception that the lesbian, in rejecting the role of object of exchange between men, exceeds the phallic fantasy of woman as specularized Other.[90] This is particularly relevant to the scenarios of spectral visitation discussed in Chapter 3 and to the vampire narratives examined in Chapter 4. The concept of excess often finds expression in lesbian Gothic in images of the grotesque body. The contrast that Mikhail Bakhtin draws between the classic body, its opaque surface signifying 'a closed individuality',[91] and the grotesque body, its protruding limbs and organs transgressing the limits between the individual and the world, is, of course, pertinent to Gothic in general. The fanged image of Dracula, the repulsive simian form of Hyde and the hunchback, hook-nose image of the witch all furnish vivid examples of the grotesque and the excess which it denotes. Reference to the grotesque body in lesbian Gothic, in addition to denoting the breakdown of the constraints imposed by the rational and the movement into the fluid, undifferentiated realm of fantasy and the unconscious, can also signify, as de Lauretis argues in her discussion of lesbian representation, the transgressive power of femininity and lesbian/queer sexuality. An emphasis on the grotesque body, it is interesting to note, is reflected in works of lesbian Gothic not only in their content but also in their style and narrative structure. In Ellen Galford's *The Fires of Bride* and Schulman's *After Delores* it finds expression in a proliferation of story lines and alternative viewpoints, while in the comic texts of Scott and Livia it manifests itself in sudden outbursts of witty parody and zany humour.

Another feature that furnishes a link between the works of lesbian Gothic discussed in this study is the representation of alternative family formations and structures, often anticipating or reflecting a queer viewpoint. Sedgwick sees the aim of the queer movement as the disengaging of sexual/social ties from the biological family unit to which they have traditionally been restricted, along with the creation of alternative attachments and groupings.[92] Gomez, Martinac and Schulman develop these ideas in fictional form, creating a fantasy blueprint for alternative ways of living.

Alternative familial forms and social structures furnish the site where the lesbian achieves self-definition and emotional fulfilment. As a result, they are frequently associated in lesbian Gothic with her quest for identity. They are also related to the lesbian subject's search for origins, both individual and communal. Indicative of the importance that the search for 'family' and origins assumes in texts of this kind is the way in which fantasies relating to birth, seduction and parental relations, in some cases parodying and recasting the Freudian primal fantasies, recur in novels and stories.[93] The interest that the theme of the individual's search for origins holds for writers of lesbian Gothic is also reflected in the frequency with which the texts they create move into the terrain of historical narrative. In fact, many of the novels and stories discussed in this study take the form of innovative fictions of history. They utilize Gothic as a vehicle for both recreating images of the lesbian past and discussing the fascination which investigating and reconstructing lesbian history holds for women. They also comment on the problems of misinterpreting or idealizing the past to which such fascination can give rise.

GOTHIC, FICTIONS OF HISTORY AND THE LESBIAN PAST

The appropriation of themes and structures from historical narrative which is a prominent feature of lesbian Gothic is, of course, a phenomenon which is by no means new. From its advent in the eighteenth century Gothic has been imbued with an aura of the archaic and the ancient. With the aim of promoting these attributes, early examples of the genre such as Walpole's *The Castle of Otranto* (1764), in addition to utilizing a medieval setting comprising turretted castles and cloistered monasteries, sometimes present themselves to the reader as translations from earlier documents or as fragments of a collection of partially destroyed manuscripts.[94] Walpole and Radcliffe utilize earlier periods as a fantasy arena where crimes of violence and power struggles among aristocratic families are enacted and scenarios of female entrapment and suffering take place. Works published subsequently develop the historical associations of the genre in different ways and with varying degrees of intellectual and stylistic sophistication. Novels and stories focusing on the fortunes of the ancient house (both in the sense of the building itself and of the family living there), such as Nathaniel Hawthorne's *The House of the Seven Gables* (1851), Poe's 'The Fall of the House of Usher'.(1839) and M.R. James's 'The Ash Tree' (1931), trace a sequence of intergenerational mishaps and crises in which the sins of the father are visited upon the sons – in some cases, the daughters too! The chain of evil in these and other narratives frequently originates in a curse imposed on the founding father which neither he nor his descendants are able to exorcize.

The ghost story tends to take a different approach to history, one which is personal and psychological in emphasis. Foregrounding the operations of memory and the complex displacements which it effects, writers explore the anxieties and terrors generated by 'the return of the repressed'. In Henry James's 'The Turn of the Screw' (1898) and Walter de la Mare's 'Out of the Deep' (1923) the protagonist's encounter with representatives of the spectral world plunges her/him into a disturbing episode from the past involving a traumatic confrontation with doubles and mirror images. The evocation of earlier periods of history in the ghost story often concentrates on events of a fearful, grisly nature and assumes a visionary and visual aspect. The protagonist in M.R. James's 'A View from the Hill' (1931), on looking through a pair of binoculars whose lenses are constructed from dead men's bones (unbeknown to him), sees an image of the surrounding landscape as it was in the Middle Ages, complete with gibbet and rotting corpse.

Horror fiction and film also appropriate historical themes, social as well as personal, reworking in popular terms the motifs and strategies employed in classic texts. In the field of fiction King's *Pet Sematary* (1983) and John Saul's *Nathaniel* (1984) transfer to a present-day location the theme of the evils of parental inheritance. Both represent family history as a chain of macabre events that escalate in violence and anguish with the passing of the years. Anne Rice in *Interview with a Vampire* (1976) exploits the legendary longevity of her vampire heroes to create vignettes of sexual and social decadence in nineteenth-century New Orleans. In film, the motif of the long-term effects of the individual's acts of violence and the influence it has on future generations is reproduced in *Hands of the Ripper* (1971), which portrays the murderer's hands continuing to kill after he himself is dead, and in the violent rampages of Freddie in *A Nightmare on Elm Street* (1984) and the sequels it has generated. Meanwhile *Day of Wrath* (1943) and *Witchfinder General* (1968) transform the witch-hunting eras of the past into an arena for staging the horrific consequences of persecution and sexual repression.

Writers of lesbian Gothic similarly exploit and manipulate the connections between Gothic and historical fiction. They develop, in fact, many of the strategies and motifs that writers and film directors conventionally employ to articulate the links between the two genres. Brown's *The Haunted House* recasts, from a psychological viewpoint, the motif of parental disturbance and the destructive effect it has on the members of the younger generation and the relationships they form. Hanrahan's *The Albatross Muff*, in recreating the stifling atmosphere of Victorian family life and its oppressive implications for women, creates a variation on the narratives of female entrapment associated with Radcliffe and Charlotte Brontë. Zanger's *Gardenias Where There Are None* appropriates from the classic ghost story themes of memory and the protagonist's encounter with a spectral double from the past. In *The Gilda Stories* Gomez utilizes the longevity of her vampire protagonist as a vehicle to create images of African-American history. These writers, however, rather than merely reproducing motifs from earlier texts, utilize the interrelation between Gothic and historical narrative to explore issues of particular interest to the lesbian/queer reader. The vivacity and inventiveness with which they develop the historical dimension of the genre reflect the importance that the recovery and reconstruction of the past, imaginative as well as scholarly, assumes in lesbian culture and politics.

As theorists observe, one of the problems confronting the woman who identifies as lesbian or bisexual in hetero-patriarchal society is a sense of deprivation at being denied a history and the sense of identity which it promotes. Martha Vicinus maintains, in fact, that 'for lesbians today the most important and controversial questions concern the origins of an individual and a group identity',[95] while Gabriele Griffin remarks on 'the sense expressed by many lesbians in the 1970s that they had no sustained history constructed by themselves'.[96] Griffin regards access to history as particularly important for those women who, as is the case with lesbians, are relegated to the social margins and have little control over the dominant discourses. The sense of deprivation to which she refers was understandably at its most acute in the early years of the lesbian movement, when little attempt had been made to chart and document the lesbian past. It played, in fact, an instrumental part in promoting the growth of lesbian historical studies.[97] This discipline, far from remaining stationary, has undergone a series of significant modifications and shifts of emphasis in the course of the past twenty-five years.

In the 1970s, when a focus on lesbian 'heroines' was in fashion and the study of lesbian history at its most elementary and intellectually immature, researchers concentrated on investigating the lives of 'special individuals'. They frequently lacked a training in historical methodology and, as Vicinus admits, were 'more concerned with finding heroines than with uncovering the often fragmentary and contradictory evidence which must make up the lesbian past'.[98] While eager to theorize lesbianism within feminist parameters, they paid little attention to its sexual dimension and were, on the whole, unaware of the changes that had occurred over the centuries in constructs of female sexuality.

In the present era of the 1990s, however, the study of lesbian history has moved on apace, acquiring a new degree of rigour and complexity. Poststructuralist thought, by alerting attention to the part played by viewpoint and interpretation in accounts of the past, has problematized the concept of historical 'objectivity' and knowledge. As well as questioning the conventional separation between the discourses of history and literature, it has exposed the partisan nature of historical records and alerted attention to the ideological usage that theorists and politicians make of them.[99] Advancements in social-constructionist theory have also influenced the study of lesbian history. By questioning the validity of transhistorical identities such as 'woman', 'lesbian' and 'black', theorists have alerted attention to the fact that they are cultural constructs. They have also promoted an awareness of the political uses to which researchers put them. As Zimmerman observes, summing up these ideas, 'All notions of the lesbian – whether essentialist or anti-essentialist, universal or socially constructed – are themselves products of particular historical discourses and serve specific political and theoretical purposes'.[100] As a result of these developments, present-day students of lesbian history show little interest in searching the past for role models or 'special individuals', as their predecessors did in the 1970s. Some, such as Vicinus, investigate questions relating to lesbian sexual identity or explore the different forms which relationships between women took in earlier periods.[101] Others, like Jennifer Terry, influenced by the work of Michel Foucault, examine the ways in which women who formed primary relationships with members of their own sex were classified as deviant by the dominant culture. They also document incidents of resistance on the part of individual women or the lesbian/feminist community in general.[102]

The modifications and transformations that have occurred in lesbian historical studies have understandably influenced the treatment of history in lesbian Gothic. The novels and stories discussed in this study differ considerably in the approach to history that they adopt and in the narrative strategies they utilize to represent it. Allard's *Légende*, published in the early 1980s and employing the format of the feminist confessional narrative, offers the reader a set of exemplary role models and claims to give her a transparent window on to the past. Galford's *The Fires of Bride*, published some years later, in contrast adopts a more sophisticated postmodern approach. By interweaving realist and fantasy episodes, and portraying characters living in the twentieth century engaging in historical research and archeological excavation, Galford creates an interplay between historical and literary discourses. She positions the reader into perceiving that our images of the past are cultural constructs, reflecting contemporary prejudices and ideals. Livia's *Minimax*, an example of comic Gothic, displays a similarly postmodern parodic stance. Livia playfully compares present-day constructs of lesbianism, including British lesbian-feminist and Californian New Age, with the roles that flourished in early twentieth-century Paris. She teases out their connections and discontinuities and foregrounds the element of performativity which they display.

Discussing the treatment of history in postmodern fiction, Linda Hutcheon describes writers as 'reshaping material (in this case the past) in the light of present'.[103] In fact, she sees what she terms 'this interpretative process' as typifying postmodern narrative practice. Writers of lesbian Gothic take a similar course, utilizing the reconstruction of episodes from the lesbian past to address and publicize present-day cultural and political issues. Hanrahan encodes radical feminist concepts of sisterhood in the image of nineteenth-century family life she creates in *The Albatross Muff*, while Martinac in *Out of Time* utilizes the 1920s social context from which her spectral visitors hail to explore different forms of the lesbian/feminist community. Winterson is yet another writer who employs the reconstruction of the past as a vehicle for discussing present-day interests and concepts. In *Sexing the Cherry* she models the perceptions and lifestyles of her seventeenth-century characters on queer ideas of sexuality and subjectivity.

Like Victor Frankenstein's monstrous progeny, the development of Gothic has been by no means trouble free but has been beset, more often than not, by conflict. From the moment of its advent in the eighteenth century, the genre has been the target of controversy on moral, ideological and stylistic grounds. Although today it is a popular topic of study in university departments of literature and film, even its staunchest admirers agree that, from a literary point of view, it is eccentric and bristles with anomalies and contradictions. William Day argues that, regarded in terms of genre, Gothic is reactive and inauthentic. He points out that it constructs its narratives by parodying other fictional forms, purloining and recasting fragments from the realist novel and the romance,[104] in a manner resembling the piecemeal way in which Frankenstein assembled his ill-fated creature. Lesbian Gothic is open to even harsher criticism. It invites the accusation that, in appropriating and reworking structures and motifs from classic and popular Gothic, it is *doubly* inauthentic – a mere parody of a parody, so to speak!

Lesbian Gothic, like its more mainstream counterpart, is, one has to acknowledge, a thoroughly unorthodox, hybrid form of fiction. This, as well as accounting for the inventiveness that many of the texts exemplifying it display, explains their ability to furnish a vehicle for the ideas and perspectives of the queer movement – which are similarly unorthodox. The novels and stories on which this study focuses are, of course, by no means uniformly successful. In some, the representation of the lesbian in the role of vampire or witch, instead of serving to interrogate and deconstruct phallocentric stereotypes of the monstrous, has the reverse effect of reinforcing them, thus perpetuating existing prejudices. The texts discussed below furnish illustrations of problematic features of this kind. The majority of texts, however, employ Gothic structures imaginatively. At the simplest level of transformation the lesbian, instead of existing as an absence or silence in the narrative or being assigned the role of monster, as is often the case in the Gothic texts of the past, is credited with an identity and a viewpoint. She is permitted to emerge from the closet (or in the case of the lesbian vampire, the coffin!) and recount her own story. The tales that she tells and the adventures she encounters form the subject of the following chapters.

NOTES

1. Mary Wings, 'Rebecca Redux: Tears on a Lesbian Pillow', in Liz Gibbs (ed.), *Daring to Dissent: Lesbian Culture from Margin to Mainstream* (Cassell, 1994), p. 13.

2. Jody Scott, *I, Vampire* (The Women's Press, 1986), p. 18. Further page references are to this edition and are in the text.

3. David Punter discusses these critical approaches in *The Literature of Terror: A History of Gothic Fiction from 1765 to the Present Day* (Longman, 1980), pp. 18–21.

4. Chris Baldick (ed.), *The Oxford Book of Gothic Tales* (Oxford University Press, 1993), p. xix.

5. Sybil Korff Vincent discusses comic Gothic in 'The Mirror and the Cameo: Margaret Atwood's Comic/Gothic Novel: *Lady Oracle*', in Juliann E. Fleenor (ed.), *The Female Gothic* (Eden Press, 1983), pp. 153–63.

6. For discussion of these films see Nina Auerbach, *Our Vampires Ourselves* (University of Chicago Press, 1995), pp. 165–9.

7. Anne Cranny-Francis, *Feminist Fiction: Feminist Uses of Generic Fiction* (Polity Press, 1990), pp. 75–7.

8. Rosemary Jackson, *Fantasy: The Literature of Subversion* (Methuen, 1991), pp. 34–42.

9. Barbara Creed remarks about the film, 'Possession becomes the excuse for a display of aberrant feminine behaviour which is depicted as depraved, monstrous, abject – and perversely appealing' (*The Monstrous-Feminine: Film, Feminism and Psychoanalysis*, Routledge, 1993, p. 31).

10. Gray's novel gives a lurid account of the S&M activities of a group of urban lesbians, representing the women as manipulative and ruthless.

11. Punter observes that 'The appalling feature of this aspect of Lovecraft's writing [his focus on the monstrous] is that, reading through not only his fiction but also his letters, one realizes that the terms which he applies to his invading non-human monstrosities are precisely the same as those in which he describes members of all

American ethnic groups, with the exception of the caste of East Coast "Old Americans" to which he belonged' (*The Literature of Terror*, p. 283).

12. For reference to 'the return of the repressed' see Sigmund Freud, 'The "Uncanny" ', in Sigmund Freud, *The Complete Psychological Works*, ed. and trans. by James Strachey in collaboration with Anna Freud (Hogarth, 1955), vol. 17, pp. 217–53; and Rosemary Jackson, *Fantasy*, pp. 64–7, 114–17.

13. Critical studies appropriating a psychoanalytic viewpoint include Jackson, *Fantasy*, and Eve Kosofsky Sedgwick, *The Coherence of Gothic Conventions* (Methuen, 1980).

14. Donald A. Ringe, *American Gothic: Imagination and Reason in Nineteenth-Century Fiction* (University Press of Kentucky, 1982).

15. Punter, *The Literature of Terror*, pp. 189–90.

16. Kate Ferguson Ellis, *The Contested Castle: Gothic Novels and the Subversion of Domestic Ideology* (University of Illinois Press, 1989). See also Eugenia C. Delamotte, *Perils of the Night: A Feminist Study of Nineteenth-century Gothic* (Oxford University Press, 1990) and Ellen Moers, *Literary Women* (The Women's Press, 1978).

17. Patricia White discusses the utilization of spectral imagery in lesbian representation in film in 'Female Spectator, Lesbian Spectre: *The Haunting*', in Diana Fuss (ed.), *Inside/Out: Lesbian Theories, Gay Theories* (Routledge, 1991), pp. 142–73. Studies referring to the portrayal of the lesbian in Gothic and horror film include Barbara Creed, *The Monstrous Feminine: Film, Feminism, Psychoanalysis* (Routledge, 1993), pp. 67–72; Andrea Weiss, *Vampires and Violets: Lesbians in the Cinema* (Jonathan Cape, 1992), pp. 84–108; and Clare Whatling, *Screen Dreams: Fantasising Lesbians in Film* (Manchester University Press, 1997), pp. 79–115.

18. Wings, 'Rebecca Redux', pp. 11–33.

19. Case, 'Tracking the Vampire', *Differences: A Journal of Feminist Cultural Studies*, 3:2 (1991), 1–20.

20. 'The Blank Page' is reprinted in Margaret Reynolds (ed.), *The Penguin Book of Lesbian Short Stories* (1994), pp. 117–22.

21. Terry Castle, *The Apparitional Lesbian: Female Homosexuality and Modern Culture* (Columbia University Press, 1993), pp. 21–65.

22. For reference to the lesbian/feminist transformation of popular genres, see Helen Carr (ed.), *From My Guy to Sci-Fi: Genre and Women's Writing in the Postmodern World* (Pandora, 1989); Anne Cranny-Francis, *Feminist Fiction: Feminist Uses of Genre Fiction* (Polity Press, 1990); and Paulina Palmer, *Contemporary Lesbian Writing: Dreams, Desire, Difference* (Open University Press, 1993), pp. 63–97.

23. Patricia Duncker popularized the use of the term 'writing lesbian' in *Sisters and Strangers: An Introduction to Contemporary Feminist Fiction* (Blackwell, 1992), pp. 167–209.

24. Marilyn R. Farwell, *Heterosexual Plots and Lesbian Narratives* (New York University Press, 1996), p. 4.

25. Bonnie Zimmerman, *The Safe Sea of Women: Lesbian Fiction 1969–1989* (Beacon Press, 1990), p. 15.

26. Zimmerman, *The Safe Sea of Women*, p. 15.

27. Teresa de Lauretis, 'Eccentric Subjects: Feminist Theory and Historical Consciousness', *Feminist Studies*, 16:1 (1990), 145.

28. Farwell, *Heterosexual Plots*, pp. 12–13.

29. See Farwell, *Heterosexual Plots*, pp. 27–8; and Palmer, *Contemporary Lesbian Writing*, pp. 102–5.

30. Julia Penelope Stanley, 'Uninhabited Angels: Metaphors for Love', *Margins*, 23 (1975), 8.

31. Farwell, *Heterosexual Plots*, pp. 146–56.

32. Castle, *The Apparitional Lesbian*, pp. 61–91.

33. Charlotte Bunch, 'Not for Lesbians Only', in Charlotte Bunch and Gloria Steinem (eds), *Building Feminist Theory: Essays from Quest* (Longman, 1981), pp. 67–73.

34. Adrienne Rich, 'Compulsory Heterosexuality and Lesbian Existence', in *Blood, Bread and Poetry: Selected Prose 1979–1985* (Virago, 1987), pp. 23–75.

35. Pat Califia, 'Feminism and Sadomasochism', *Heresies* (Sex Issue) (1981), 26–33.

36. Joan Nestle, *A Restricted Country* (Firebrand, 1987), pp. 74–119.

37. Monique Wittig, 'The Straight Mind', in *The Straight Mind and Other Essays* (Harvester Wheatsheaf, 1992), pp. 21–32.

38. Judith Butler, *Gender Trouble* (Routledge, 1990), pp. 1–34; and 'The Lesbian Phallus and the Morphological Imaginary', in *Bodies That Matter: On the Discursive Limits of Sex* (Routledge, 1993), pp. 57–91. These shifts in approach are discussed by Palmer in *Contemporary Lesbian Writing*, pp. 9–36; and Bonnie Zimmerman in 'Lesbians Like This and That: Some Notes on Lesbian Criticism for the Nineties', in Sally Munt (ed.), *New Lesbian Criticism: Literary and Cultural Readings* (Harvester Wheatsheaf, 1992), pp. 1–15.

39. Eve Kosofsky Sedgwick, 'Queer and Now', in *Tendencies* (Routledge, 1994), p. 8.

40. Butler, 'Critically Queer', in *Bodies That Matter*, p. 228.

41. A focus on fantasy and on multiple roles and identities is to the fore in Butler, 'Passing, Queering: Nella Larsen's Psychoanalytic Challenge', in *Bodies That Matter*, pp. 106–85; and Sedgwick, 'Queer and Now', pp. 1–20.

42. For reference to the concept of 'the abject' see Julia Kristeva, *Powers of Horror: An Essay in Abjection*, trans. by Leon S. Roudiez (Columbia University Press, 1991), pp. 1–113; and Creed, *The Monstrous-Feminine*, pp. 8–15.

43. See Butler, *Bodies That Matter*, pp. 19–23, 223–42; Elizabeth Grosz, 'Refiguring Lesbian Desire', in Laura Doan (ed.), *The Lesbian Postmodern* (Columbia University Press, 1994), pp. 67–84; and essays by Tim David and Lawrence Knopp discussing lesbian/gay attempts to reclaim urban space in David Bell and Gill Valentine (eds), *Mapping Desire: Geographies of Sexuality* (Routledge, 1995), pp. 149–61, 285–303.

44. Zimmerman, *The Safe Sea of Women*, p. 211.

45. Cranny-Francis, *Feminist Fiction*, p. 19.

46. Jackson, *Fantasy*, p. 175.

47. Stephen King, *Bag of Bones* (Hodder and Stoughton, 1998), pp. 76–7.

48. Cranny-Francis, *Feminist Fiction*, p. 103.

49. Richard Dyer, 'Children of the Night: Vampirism as Homosexuality, Homosexuality as Vampirism', in Susannah Radstone (ed.), *Sweet Dreams: Sexuality, Gender and Popular Fiction* (Lawrence and Wishart, 1988), p. 49.

50. See the essays by Marcia Tillotson, Ann Ronald and Cynthia Griffin Wolff in

Juliann Fleenor (ed.), *The Female Gothic* (Eden Press, 1983), pp. 167–207; and Coral Ann Howells, 'The Pleasure of the Woman's Text: Ann Radcliffe's Subtle Transgressions in *The Mysteries of Udolpho* and *The Italian*', in Kenneth W. Graham (ed.), *Gothic Fictions: Prohibition/Transgression* (AMS Press, 1989), pp. 151–62.

51. See Claire Kahane, 'The Gothic Mirror', in Shirley Nelson Garner, Claire Kahane and Madelon Sprengnether (eds), *The (M)other Tongue* (Cornell University Press, 1985), pp. 336–43; and Tania Modleski, *Loving with a Vengeance: Mass-produced Fantasies for Women* (Methuen, 1984), pp. 69–74.

52. Moers, *Literary Women*, p. 91.

53. See Kahane, 'The Gothic Mirror'.

54. See William Patrick Day, *In the Circles of Fear and Desire: A Study of Gothic Fantasy* (University of Chicago Press, 1985), pp. 20–7, 54, 57; Kahane, 'The Gothic Mirror', p. 339; and Sandra M. Gilbert and Susan Gubar, *The Madwoman in the Attic: The Woman Writer and the Nineteenth-Century Imagination* (Yale University Press, 1979), pp. 358–71.

55. Creed, *The Monstrous Feminine*, p. 54.

56. See Day, *In the Circles of Fear*, pp. 86–9.

57. For reference to 'the return of the repressed' see note 12.

58. Rosemary Jackson, *Fantasy*, p. 65.

59. Freud, 'The "Uncanny"', p. 368.

60. Linda Ruth Williams, *Critical Desire: Psychoanalysis and the Literary Subject* (Edward Arnold, 1995), pp. 178–9.

61. Rosemary Jackson, *Fantasy*, pp. 65–6, 72.

62. Sedgwick, *The Coherence of Gothic Conventions*, p. 12.

63. *Ibid.*

64. Bram Stoker, *Dracula* (Oxford University Press, 1985), p. 39. For discussion of the novel's homoerotic resonances see Ken Gelder, *Reading the Vampire* (Routledge, 1994), pp. 74–6.

65. Robert Louis Stevenson, *The Strange Case of Dr Jekyll and Mr Hyde* (Penguin, 1979), pp. 68, 48. For discussion of the homoerotic/homosocial tension in the novel see William Veeder, 'Children of the Night: Stevenson and Patriarchy', in William Veeder and Gordon Hirsch (eds), *Dr Jekyll and Mr Hyde after One Hundred Years* (University of Chicago Press, 1988), pp. 107–60.

66. Jonathan Jones, 'He created the horror movie, and then his life became one', *Guardian*, Review Section, 5 September 1998, p. 18.

67. Ken Plummer, *Telling Sexual Stories: Power, Change and Social Worlds* (Routledge, 1995), pp. 27–9, 80–96.

68. Sedgwick discusses queer attempts to disengage sexual/social attachments from the biological family unit and to create new structures and groupings in 'Queer and Now', pp. 5–7.

69. Butler, *Bodies That Matter*, p. 8.

70. Fuss, *Inside/Out*, pp. 29–61. Castle too discusses the connections between spectral imagery and lesbianism. (*The Apparitional Lesbian*, pp. 1–9.)

71. White, 'Female Spectator, Lesbian Specter', p. 142.

72. Case, 'Tracking the Vampire', pp. 1–4.

73. Fuss, *Inside/Out*, p. 3.

74. Mary Daly, *Gyn/Ecology: The Metaethics of Radical Feminism* (Women's Press, 1979), p. 323.

75. Luce Irigaray, *The Irigaray Reader*, ed. Margaret Whitford (Blackwell, 1991), pp. 91, 107.

76. Creed, *The Monstrous Feminine*, p. 61.

77. Weiss discusses *Blood and Roses* in *Vampires and Violets*, pp. 92–5.

78. See Creed's discussion of the film in *The Monstrous Feminine*, p. 124; and Lynda Hart's in *Lesbian Sexuality and the Mark of Aggression* (Routledge, 1994), pp. 124–34.

79. See Bram Dikstra, *Idols of Perversity: Fantasies of Feminine Evil in Fin-de-Siècle Culture* (Oxford University Press, 1996), pp. 258–64.

80. Elizabeth Riley, *All That False Instruction* (Angus and Robertson, 1975).

81. Nancy Toder, *Choices* (Persephone Press, 1980).

82. Teresa de Lauretis, 'Sexual Indifference and Lesbian Representation', in Henry Abelove, Michele Aina Barale and David Halperin (eds), *The Lesbian and Gay Studies Reader* (Routledge, 1993), p. 144. Further page references are to this edition and are in the text.

83. Elizabeth Grosz, *Jacques Lacan: A Feminist Introduction* (Routledge, 1990), p. 175.

84. Irigaray, *This Sex Which Is Not One* (1977), trans. Catherine Porter with Carolyn Burke (Cornell University Press, 1985), p. 78.

85. Irigaray, *This Sex*, p. 76.

86. Butler, 'Imitation and Gender Insubordination', in Fuss, *Inside/Out*, pp. 13–31.

87. Butler, *Bodies That Matter*, p. 21.

88. Day, *In the Circles of Fear*, pp. 22–7.

89. For reference to these debates see Emma Healey, *Lesbian Sex Wars* (Virago, 1996), pp. 41–201.

90. See de Lauretis, 'Sexual Indifference and Lesbian Representation', pp. 149–58; and White, 'Female Spectator, Lesbian Specter', pp. 142–72.

91. Mikhail Bakhtin, *Rabelais and His World* (Indiana University Press, 1984), p. 320.

92. Sedgwick, 'Queer and Now', p. 6.

93. For reference to the part played by primal fantasies in literature see John Fletcher, 'Gender and Primal Fantasy', in Victor Burgin, James Donald and Cora Kaplan (eds), *Formations of Fantasy* (Methuen, 1986), pp. 109–41.

94. Baldick, *The Oxford Book of Gothic Tales*, pp. xvi, xvii.

95. Martha Vicinus, ' "They Wonder to Which Sex I Belong": The Historical Roots of Modern Lesbian Identity', in *Which Homosexuality? Essays from the International Scientific Conference on Lesbian and Gay Studies, Amsterdam 1987* (GMP Publishers, 1989), p. 172.

96. Gabriele Griffin, *Heavenly Love? Lesbian Images in Twentieth-Century Women's Writing* (Manchester University Press, 1993), p. 91.

97. Studies of lesbian history include Lilian Faderman, *Surpassing the Love of Men: Romantic Friendship and Love between Women from the Renaissance to the Present*

(Women's Press, 1995); Faderman, *Odd Girls and Twilight Lovers*; and Emma Donoghue, *Passions between Women: British Lesbian Culture 1668–1801* (Scarlet Press, 1993).

98. Vicinus, ' "They Wonder to Which Sex I Belong" ', p. 172.

99. Linda Hutcheon, *A Poetics of Postmodernism: History, Theory, Fiction* (Routledge, 1988), pp. 83–101.

100. Zimmerman, 'Lesbians Like This and That', p. 9.

101. Vicinus, ' "They Wonder to Which Sex I Belong" ', p. 172.

102. Jennifer Terry, 'Theorising Deviant Historiography', *Differences: A Journal of Feminist Cultural Studies*, 3:2 (1991), 55–74.

103. Hutcheon, *A Poetics of Postmodernism*, p. 137.

104. Day, *In the Circles of Fear*, pp. 59–62.

CHAPTER 2

The witch and rebellious
femininity

'The Background into which the feminist journeying spins is the wild realm of
Hags and Crones. It is Hag-ocracy.'[1]

CRONES, COVENS AND SHAPE-CHANGING

The treatment of the witch as a signifier of lesbian/feminist interests and
ideals is by no means new. Warner utilizes the motif in *Lolly Willowes* (1926)
to challenge the misogynistic image of the spinster and to explore woman's
quest for privacy and personal space, while Barnes in *Nightwood* introduces
images of supernatural possession and animal transformation, associated
with witchcraft, to foreground the lesbian's abject position in society. As the
metaphorical links that Barnes creates between the two figures indicate, the
lesbian resembles the witch in both her exclusion from mainstream society
and the threat she poses to hetero-patriarchal values and conventional
models of femininity. The contrasting images of witchcraft created by the
two writers anticipate the different approaches to the motif inscribed in
lesbian fiction today. Both emphasize its transgressive aspect but, whereas
Warner's depiction is predominantly playful, including episodes in which the
heroine expresses disappointment at the conventional attitudes of her sister
witches and the tedious nature of the Sabbath they attend, Barnes's is much
darker in tone. Reference to 'sensuous communion with unclean spirits'[2] and
surreal dreams of funerals, combined with vampirish allusions to 'women
bloodthirsty with love',[3] highlight the perverse connotations of lesbianism
and its sadomasochistic associations.

The fictional representations of the witch produced in the past twenty-five
years discussed in this chapter, while continuing to reflect these polarities,
reveal a far wider range of interpretations. Images produced in the 1970s and

the early 1980s include the fearsome portrayal of the witch in the role of archaic mother in Hanrahan's *The Albatross Muff* and Tennant's *The Bad Sister* (1971), and the benign delineation of her as mystic and poet in Allard's *Légende*. Winterson's *Sexing the Cherry* and Donoghue's *Kissing the Witch* (1997), published recently, adopt a postmodern perspective, advertising the fictionality of the motif by introducing intertextual allusions. In contrast to Hanrahan and Allard who, influenced by the utopian idealism of the radical feminist movement, treat the witch as a signifier of a separate cultural space where women can pursue their desires unimpeded by male control, Winterson and Donoghue depict her as a construct projected upon women by hetero-patriarchal culture and individual men. They portray their female characters either becoming entrapped within its confines or cannily exploiting it for their own ends. Galford's *The Fires of Bride* reflects a similarly postmodern stance. Subjecting the motif to humorous parody, Galford utilizes it to comment playfully on lesbian/feminist concepts of female assertiveness and women's community.

An important source of inspiration for writers working in the 1970s and the early 1980s – which helps to explain the popularity the motif acquired in lesbian culture during these years – is the image of the witch created by the radical feminist movement. As Daly's *Gyn/Ecology* (1978) illustrates, the witch played an important role in the iconography of the movement as a signifier of those attributes, such as strength, independence and commitment to lesbian sisterhood, which patriarchy seeks to repress by recruiting women into heterosexual relations and encouraging them to conform to a docile model of femininity. Daly dedicates her study to her sister 'Hags, Harpies, Crones' (xii) and, creating her own inimitable blend of theory and myth, invites the reader to liberate 'the Wild Witch within her' by accompanying her on a journey intended to inspire 'the Lesbian Imagination in All Women'.

The witch also features in Daly's writing as a signifier of marriage resistance. Refusing to be confined within the domestic sphere to which women have traditionally been relegated, she sallies forth and creates her own woman-identified space, social and psychological. Her powers of shape-changing are interpreted by Daly as representing woman's ability to transform her psyche and experiment with new lifestyles and art forms. By creating a separatist community and experimenting with new linguistic structures, women, Daly maintains, can liberate themselves from the oppressive influences of patriarchal culture (pp. 330–1).

Daly's celebratory portrayal of the witch as a lesbian feminist icon is exhilaratingly heady stuff and understandably influenced many writers of fiction. Her representation of the witch as the signifier of a separate female sphere where women, having liberated themselves from male control, can create their own individual culture established the pattern for the treatment of the motif in novels and stories. Michèle Roberts employs the term 'witch' in *The Visitation* (1983) as a synonym for 'feminist' and treats the coven to which she belongs as an image for women's community and the consciousness-raising group that forms its nucleus.[4] She portrays her heroine Helen as participating in a group of this kind. The witch motif, as well as linking the female characters socially, also connects them on a psychic plane. Helen's kindly grandmother who, when alive, lends a sympathetic ear to her problems, materializes in her fantasies after her death in the guise of a benevolent witch. Helen senses her spirit hovering protectively in the air, watching over her.

Aileen La Tourette and Sarah Maitland are two of the first writers of fiction associated with the radical feminist movement to interpret the witch in a specifically lesbian light. Their representation in their jointly produced collection 'The Wedding Stories' (1984) reflects the influence of Daly. Topics on which 'The Wedding Stories' focus include lesbian resistance to the institution of marriage and the difference between the ugly caricature of the hag which male-supremacist culture misogynistically constructs and the spiritual beauty of the 'strong, creative women'[5] on whom men project it. Marriage resistance is, in fact, 'The Wedding Stories' central theme – one which in the concluding stages takes a dramatic form. Frances, the prospective bride, escapes from the altar in the nick of time, aided and abetted by her lover Jane. The latter makes an unexpected entry at the wedding banquet wearing a witch's mask and, disrupting the festivities, invites her to dance. The episode concludes with the two women defying convention and, to the astonishment of the groom and wedding guests, eloping together.

The portrayal of the witch in 'The Wedding Stories' displays other connections with Daly's representation. Like Daly, La Tourette and Maitland utilize the term 'witch' in two different ways: in a political sense as a synonym for 'lesbian feminist' and in a psychological one as a metaphor for the attributes of strength and rebelliousness which they believe women who identify as lesbian display. 'The Wedding Stories', like *The Visitation*, illustrate the revivifying effect that the radical feminist movement had on the motif of the witch, imbuing it with strongly lesbian/feminist associations and transforming it into a vehicle for the treatment of contemporary interests and ideas.

THE WITCH AS RADICAL FEMINIST ICON

Both *The Visitation* and 'The Wedding Stories' treat the motif of the witch relatively simply. Their representation is of interest more from an ideological than a literary viewpoint and, even taking into account the varied definitions of the genre that have emerged over the years, neither really merits the designation 'Gothic'. In contrast Hanrahan's *The Albatross Muff* and Tennant's *The Bad Sister* approach the motif in a considerably more complex manner and employ themes and structures that are typically Gothic in character. The fictions that the two writers create involve the reader in negotiating contrary versions of reality and value schemes. As is the case in earlier works of Female Gothic such as Shelley's *Frankenstein* (1818), they utilize multiple narrators and points of view and create a web of intermeshing storylines.[6] The fantasy world to which they introduce the reader is characterized by reference to the paranormal and by the blurring of the boundary between the mundane and the surreal.

The two novels are, in fact, very different in both location and ideological perspective. Whereas *The Albatross Muff* is set in the nineteenth century, the action of *The Bad Sister* takes place in the 1980s. Unlike Hanrahan, who wholeheartedly endorses radical feminist values, Tennant adopts a viewpoint that is ambiguous and difficult to define. Though clearly fascinated by radical feminist culture and social formations (the women's commune in particular) she treats them, on occasion, in an anti-feminist and even lesbophobic light. However, despite these differences, the two novels reveal significant points of affinity. Both base their portrayal of the witch on the 1970s radical feminist image. *The Albatross Muff* represents her challenging patriarchal constructs of femininity and motherhood, while *The Bad Sister* associates her with feminist community. And, in addition to reflecting the influence of radical feminism, both novels respond fruitfully to the psychoanalytic interpretations of the witch proposed by Creed and Catherine Clément. Instead of portraying the witch in a consistently heroic light as Daly tends to do, these two theorists foreground the intriguing contradictions she embodies. Clément in 'The Guilty One' describes her as an antiestablishment figure who lives on the margins of society and is bisexual. She associates her, on account of the connection she reveals with the feminine dimension of the Imaginary,[7] with the figure of the hysteric and emphasizes, in keeping with this, the unstructured and, ultimately, ineffectual nature of the acts of rebellion she performs.[8] Creed, interpreting the witch in the context of the Kristevan theory of the abject, relates her to the mythical figure of the archaic mother. The latter, Creed emphasizes, is a menacing figure who threatens to destroy the offspring which her womb brings forth. In this respect she epitomizes woman's contrary powers of generation/annihilation.[9]

Two features of Clément's theorization are particularly relevant to Hanrahan's and Tennant's novels. The first is her association of the witch with the figure of the hysteric as defined by Freud and her identification of her, as a result, with what she calls 'the subversive weight attributed to the return of the repressed'.[10] The repressed, as Clément defines the concept, is not only gendered in that it encompasses transgressive fantasies and desires stemming from the feminine dimension of the Imaginary, but also carries connotations of class. Clément associates it with the proletariat and its oppressed economic position. Hanrahan and Tennant interpret the witch in a similarly complex manner, portraying her as exemplifying a repressed dimension of existence, both sexual and social. The witch features in the novels of the two writers as an uncanny presence who haunts and disrupts the fragile security of male upper-class society. However, the precise significance of this disruption remains, in both their works, ambiguous. Its effectiveness is undermined by the fact that as well as being temporary it takes place on a purely personal level and has an air of fantasy about it. It thus represents, as is the case in Clément's theoretical account, an example of 'protest' rather than 'revolution'.

The second feature of Clément's account of the witch that is pertinent to the narratives of Hanrahan and Tennant is her reference to the hysteric as the witch's daughter.[11] The witch and the hysteric are related, Clément maintains, by the fact that both rebel against patriarchal conventions of femininity and have a destabilizing influence on society. Hanrahan and Tennant envision a similar connection between the two figures. Indicative of this is the way that they position the female character to whom they assign the role of witch in a maternal relationship to a younger woman who, like the hysteric, is bisexual and emotionally unstable.[12] As is often the case in Female Gothic, the two writers describe the maternal as alternating between the nurturing and the menacing. In consonance with this, they assign to the witch, at certain key points in the narrative, the ambiguous persona of archaic or phallic mother. She unexpectedly shifts from being a benevolent figure who generates and nurtures life to acting as the instrument of its destruction.

The most important role that the witch performs in *The Albatross Muff* and *The Bad Sister* is to introduce her 'daughter' hysteric to the world of Gothic fantasy. This, critics explain,[13] is a paranormal realm characterized by the breakdown of the borders between the familiar and the unfamiliar, where personal identity disintegrates and the integrity of the self starts to waver and collapse. The individual, on entering it, experiences a process of enthralment in which emotions of fascination and desire conflict with fear.[14] The movement into this realm, as is often the case in Gothic narrative, is heralded in the two novels by the sudden proliferation of images relating to shape-changing, doubling and the grotesque body. In addition to furnishing an occasion for the analysis of female subjectivity, its representation gives the two writers the opportunity to explore the theme of woman's quest for origins and 'family'. The witch, in introducing her daughter to this realm, is portrayed as initiating her into an alternative family structure. This takes the form of a mother/daughter dyad in which, as is the case in the infant pre-oedipal stage, male intervention plays no part. In constructing this myth of origins, both novels, as we shall see, introduce scenarios that re-enact fantasies of birth and seduction from a female viewpoint.

The Albatross Muff is unusual for the 1970s in that it advertises itself to the reader as a lesbian fiction not by treating the theme of 'coming out' or by focusing on sexual relationships between women but by utilizing a strategy which, as well as being strongly political, is more subtle. It gives a trenchant critique of codes of compulsory heterosexuality and their oppressive effect. Nineteenth-century London, the location in which Hanrahan sets her novel, allows ample scope for this, also providing a space for an analysis of inequalities relating to class. References to class tension, both explicit and covert, pervade the text. Hanrahan refers to the Chartist Riots of 1848 and describes London itself in terms of the divisions between rich and poor. Her description of the poverty-stricken districts of the city as a 'nightmare other-England'[15] peopled by beggars and pickpockets, where members of the upper class fear to venture, while recalling Charles Dickens' representation of the derelict areas of London, also carries connotations of Karl Marx's famous reference to the spectre of the proletariat which he envisaged haunting England.[16] Hanrahan transforms these borrowings from male writers, utilizing them to create a narrative that is emphatically lesbian/feminist in tenor. It illustrates the oppressive effect on women of the upper-class constructs of marriage and motherhood current in Victorian England and the ideology of female self-sacrifice underpinning them. In exposing the way in which these constructs entrap and, in some cases, destroy the female characters, Hanrahan inverts hetero-patriarchal values by assigning to them the role of 'monster' which anti-feminist films, such as *Basic Instinct* and *Fatal Attraction*, attribute to the lesbian or the single woman. Pregnancy and childbirth carry connotations in the novel not of life and emotional fulfilment, as is the case in fiction with a masculinist viewpoint, but of physical deformity and death. The heroine Stella describes her pregnant body as discoloured and monstrous: 'all pale with blue marks on her stomach' (p. 119). She fantasizes about giving birth not to 'a proper baby' but to 'a little black monkey that crouched inside her' (p. 185). In problematizing the conventionally positive associations of motherhood and birth by representing them as a source of danger and death, Hanrahan develops a popular topos in Female Gothic. Victor Frankenstein associates the creature he constructs with a 'workshop of filthy creation' [17] and rejects him in a fit of loathing. Esther, the narrator of Sylvia Plath's *The Bell Jar* (1963), identifies babies with the death of her creative talent as a poet. She is horrified, rather than impressed, by the scene of childbirth which her boyfriend Buddy forces her to witness.[18]

The emphasis on sickness and death that pervades *The Albatross Muff* is introduced in the opening chapter, with the account of the return of the ten-year-old Stella to England from the Australian colonies in the company of her mother and her nursemaid Moak. On the voyage home Stella experiences nightmares occasioned by her father's violent death in the bush and, on settling in London suburbia, quickly becomes aware of the injurious effect that sexual reproduction and family life have on women. On watching Pensa, her mother's friend and the wife of William Hall, reduced to the role of invalid by a series of miscarriages and difficult births, she thinks grimly, 'Marriage hadn't agreed much with Mama when she'd had it in New South Wales, but this was worse. Mrs. William Hall was so pale and sickly ...' (p. 58). Pensa, she notes, is reduced to lying like 'a limp rag-dolly on her couch' (p. 87), as trapped 'as a caged canary' (p. 42). Stella's childhood perception of the destructive effects of pregnancy and childbirth turns out to be prophetic. On reaching adulthood, she suffers a temporary breakdown and, on recovering, herself becomes prey to these 'monsters'. When Pensa dies from complications relating to childbirth, Stella embarks on a relationship with William Hall and unwisely agrees to become his second wife. She dies shortly afterwards in circumstances ironically similar to her predecessor's.

One of the few female characters in the novel to escape destruction by the 'monsters' of marriage and childbirth is Pensa's daughter Edith. Edith is Stella's childhood friend and becomes, for a brief period in her teens, her lover. She holds a similarly poor opinion of marriage and childbirth. Rejecting the mystificatory myth of 'baby in a rose bud' (p. 34), which adults attempt to palm off on children, she recognizes that 'getting born was nasty, and meant Mama losing blood and the bedroom full of smells' (p. 34). Babies, she perceives, rather than necessarily being 'a well spring of pleasure, a messenger of peace and love' (p. 146), as people conventionally make them out to be, can be aggressive and predatory. Her little brother Johnny sucks at her mother's breast with vampirish vigour, further weakening her health. Edith escapes the fate of Pensa and Stella and avoids death from childbirth less as a result of any act of self-assertion on her part than because her face is disfigured by a deformed lip. This blemish deters prospective suitors, making her, in terms of the specular economy of bourgeois Victorian society, unmarriageable. In the male-dominated world of Victorian England that Hanrahan describes, Edith exemplifies female independence. She eventually leaves home and earns a living by utilizing her gifts of imagination as a creative writer. Lesbian relationships and a literary career are depicted by Hanrahan, in typically radical feminist manner, as a means for woman to liberate herself from male control and escape the oppressive lifestyle and physical dangers that family life and childbirth involve.

At the centre of this narrative of female entrapment is the mysterious figure of Moak, the nursemaid who accompanies Stella and her mother on the voyage from Australia and settles with them in London. Positioned in the text as a signifier of 'the repressed' and the disturbing tendency it reveals to 'return', Moak has many of the attributes traditionally associated with the figure of the witch. In addition to carrying a hare's foot in her pocket and recognizing the inauspicious nature of the killing of some albatrosses on the voyage home, she typifies the abject and is an agent of social destabilization. Her origins, regarded from a white, middle-class viewpoint, are thoroughly disreputable. She has foreign blood in her veins, was formerly a convict and, as Stella discovers on the voyage home, has little regard for sexual propriety. As the narrative progresses, she becomes increasingly associated with the woman-identified domain of mother/daughter relationships and the contradictions of vulnerability/power that they epitomize. Although her mixed racial origins and working-class position make her socially and economically marginal, the authority she wields in the private sphere of the home as nurse and surrogate mother amply compensates for this. In Stella's eyes it gives her powers verging on the magical. Hanrahan's decision to assign to Moak the persona of witch illustrates her understanding of the contradictory position which, as feminist theorists illustrate, the nursemaid and the servant girl occupy in capitalist patriarchy. The two represent, as Clément and Hélène Cixous point out, 'the hole in the social cell'[19] of the upper-class family unit, the chink in the armour of bourgeois propriety where forces of social and sexual disorder can creep in. Jane Gallop, elaborating this interpretation, describes the nursemaid as 'a threshold figure'[20] since she exists both within the family and outside it. Though socially inferior and excluded from the privileges which her upper-class employers enjoy, she nonetheless resides, as Gallop perceives, 'at the heart of the family, in the cell nucleus. She is so much a part of the family that the child's fantasies (the unconscious) do not distinguish between "mother or nurse".'[21]

Gallop's account of the nursemaid's ambiguous social position precisely sums up the role that Moak occupies in relation to Stella and her mother – and Hanrahan subtly teases out the contradictions which her situation reflects. Like the proletariat, on whose labour upper-class society depends, Moak's presence, while vital to the material welfare of the two women, is simultaneously a source of fear. Like the streetsellers and beggars who people the streets of 'the nightmare other-England' (p. 112), she arouses in Stella a mixed response of fascination and repulsion. She makes no effort to conform to ladylike standards of dress or behaviour and is justifiably accused of being 'dirty and most dreadfully untidy' (p. 17). Yet Stella enjoys an emotional warmth in her relationship with her which her involvement with her mother lacks. Moak's tendency to transgress acceptable limits of gender, race and class, along with the attraction she holds for her young charge, is encapsulated in the naïvely ambiguous compliment the latter pays her:

> Moak was better than Mama. She was big and had a man's smell. Her skin was as brown as a gypsy's. Moak was a dark lady; though she wasn't a lady, according to Mama's standards ... (p. 13)

The contrary roles that Moak plays as agent of nurture/destruction and instrument of life/death form the basis of the novel's story line. Acting as Stella's protector, she defends her from the abusive attentions of one of her mother's male admirers. When, shortly after arriving in London, she is dismissed from the post of nurse on account of becoming pregnant, she vows, despite her enforced separation from Stella, to continue to protect her with 'her web of love' (p. 110). Stella, however, interprets her words as a threat rather than a promise. She feels increasingly guilty about her relationship with Moak and, when her baby brother falls sick and dies, suspects her of being responsible for his demise.

Moak's witch-like status is registered in the text in a variety of ways. Imagery carrying connotations of the abject and the Bakhtinian concept of the grotesque body is important in this respect. On the voyage from Australia

Moak, as suits her working-class status, is relegated to the 'below stairs' (p. 14) section of the ship. This, as well as being the province of the common members of crew, represents, on account of its enclosed, box-like shape, the 'lower' female faculties of sex and procreation. Stella, who is intrigued by its disreputable associations, vividly describes it as 'an animal world, where men took their pants down and bits of chaff stuck to your clothes' (p. 14). This 'below stairs' domain furnishes the setting for Moak's performance of a perversely sexual enactment of birth and breastfeeding. Stella, on visiting her there, finds her not, as she had expected, ministering to her baby brother but enjoying an illicit encounter with a 'baby' of a different kind:

> Moak already had her baby. And he was sucking at her titty hanging out; his carrot hair ... mixed with her skin and the clothes she wore under her dress. The clothes were secret. They were only revealed to Stella when it was night, and time for bed.... Her throat was stuck with noises. Carrots sucked on. He was rude, with his rump displayed. (p. 13)

This act of sexual licence that Stella, positioned by Hanrahan in the role of voyeur, watches Moak perform with a member of the crew illustrates the importance which woman's quest for origins assumes in the novel. The episode re-enacts a Freudian primal fantasy, bringing together displaced images of birth and nurture with the scene of parental intercourse in which the child surreptitiously watches its parents engage in sexual relations.[22] It symbolically foregrounds the sense of conflict and uncertainty that Stella feels about her own origins, torn as she is between feelings of commitment to her respectable bourgeois biological mother and her disreputable surrogate mother Moak.

This decidedly earthy portrayal of Moak illustrates the role that imagery relating to the grotesque body plays in the text. As well as exemplifying the protuberances and inarticulate grunts of the body in its grotesque manifestation, it brings together two key examples which Bakhtin himself cites: sexual intercourse and childbirth.[23] The representation of Moak in these terms foregrounds her role as agent of transgression – social, sexual and racial.

Similarly transgressive in emphasis, though very different in mood, is the portrayal of Moak in the majestic role of archaic mother, the persona which she assumes in Stella's imagination on the night of her baby brother's death. Looking back on the event, Stella is uncertain whether to regard it as fact or fantasy. She comments, 'Sometimes she was sure it had been a dream. The picture of Moak coming across the nursery – so big, with her cloak folded like albatross wings around her' (p. 73). In taking on the appearance of archaic mother, Moak is temporarily transformed into a figure of immense power associated with the primeval forces of night and death. The archaic mother signifies, according to Creed, 'the pre-phallic mother, the being who exists prior to the knowledge of the phallus, the mother as originating womb'.[24] In her contrary roles of agent of procreation/destruction, she epitomizes 'the point of origin and of end' (p. 17).

Moak makes a second appearance in this role in the concluding pages of the novel. Leaving the squalid cellar where poverty forces her to dwell and once again disrupting the tranquillity of the upper-class world, she makes her way through the genteel suburbs to wreak vengeance on the individual whom she regards as responsible for her 'daughter' Stella's death – Mr William Hall. Edith, who at Stella's request has summoned her to the deathbed, is astonished by the metamorphosis she has undergone and by the power she appears to wield. She comments, 'Moak was so much possessed by magic, that anything might be true.... Queer and brown and foreign, hate – or was it love? – had made her strong' (p. 203).

This description exemplifies the contradictions of love/hate, the mundane/magical which Moak, a disturbingly powerful creation, embodies. Hanrahan's portrayal of her and the ideological significance which it inscribes are particularly innovative since, while exemplifying the radical feminist emphasis on female strength and sisterhood, they also anticipate the focus on a multiplicity of transgressive identities and the problematizing of the division between homosexual/heterosexual identifications that characterize present-day queer politics. Moak transgresses convention, sexually, socially and from the point of view of race. Her attitude to sex eludes categorization since, while engaging in sexual relations with men herself, she nonetheless recognizes the physical and psychological dangers they pose to women. She disapproves of Stella's relationship with William Hall, perceiving the threat it represents to her life, but endorses the lesbian attachment she forms with Edith. In reconciling these apparent contradictions, Moak makes an appropriately complex centre for Hanrahan's Gothic fiction of history.

Tennant's *The Bad Sister* is of interest both in its own right and for the thematic affinities that it reveals with *The Albatross Muff*. In exploring the connections between the witch and the hysteric, Tennant, like Hanrahan, relates the two figures to a repressed dimension of existence which, in addition to being defined as feminine, carries proletarian associations. She portrays the witch and her 'daughter' hysteric linked in a passionate relationship, in which the former introduces the latter to a dangerously seductive fantasy realm where the borders between self and Other waver and collapse. However, these general similarities between the two novels serve chiefly to highlight the ideological differences they display. In contrast to Hanrahan, whose stance is explicitly feminist and who utilizes Gothic conventions both to expose the oppressive nature of patriarchal constructs of femininity and to affirm the value of lesbian and queer perspectives, Tennant's attitude shows signs of confusion. In utilizing Gothic conventions to interrogate the phallocentric representation of woman as Other, she falls into the trap of reproducing and re-enforcing homophobic and misogynistic stereotypes rather than challenging them.

As is illustrated by her subsequently published novel *Two Women of*

London: The Strange Case of Ms Jekyll and Mrs Hyde (1989), which creates a female version of Stevenson's famous work, Tennant specializes in the art of Gothic parody and pastiche. *The Bad Sister* also recasts, though in a manner which is less explicit, a classic Gothic text: James Hogg's *The Private Memoirs and Confessions of a Justified Sinner* (1824).[25] Hogg's story of the two brothers George and Robert, who, though born of the same mother, were, to judge from the rumours relating to their birth, sired by different fathers, is transformed by Tennant into the story of the two Scottish half-sisters Ishbel and Jane. Ishbel is the legitimate daughter of a member of the aristocracy and, as befits her social status, is conventionally feminine and charming. The illegitimate Jane, on the contrary, as her mother's adoptive surname 'Wild' signals, is aggressively antisocial and rebellious. Gil-Martin, the diabolic figure who, in Hogg's novel, plays the role of Robert's uncanny shadow and partner in crime, also makes an appearance in *The Bad Sister*. Tennant assigns to him, in fact, two different personae. He furnishes the inspiration for the character of Meg, the witch-like leader of the radical feminist commune to which Ishbel and her mother belong. In inveigling Jane into the unstable, transgressive world of Gothic fantasy and assisting her in the attempted murder of her half-sister Ishbel, Meg behaves in a similarly manipulative manner to Hogg's Gil-Martin who, we are led to believe, assists Robert in the murder of his half-brother George. In addition to furnishing the inspiration for Meg, Gil-Martin also appears in *The Bad Sister* under his own name, as a supernatural figure whom Meg creates by magic means. Jane alerts attention to his role in this respect when she refers to Meg's ability 'to conjure him from air, from leaves, from atoms, from water and fire ...'.[26]

One of Tennant's aims in *The Bad Sister*, as the novel's title suggests, is to interrogate the terms 'sisterhood' and 'sister', revealing them to be the site of different meanings and discourses. Like Hanrahan, she utilizes the conventional Gothic device of introducing narrators with different viewpoints and employs the dialogic perspective in which it results to question unitary ways of seeing. This, as well as introducing a note of uncertainty regarding the credibility of certain events recounted, prompts the reader to interpret the relationship between the sisters on two different planes. In social terms, Jane's obsessive hatred for her half-sister Ishbel and the attempt she makes to murder her reflect feelings of envy for her privileged lifestyle. However, Tennant's introduction of the motif of the double and her reference to Jungian ideas of androgyny also encourage us to see the relationship between the two women in a psychological light. From this viewpoint, Jane's attempted murder of Ishbel represents a symbolic bid to rid herself of the conventionally 'feminine' aspect of her own psyche, the aspect which she resents as subservient and conformist. Relevant here is her observation that 'The Muse is female, and a woman who thinks must live with a demented sister. Often the two women war, and kill each other' (p. 63). As well as reflecting different dimensions of reality, the murder of

Ishbel is ambiguous in other ways. Uncertainty exists as to whether or not it actually takes place, since it can be interpreted either as an actual event or as a figment of Jane's hysterical imagination.

In enacting the role of uncanny shadow and evil influence that she inherits from her connection with Hogg's Gil-Martin, Meg is instrumental in encouraging Jane's antisocial behaviour and murderous tendencies. By controlling her fantasy life, she initiates her into a realm of magic and transformation described in terms of witchcraft. Like the sorceresses and shamans to whom Clément refers in her theorization of the witch, who claim to have made 'fictitious voyages, transitions between the here and the beyond',[27] Jane experiences fantasies of flying and exotic voyages. She dreams of 'flying on my broomstick' and 'floating into the black night until I banged up against the stars' (p. 35). Meg also confers on Jane powers of physical transformation. As a result, Jane becomes proficient in the art of gender-bending, shifting to and fro between feminine and masculine personae. Commenting on the role she plays in exemplifying the new breed of woman produced by the Women's Movement, she boasts, 'I was unplaceable perhaps, a new genetic pattern like a neon sign in cuneiform, something ancient and known and at the same time infinitely strange' (p. 37). The mermaid and the siren, mythical figures employed by *fin-de-siècle* writers and artists to represent the monstrosity and degeneracy of the lesbian and the 'new woman',[28] are two other personae that Tennant assigns to Jane.

Jane's paranormal adventures take place against the backdrop of a modern version of the Gothic city and Tennant represents its inhabitants in a distinctly surreal light. The women lodging at the refuge in the vicinity of Jane's London flat reveal 'the unacceptable disfigurement' of 'great lakes of blue bruise on their faces and arms' (p. 35) and are contemptuously described as 'having the foolishness not to stop themselves from being beaten up'. The lesbians who visit the club adjacent to the refuge are represented, more bizarrely still, as displaying 'breasts which meet like soft pillows as they dance' (p. 3). Images of this kind present us with difficulties of interpretation. It is possible, of course, to read them as reflecting Jane's scornful view of women who are less adventurous than herself in exploring paranormal dimensions of reality. However, the fact that nowhere in the novel are they qualified or countered makes them problematic. They reproduce misogynistic stereotypes of femininity, portraying woman/lesbian as a form of monstrous spectacle. They illustrate, in this respect, the difficulties that confront the writer who attempts parodically to rework the grotesque images which patriarchal culture projects upon women. Rather than redefining the boundaries of the abject, she may end up reinforcing them and perpetuating, unchanged and unchallenged, existing prejudices.

Problems of a similar kind occur with Tennant's portrayal of Meg in the role of radical feminist. Tennant associates her, somewhat predictably, with the colour red, denoting blood and passion. Blood carries connotations of childbirth, murder and vampirism – and Meg reveals connections with all three. The sitting-room in her Chelsea home is ominously described as a 'forbidding dark red box' (p. 85), while the red décor of the radical feminist commune over which she presides recalls locations in earlier Gothic novels where performances of rebellious femininity are staged. One of the most famous is, of course, 'the red room' in Brontë's *Jane Eyre*, where the eponymous heroine is incarcerated as a punishment for relinquishing self-control and indulging in an outburst of temper. The decadence and claustrophobia of the settings in which Meg appears, and the way they reflect and accentuate her witch-like status, also resemble the locations which Robin frequents in Barnes's *Nightwood*. Robin's representation, in fact, looks forward to Meg's portrayal. She anticipates Meg in being described in terms of witchcraft, inhabiting a transgressive, twilight world of lesbian eroticism, and revelling in the abject role of outcast that society assigns to her.

In *The Bad Sister*, as in *The Albatross Muff*, the entry of the witch and her 'daughter' hysteric into the Gothic world and the transformations to which it gives rise are accompanied by the parodic enactment of fantasies of birth and seduction. Two episodes are particularly important in this respect. The first, which foregrounds the anxieties Jane experiences about her role as illegitimate offspring, centres on a party that she attends as a child at the home of her half-sister Ishbel. The children embark on a game of hide-and-seek and Jane and Ishbel conceal themselves in a cupboard in the master bedroom. Jane, in words evoking a fantasy of the return to the womb, describes how 'we ran down the dark passage as if we were trying to bury ourselves right in the centre of the house', eventually taking refuge in the cupboard 'under Ishbel's mother's skirts'. Here the two girls huddle so close together that, as Jane expressively puts it, emphasizing the blood tie which unites them, 'We could have been sewn together' (p. 113). The bedroom, however, is out of bounds to the children and the game concludes disastrously with Jane's humiliation. On attempting to extricate herself from the womb-like interior of the cupboard, she accidentally catches hold of one of the garments on the rail and finds herself 'standing in the bright light in the act of stealing Ishbel's mother's dress' (p. 114). The account she gives of her entry into the external world of the revellers, with its emphasis on humiliation and illicit deeds, uncannily repeats the circumstances of her actual illegitimate birth. It reproduces, in displaced form, the feelings of shame she experiences as a result of her socially disreputable origins.

The second enactment of the fantasy of birth which Tennant introduces is sexual in character. It reflects Jane's desire to be reborn into the empowering lesbian-feminist 'family' which Meg, with her associations of witchcraft and her role as commune leader, epitomizes. She describes how Meg, having enticed her into her Chelsea flat, seduces her and, adopting the role of phallic mother,[29] creates her anew in her own witchy image. She observes that, during the event, 'Meg's face had become huge above me. It blotted out the light, anonymous as the memory of a mother's face. From the side of the vast head sprung her snake-like locks ...' (pp. 85–6). The contrary powers of creation/destruction that the phallic mother enjoys are exemplified by the act of vampirish penetration which Meg performs as, with 'teeth long and white and pointed as stalactites', she punctures Jane's neck and draws forth two 'scarlet lozenges' of blood. She looks, Jane notes, like a 'woman who had given birth, where there is exhaustion, and blood and sweat' (p. 87).

Tennant's portrayal of Meg in the role of phallic mother invites comparison with Hanrahan's representation of Moak in the guise of archaic mother in the *Albatross Muff*. Significant differences emerge, however, between the writers' treatment of the two characters. Hanrahan depicts Moak in a multidimensional manner and emphasizes the contradictions of power/powerlessness that she displays. She juxtaposes references to Moak's symbolic significance with passages of naturalistic description which, by foregrounding her impecunious outcast position, furnish her with a convincing social context and foreground her humanity and pathos. Tennant, on the contrary, gives Meg no tangible social context and ascribes to her few vestiges of humanity. Meg appears, as a result, distinctly one-dimensional. Though credible enough in the the role of wicked witch, as a portrayal of a 1970s radical feminist she strikes the reader (this one at any rate) as a misogynistic caricature. Existing largely on the plane of fantasy imago, she reproduces and perpetuates the all-too-familiar stereotype of the lesbian as example of 'the monstrous-feminine'.

CULTURAL FEMINIST APPROACHES: FEMALE CREATIVITY AND THE WORLD OF NATURE

The motif of the witch, while remaining popular in the lesbian fiction of the 1980s, underwent a shift of interpretation during this period. In addition to denoting attributes of female strength and sisterhood, it became increasingly associated with the emphasis on woman's relationship with the natural world and the focus on her gifts of imagination and creative abilities promoted by the cultural feminist movement.[30] As is illustrated by Allard's *Légende*, a lesbian feminist version of the historical romance set in the coastal area of Brittany, Gothic narrative, particularly the strand known as 'Female Gothic' which foregrounds woman's complex fantasy life and her access to the psychic, makes an appropriate vehicle for articulating ideas of this kind. The belief that women will achieve fulfilment by developing typically feminine attributes of sensitivity and intuition and by engaging in creative writing is reflected both in the novel's content and in its fluid imagistic style.

Like Hanrahan and Tennant, Allard identifies the witch with a separate feminine dimension of culture that patriarchy seeks to repress. However, instead of representing her as a fearsome figure who destabilizes social and familial relations, as her two predecessors do, she emphasizes her creative abilities and her connections with the natural world. The two generations of women to whom Allard assigns the role of witch reveal affinities with Clément's theoretical account. On visiting the desolate locations that furnish the inspiration for their poetry, they find themselves, like the witch whom Clément describes, 'in impossible places, in bramble forests, on the heath ...' They also occupy, like her, a marginalized social role. From 'this position outside the family' they 'derive two gifts – the illuminism of lucid madness which, depending on its extent, is poetry' and 'second sight, a sharp penetration, speech both innocent and cunning'.[31]

Clément's reference to the contradictions that the witch embodies also sheds light on Allard's portrayal. On the one hand, as Clément emphasizes, the witch's connections with the realm of the Imaginary are emotionally empowering and make her a disruptive presence in society. On the other hand, however, because she is isolated and has no rational programme for social change, she is unable to defend herself against persecution and her acts of protest thus prove ineffectual. Allard's characters display similar contradictions of power/powerlessness. Though they challenge patriarchal control by creating a private space where lesbian partnerships and female culture can temporarily flourish, fear of reprisal from the local community forces them to keep this space secret. Both they themselves and the artifacts that represent them are eventually destroyed by the forces of hetero-patriarchy.

The emphasis on female entrapment and persecution which informs *Légende* relates the novel, as is the case with Hanrahan's *The Albatross Muff*, to the Gothic view of history as a sequence of oppressive events centring on the milieu of the family or local community. However, in contrast to Hanrahan, who exploits the links between Gothic and historical narrative to explore women's entrapment by the institution of marriage in an urban context, Allard utilizes it to represent the lesbian couple's struggle for survival in a rural setting. In keeping with the cultural feminist emphasis on the natural world that the novel encodes, she associates the two lovers, who are the focus of interest in the first half of the narrative, with the elements. Aurélie, a native of Brittany, has access, like her mother before her, to the occult. She draws the inspiration for her visions and the poetry in which she expresses them from the *menhirs*, a mysterious group of standing stones associated by the locals with pagan sacrifice and magic. Philippa, on the contrary, occupies the role of 'stranger' and displays links with the sea. She is raised as an orphan in the port of St Malo and, on discovering that her father was a British sailor, determines to emulate his way of life. She dresses as a man and succeeds in gaining employment on a ship. However, on discovering during the voyage that the crew has contracted a fatal disease, she decides that she has had enough of nautical life and leaps overboard. In an episode signifying a symbolic rebirth, she is washed up on the coast of Brittany where she is discovered by Aurélie who, in typically romantic manner, takes her home and nurses her back to health. The two women fall in love and embark on a relationship. In order to keep their union secret from the prying eyes of the villagers, Philippa continues to pass as a man and participates with Aurélie in a wedding ceremony. The relationship between the two women represents, on a symbolic plane, the union of earth and water. Philippa's connections with the sea relate her to characters from legend and fairy-tale such as the merman and Hans Christian Andersen's Little Mermaid. She moves, like them, from one element to another and, despite her efforts to accommodate the customs of her host community, continues to be regarded by the Brittany peasants as a foreigner. When, after some years, the fishing fleet to which she belongs is destroyed in a storm, she perishes with her fellows and is reclaimed by the waves whence she came. Aurélie too, on account of her reputation for witchcraft, is distrusted by her neighbours and is treated as suspiciously Other. Broken-hearted by Philippa's unexpected death, she loses the will to live and commits suicide by throwing herself from the headland. The villagers, assuming the couple to be man and wife, celebrate their fidelity by erecting a statue in their memory. This expression of public admiration is, however, short-lived. When, some years later, they inadvertently discover the truth about the couple's lesbian identity, they express their anger at this violation of convention by destroying the statue and casting it into the sea.

However, the story of Aurélie and Philippa, imaginative though it certainly is, is not the only focus of narrative interest since the novel concentrates, in fact, not on one pair of lovers but two. In addition to representing the partnership between Aurélie and Philippa, in the second half it deals with the attachment that develops between Aurélie's niece Mimi, whom she raises as her own child, and Adèle, the daughter of a neighbour. Mimi resembles Aurélie in that she writes poetry and possesses the gift of second sight. She employs her extrasensory gifts to gain access to past events and, in picturing Aurélie's and Philippa's initial meeting on the shore, celebrates the telepathic bond that unites her to them. Introducing a typically cultural feminist reference to female intuition and symbiotic bonding, she comments, 'It took that uncanny faculty of ours, that ability to become a part of each other's minds, for me to know what had happened that morning in the cove ...'[32]

Légende, as well as being of interest in terms of the encoding of cultural feminist values, also merits discussion from the viewpoint of its reworking of genre. The blood tie linking the two couples whose adventures Allard recounts, along with the generation gap separating them, as well as giving the novel an historical emphasis, transforms it into a lesbian version of a fictional genre conventionally popular with women writers and readers. This is the family saga. The saga, as Christine Bridgwood points out, while revealing similarities with the romance, differs from it in 'its lack of drive towards narrative closure'.[33] Instead of being organized around 'a few moments of transcendence (the first glimpse of the hero, the first sign of his admiration in the gaze, the kiss)', it treats the experiences of several different generations of women. In this respect, it is 'structured as a long-term process' (p. 168).

In employing the family saga as a vehicle for tracing the development of lesbian relations through two generations of women, Allard radically transforms the heterosexual values that it traditionally encodes. The version of the saga that she creates celebrates not the patriarchal family unit, dominated by a man, but an alternative lesbian unit composed of four women. It centres not on the family tree but on a communal network extending through time of a more radical kind, one which provoked controversy among feminists in the 1980s. This is the concept of lesbian continuum, formulated by Adrienne Rich.

Lesbian continuum and the cluster of ideas relating to it constitute in many respects an admirable frame for the construction of lesbian historical fiction – particularly the version with Gothic affiliations which Allard herself writes. In challenging the narrowly sexual definition of the sign 'lesbian' accepted by the sexologists and the medical profession, and expanding it to include other forms of woman-identified experience such as female friendship and camaraderie that are not overtly sexual, Rich explicitly refers to woman's relationship with the past. She describes lesbian continuum as encompassing 'a range – through each woman's life and throughout history of woman identified experience'.[34] In fact, one of the attractions that the theory of lesbian continuum held for lesbian feminists at the time was that, rather than relegating women to a temporal vacuum, it acknowledges the fact that they do have a history. However, Rich's treatment of lesbian history, though useful in the sense that it credits women with a past, lacks intellectual rigour. It has been criticized by Ann Ferguson for treating 'lesbian identity as a transhistorical phenomenon' and ignoring the fact that this identity, as we conceive it today, is relatively recent in origin.[35] However, the very lack of precision in Rich's treatment of history, which theorists and researchers find problematic, proves an asset to the creative writer. It permits scope for her play of imagination and leaves her free to fill in the gaps in Rich's account by creating her own fictional version of events. Allard exploits this imaginative licence to the full. Utilizing the concept of lesbian continuum as a framing device for her text, she creates a Gothic narrative-cum-fiction of history which traces the transmission of visionary powers and literary creativity from one generation of women to another.

In depicting the two lesbian couples whose adventures she recounts, Allard teases out both the differences and the similarities which their lifestyles display. In contrast to Aurélie and Philippa who, in order to conceal the sexual nature of their partnership from the villagers, have to pass as man and wife, Mimi and Adèle, living in a later period, are able conceal their relationship under the guise of friendship. And unlike Aurélie, who keeps the poems she writes to herself and has no thought of publishing them, Mimi takes the step of contacting a Parisian publisher and, with Adèle's encouragement, becomes in time an established writer.

However, in this decentered text with its collage of interweaving voices and narrative lines, it is the affinities between the two couples rather than the differences that achieve prominence. Their lives mirror one another in a number of ways. The partnerships of both, as well as suffering from a lack of social recognition, are disrupted by a series of violent events. These include Philippa's death at sea, Aurélie's suicide, the destruction of the statue erected in the couple's memory by the villagers, angered by the discovery of their lesbianism, and the mutilation of Adèle's portrait by her mother, outraged for similar reasons. The consequences of these acts of violence are registered in symbolic terms. References to the demolished statue and the mutilated portrait merge to become a metaphor for Aurélie's corpse lying broken on the rocks where, in her suicide leap, she fell. Their accumulative effect is to portray the four women as victims of provincial bigotry and persecution.

In tracing the affinities and connections between the four characters around whom her narrative revolves, Allard reworks certain motifs familiar to the reader from the tradition of Female Gothic. The most important is the representation of woman as Other. The significance that Allard assigns to the concept, as suits her cultural feminist viewpoint, is ambiguous and double-edged. As a projection imposed on woman by a misogynistic culture, it is recognized as oppressive but, as an affirmation of her unique creative abilities and a strategy to promote a separate female cultural sphere, it is also depicted in a positive light. Several different forms of marginalization and 'otherness' are explored in the novel: sexual, social and racial. They are illuminated by reference to Kristeva's discussion of the concept of the foreigner in *Strangers to Ourselves*. In the concluding section of her study, where she refers to Freudian theories of the unconscious and the uncanny, Kristeva states, 'The foreigner is within me, hence we are all foreigners.'[36] Allard arrives at a similar conclusion – and the quotation furnishes an appropriate epigram for her novel.

Imagery of sea and mist, as du Maurier's *Rebecca* and Susan Hill's *The Woman in Black* (1983) illustrate, is a common feature in Female Gothic. Allard employs it not only for atmospheric effect and to evoke an air of mystery but also to link the subjectivities of the various characters whom she portrays. She utilizes it to relate their internal emotions to their external environment, and to connect present-day occurrences with past events. These different uses come together in the episode in which Mimi, her eyes misting over with tears at the thought of the suffering that Aurélie and Philippa endured in the past, remembers that 'It was a misty morning when Philippa had first come to the cove' (p. 21). Mist is further associated with the visits that Aurélie pays to the *menhirs* and the visions they inspire in her.

The impression that *Légende* gives of a continuum of woman-identified experience connecting two generations of women is accentuated by the spiralling structure of the narrative and by the strategies of repetition that Allard introduces. Key events, such as Philippa's arrival on the Brittany coast, are recounted from more than one perspective, while the situation of Mimi, the representative of the present generation, frequently echoes that of her predecessors. For example, the reference she makes to her spring cough acts as a device to plunge the reader back in time to Philippa's account of the cough which she developed as a result of the epidemic she encountered on board ship.

By constructing an interplay of voices linking two different generations of women, Allard creates a text which, in terms of the cultural feminist aesthetic operating in the period of its publication, can be described as typically 'feminine'.[37] It is one in which the past and the present, the internal and the external, symbiotically merge and interact. As the title she selects for her novel signals, she aims to fashion not a realist account of the lesbian past but a *legendary* one: a history, to quote Clément's essay, 'of legend and myths – a history arranged the way tale-telling women tell it'.[38]

POSTMODERN FABLES: MASQUERADE AND MIMESIS

In 1983, the year prior to the publication of Allard's *Légende*, a novel focusing on the figure of the witch by a writer famous for her vivid representation of women's oppressed position in present-day society appeared in print: Fay Weldon's *The Life and Loves of a She-Devil* (1983). Weldon's portrayal of the witch is postmodern in style and was to establish the pattern for the treatment of the motif in the years ahead. By parodically reworking images appropriated from fairy-tale, she creates a controversial study of female initiative and self-invention, illustrating woman's ability to manipulate and exploit male-defined images of femininity. Though making only minor reference to lesbianism, the novel is relevant to the portrayal of the witch in the lesbian texts published in the late 1980s and the 1990s.

The Life and Loves of a She-Devil recounts the strategies which Ruth Patchett, eponymous she-devil and self-styled witch, uses to gain revenge on her rival in love Mary Fisher, a writer of romantic fiction who has usurped the affections of her husband Bobbo. Ruth also aims to win back her errant husband since, despite his infidelity, she continues to love him. Ruth's strong-jawed face with its hooked nose, along with the powers of shape-changing that she displays – the latter achieved in this twentieth-century fairy-tale not by magic but by means of role-play and cosmetic surgery – both relate her to the image of the witch. The havoc that she wreaks in the lives of Bobbo and his mistress also corresponds to the kind of destructive activities the witch allegedly performs. By adopting a series of different personae, including a member of a lesbian feminist commune, Ruth ingeniously contrives events so that Mary is reduced to penury and illness while Bobbo spends a period in gaol. Having successfully executed her plan of revenge, she turns attention to the second stage of her scheme: retrieving Bobbo's love. Registering as a patient at a clinic in California, she persuades the surgeons to transform her heavily built figure with its witch-like countenance into a replica of the petite and ultra-feminine Mary. The stratagem is successful. The novel concludes with Ruth, having completed her act of self-metamorphosis, living contentedly with Bobbo in the romantically situated high tower where Mary, now conveniently deceased, previously resided.

However, though acknowledging Ruth's achievement and the initiative and will power which it requires, Weldon portrays her reconstruction of her persona in a decidedly equivocal light. She foregrounds the triumph of art over nature, culture over biology, which it signifies but simultaneously emphasizes the high price that Ruth pays in return. Ruth's act of self-transformation, in addition to involving her in financial expense and physical pain, can be criticized as anti-feminist since, in altering her looks to conform to Bobbo's tastes, she accepts the dominance of the male gaze and endorses rather than challenges male-defined images of female beauty.

Weldon's fable of female self-invention and transformation is open to different interpretations. As well as illustrating twentieth-century woman's rejection of essentialist notions of identity and illustrating her ability to recreate herself in different roles and guises, it foregrounds the power which, even in the present feminist era when women might be expected to define their own interests and values, the binary stereotypes of angel/monster, beautiful heroine/ugly witch continue to exert on their lives. The petite and pretty Mary, since her appearance conforms to masculine expectations of beauty, is successful both socially and sexually. She is, as Ruth enviously remarks, 'accustomed to love'.[39] Ruth, in contrast, on account of her unfeminine appearance and her refusal to passively accept her husband's infidelity, is typecast as a she-devil and witch. Ironically, it is Bobbo who first refers to her in these terms. It is he who unwittingly gives her the cue to adopt the role of she-devil and exploit it for purposes of revenge. Having done her best to be a good wife and mother, Ruth unexpectedly changes tack and determines 'to give hate its head' (p. 43). As she sardonically remarks, 'Peel away the wife, the mother, find the woman, and there the she-devil is' (p. 44). She-devil and witch are, of course, not the only roles with which Ruth experiments. In remodelling her body into a replica of the pretty, petite Mary, she also exploits the contrary one of angel.

Weldon's representation of Ruth's manipulation of male-defined roles and stereotypes of womanhood responds fruitfully to Irigaray's theory of masquerade and mimesis. Basing her analysis on the discussion of femininity by the 1930s analyst Joan Riviere, Irigaray describes the feminine masquerade as the acting out by the female subject of a series of male-defined roles and scripts; she comments:

> I think the masquerade has to be understood as what women do in order to recuperate some element of desire, to participate in man's desire, but at the price of renouncing their own. In the masquerade they submit to the dominant economy of desire in an attempt to remain 'on the market' in spite of everything.[40]

Irigaray, however, does not leave the matter there, with woman relegated to the position of the passive victim of male scripting. She proposes a strategy that the female subject can employ to challenge and exploit male-defined roles and identities. She terms this 'playing with mimesis'.[41] Woman, Irigaray argues, by parodically mimicking conventional images of femininity and introducing into her performance an element of excess, can expose the artifice and inauthenticity of these images. In this way, she can resist male control and hopefully achieve a degree of agency. Ruth, in enacting the roles of monster/angel and carrying her performance to extremes, creates an inventive variation on this strategy.

The utilization of the motif of the witch to expose the stereotypes and fantasy images which masculinist culture projects upon women and to explore the female subject's attempt to negotiate them is also a feature of lesbian fiction from the late 1980s and the 1990s. This approach to the motif contrasts with that adopted by the earlier writers Hanrahan, Tennant and Allard. Instead of employing it to represent a separate female cultural space which, however fragile and temporary, allows women to pursue their desires relatively unimpeded by male interference and control, writers publishing at the present time, such as Winterson, Donoghue and Galford, utilize it to explore the misogynistic or idealizing images of femininity that phallocentric culture projects upon women, along with the female subject's attempts to subvert or exploit them. This approach agrees, in conceptual terms, with the poststructuralist view articulated by Fuss[42] and Butler,[43] that lesbian/feminist culture, rather than being a 'free space' where women are exempt from phallocentric control, is inextricably related to a phallocentric economy. Fuss criticizes Wittig for maintaining that 'a lesbian is innocent and whole, outside history, outside ideology'.[44] From this point of view, masculinist attitudes and conventions are perceived to be all-encompassing. In consequence, any act of resistance to them has to take place from within, rather than outside, their parameters. This perception, as well as being integral to Irigaray's concept of mimesis, is implicit in Butler's theorization of gender and performativity.

Winterson's *Sexing the Cherry*, in illustrating the contrary uses to which the image of the witch can be put, exemplifies this poststructuralist point of view. Winterson employs the motif both to examine the oppressive effect of misogynistic/homophobic stereotypes of femininity and to explore women's efforts to negotiate and rework them. The novel is a work of postmodern fantasy which interrelates different generic conventions, including picaresque romance, seafarer's yarn and Gothic fable. It juxtaposes and interweaves two main narrative lines: the Dog Woman's story relating her experiences in seventeenth-century London and the story that her adopted son Jordan recounts which focuses on voyages to fantastic countries, both geographical and speculative. While differing in location and imaginative range, both narratives inscribe a queer perspective and introduce imagery relating to the grotesque body. Lesbianism does not enjoy a privileged position in the novel but is treated as one of a number of transgressive sexualities, including homosexuality, bisexuality and sadomasochism. Transgressive heterosexual passions are also foregrounded, as is illustrated by Jordan's infatuation with the mysterious dancer whom he encounters in the course of his travels and his admission that he is uncertain whether she is real or a figment of his imagination. In a sentence illustrating the fluid interaction between self and Other that characterizes Winterson's treatment of subjectivity, he asks himself, 'Was I searching for a dancer whose name I did not know or was I searching for the dancing part of myself?'[45]

  The image of the witch achieves prominence in both stories. Jordan's narrative, employing the 'box within boxes' structure that contributes to the novel's intricacy of design, introduces a digressive set of tales which simultaneously develops and subverts, from a lesbian/feminist viewpoint, the story of 'The Twelve Dancing Princesses' from the collection of the brothers Grimm. In contrast to the Grimms' version, which is recounted by a male narrator, the princesses relate their own histories. And instead of portraying themselves living happily ever after with their husbands in marital bliss, they emphasize the oppressive aspects of marriage and describe their efforts to escape from male control. Rapunzel's story, which Winterson appropriates from another fairy-tale, typifies this ideological inversion, illustrating the persecutory use that society makes of the construct of the witch. She tells Jordan that she was not imprisoned in a tower by a wicked witch, as is the case in the traditional version, but chose to live there of her own free will with a lesbian partner. Her partner did not identify as a witch. On the contrary, it was Rapunzel's family who, consumed with homophobic hatred, projected the epithet upon her; as Winterson observes, they 'were so incensed by her refusal to marry the prince next door that they vilified the couple, calling one a witch and the other a little girl' (p. 52). The sealing of the door to the tower which, in the traditional version of the tale, is the method the witch employs to keep Rapunzel prisoner, becomes, in Winterson's version, an act of self-defence on the part of the lesbian couple. It is notably unsuccessful. The story concludes on a grim note, with the prince forcing an entry into the tower through the window. Having tied up Rapunzel, he forces her to watch her partner being blinded in a field of thorns, an act of brutality that signifies sexual castration in symbolic terms. It is a vindictive act of revenge, reflecting man's resentment at the lesbian subject's ability to usurp his place and to achieve sexual pleasure independent of male control.

  Rapunzel's account of the persecutory uses which homophobic society makes of the construct of the witch is counterbalanced by the very different treatment the Dog Woman affords the motif. This, though disturbing in the initial stages, has an optimistic outcome. With her gigantic stature and enormous mouth, large enough to hold six oranges, the Dog Woman has personal experience of the oppressive effect of abusive epithets and stereotypes. She commences her story by explaining that, as is the case with the naming of Rapunzel's lover, the appellation 'Dog Woman' is not of her own choosing but has been foisted upon her by other people. While ostensibly denoting her occupation as a dog-breeder, it also reflects, more unpleasantly, society's cruel response to what it regards as her grotesque appearance. Her father, regarding her as a monstrosity on account of her exceptional size, attempted to sell her to a freak show when she was a child. And, as she sardonically remarks, she does not go to church on Sundays but obediently follows the priest's injunction that 'gargoyles must remain on the outside' (p. 14). However, rather than collapsing under the weight of this oppressive treatment, the Dog Woman manipulates the image of monstrosity that society projects upon her, utilizing it for purposes of self-assertion. From a playful point of view, she employs her immense strength to toss an elephant in the air, while on a more serious plane she wages a private war against the repressive effects of Puritanism, picking up its male representatives by the scruff of the neck 'the way a terrier does a rat' (p. 88). Winterson's complex treatment of the Dog Woman's subjectivity, combined with her celebratory portrayal of her physical exploits, transforms her from an example of monstrosity and abjection to an image of female heroism. The Dog Woman's sexuality, it is interesting to note, anticipates present-day attitudes, since, in eluding precise categorization and reconciling contraries, it merits the term 'queer'. Though forming a strong attachment to Jordan and admitting that she would have liked to have had a child of her own, she simultaneously problematizes heterosexual relations. Her description of her one and only experience of sexual intercourse, a bizarre event in which her male partner, on account of her vast size, admits to feeling 'like a tadpole in a pot' and is reduced to 'burrowing down the way ferrets do' (p. 107), has the effect of defamiliarizing the sex act. Rather than making her appear ridiculous, as would be the case in an anti-feminist narrative, it makes both the act and her male partner look absurd. It also wittily parodies the misogynistic fantasy of the *vagina dentata*. Winterson's heroic representation of the Dog Woman and the radical re-evaluation of the image of female monstrosity that it achieves successfully challenge misogynistic prejudices. It contributes, in this respect, towards renegotiating the boundaries of the abject.

Donoghue is another writer who, as the title of her collection *Kissing the Witch* indicates, focuses on the lesbian revision of the fairy-tale and utilizes tactics of postmodern parody to transform the image of the witch. 'The Tale of the Kiss', in representing the peasant girl narrator deliberately assuming the role, investigates strategies relating to mimesis, teasing out the problems and contradictions that confront the woman who attempts to experiment with them. It also explores the power relations and acts of deception which such strategies can involve. The narrator, determined to resist woman's traditional destiny of marriage, leaves her parents' home in the village and takes up residence in a derelict cave overlooking the sea. Expecting the villagers to ostracize her, she is surprised when gifts start appearing at the mouth of the cave and people seek her out to ask her advice on personal problems. Recognizing that 'It is a witch they were wanting',[46] she decides to fulfil their expectations and act the part. Covering her head with a black scarf to conceal her youthful appearance, she hands out potions to the sick, counsel to the anxious and punishments to the guilty. On contemplating the power that the role of witch confers on her, she astutely perceives that it is not of her own making but has been assigned to her by the villagers themselves. While doing her best to exploit it, to 'shape it and conceal it and flaunt it and use it' (p. 213), she recognizes the ironic truth that 'It was power these scaly-fingered fishwives and their husbands could have used themselves, if they'd only known how, but instead they told themselves how helpless they were, and came and laid power at my feet' (p. 214).

The narrator is, on the whole, content with her solitary existence and with the authority the role of witch enables her to exercise – that is, until one day a beautiful red-haired girl arrives at the mouth of the cave seeking her help in achieving independence from her family. The narrator succeeds in persuading the girl's parents to allow her to lead the lifestyle of her choice and, when asked by the girl what she demands in return, rashly replies, 'A kiss'. To her surprise, the girl braves the dangers attendant on kissing a witch and grants her request. However, in so doing she introduces a new sense of frustration and dissatisfaction into the narrator's life. As the latter comments, 'On the whole I am inclined to think that a witch should not kiss. Perhaps it is the not being kissed that makes her a witch: perhaps the source of her power is the breath of loneliness around her' (p. 81).

In this instance the strategy of mimesis, though recognized to be a source of female power, is discovered to conflict with the individual's personal happiness. The authority the role of witch confers fails in the long run to compensate for the emotional isolation which its performance involves. The story concludes on a romantic note with the narrator admitting that she misses the girl and that, as a result, is no longer content to live alone. She decides to follow her to the village and, sacrificing her independence and authority, invite her to live with her. She recklessly determines, 'I would give her my heart in a bag and let her do with it what she pleased. I would say the word "love"' (p. 227).

In concluding the story with reference to the narrator's discovery of her love for the girl and her decision to relinquish her solitary way of life and seek her out, Donoghue imaginatively interrelates old and new fictional forms. She creates a fairy-tale version of the lesbian 'coming out' story.

The postmodern representation of the image of the witch as a cultural construct that, though frequently utilized for purposes of persecution, can be manipulated and exploited by women to personal advantage, is also a feature of Galford's *The Fires of Bride*. *The Fires of Bride* is the first example discussed in this study of that paradoxical fictional form, a comic Gothic text. Comic Gothic, as critics observe,[47] subverts and undermines the conventional expectations of the genre in that instead of arousing feelings of terror and fear it releases these emotions in humour. Humour and laughter have a reassuring effect on the reader, signalling that the protagonist will triumph over adversity and that, whatever setbacks s/he encounters *en route*, events will turn out happily in the end. Lesbian versions of comic Gothic, such as the novels of Galford and Scott, do not employ humour in a random fashion but utilize it satirically, for ends relating to sexual politics. They direct it at carefully chosen targets, such as the contradictions of heterosexist attitudes or the intricacies and absurdities of lesbian codes of behaviour.[48] In *The Fires of Bride*, it is hetero-patriarchal perspectives, along with the excessive idealism of the radical feminist movement, which Galford subjects to playful ridicule. She also parodies Gothic conventions and critiques the stereotypes of femininity associated with the genre, concentrating particular attention on the figure of the witch.

The action of Galford's novel takes place on Cailleach, an imaginary isle off the coast of Scotland contemptuously described by an unappreciative Lowlander as 'a miserable hole, the outermost island of the Utter Utter Hebrides'.[49] In Gaelic Cailleach means 'the Crone', a word recalling the radical feminist terminology of Daly. It furnishes a suitably eerie location for Galford's narrative, providing scope for the conventional Gothic stage set of ancient castle, ruined convent and mysteriously swirling mist. The island, as its name signals, represents a woman-identified space where women, in accord with radical feminist and cultural feminist values, can create their own community and way of life, relatively free from hetero-patriarchal intervention. However, the emphasis which Galford places on the island's fantasy aspect serves to locate it in the realm of utopian fiction, thus preventing the reader from taking it and the events which occur there too seriously. She opens the novel by sketching three different cultural scenarios for which it might furnish the setting: 'Gothic thriller', 'late Victorian romance' and 'wicked caper movie' (p. 31). This self-conscious gambit has the effect of foregrounding the fictionality of the island. It also serves to situate Galford's novel in the context of the lesbian/feminist transformation of popular genres and to prepare the reader for the fantastic events and the parodic treatment of Gothic conventions which lie ahead.

A cultural feminist focus on female creativity is strongly in evidence on Cailleach. The women who live there or visit the place, whose intertwining stories comprise the narrative, are all writers, artists or mystics. Lizzie, the heroine of the frame story, works for Caledonian Television. She visits Cailleach with the aim of interviewing the locals and producing a feature on the place. Maria, whom she encounters in the course of her travels, is an artist and has psychic powers. In achieving access to the island's turbulent past, she discovers that she has a double in an earlier period of history. This is the eleventh-century nun Mhairi who entered the local convent in order to avoid being coerced into an oppressive marriage. After taking her vows, she found an outlet for her artistic talents by illuminating religious manuscripts. She devoted her brief life to making copies of the Book of Bride, an apocryphal gospel recounting the life of the female twin of Jesus Christ that the orthodox Catholic Church dismisses as heretical. The figure who mediates between the three women, persuading Maria to visit the island, introducing her to Lizzie and unearthing a copy of Mhairi's Book of Bride, is Catriona, clan chieftain and, as becomes apparent from her high-handed and eccentric behaviour, resident witch. Catriona owns the castle that dominates the island and, exploiting her reputation for witchcraft, inveigles Maria into a love affair and introduces her to the pleasures of Cailleach. These include fantasies induced by the local malt, a sightseeing tour of the island in an ancient Land Rover and an invitation to an exceptionally rowdy clan-gathering.

Catriona is a vehicle for Galford's playfully satiric treatment of motifs relating to witchcraft, both traditional and radical feminist in association. The witch as a representative of the abject, who lives in a dirty house full of 'filthy secrets',[50] is humorously parodied in the description of Catriona's turret room, where she sleeps surrounded by bookcases crowned with stuffed herring gulls, cases of Little Arctic butterflies and boxes overflowing with ancient manuscripts. The powers of shape-changing traditionally ascribed to her are also treated humorously. On first experiencing Catriona's hospitality, Maria confesses to regarding her as a cross between Circe and the witch of Nordic fairy-tale. She is scared that her uncanny hostess will transform her 'in classical vein into a squealing pig, penned up in a sty with other bewildered ex-dinner guests' or serve her up, in fairy-tale manner, as 'a tidbit on a baking tray on the scrubbed wooden table in the castle kitchen' (p. 41). Although these particular events turn out to be fanciful, Catriona succeeds in performing other acts of transformation which, though not achieved by magic, are of key importance. As well as engineering Maria's visit to Cailleach, she persuades her, by dint of bribery and bullying, to return to the career of artist which, due to financial insecurity and lack of recognition, she has temporarily renounced. And, in an episode resembling Merlyn's duel with Madame Mim in T.H. White's The Sword in the Stone (1938), she utilizes her skills of shape-changing to vanquish her arch-enemy the Reverend Murdo MacNeish. This repressive personage is a member of the Second Schismatic Independent Kirk of the Outer Isles and, as is signalled by his attempts to suppress Catriona's vigorous love life, occupies the role of killjoy and homophobe in the narrative.

Galford's portrayal of Catriona's exuberant personality and vivacious love affairs gives her the opportunity to comment humorously on radical feminist images of womanhood. She simultaneously celebrates and pokes fun at the image of the radical feminist hags and crones whom Daly delineates. While emphasizing the strength and resourcefulness of the women who inhabit Cailleach, she also exposes their egocentricity and obstinacy and, by focusing attention on their competitiveness and feuding, illustrates the fragility of feminist ideals of sisterhood. Cultural feminist concepts of female spirituality and psychic power which flourished in the early 1980s and are unequivocally celebrated by Allard in Légende are likewise subjected to playful ridicule.

The Fires of Bride is exceptionally close-knit in structure, an effect achieved by Galford's skillful manipulation of the traditional Gothic device of employing multiple narrators and points of view. The novel's opening line, brusquely voiced by Lizzie's boss at the Caledonian Television Centre, 'Next item on the agenda: Forward Planning. I'm afraid the time has come for us to do another story on the Outer Hebrides ...' (p. 3), introduces the reader to an accumulative network of interlocking stories, recounted both by the main characters and subordinate ones. Records of the history of the island painstakingly inscribed by Catriona's seventeenth-century ancestors, Maria's stories of her left-wing parents and, at the heart of the novel, the apocryphal history of Saint Bride herself are some of the most memorable narratives. In fact, the isle of Cailleach positively blossoms with stories. Some, such as Catriona's anecdote about the native sheep with 'front and back legs of different sizes – evolved for hill-walking' (p. 44), merit the adjective 'tall'. Others remain untold but are tantalizingly hinted at, as Maria discovers when, studying a map of the island, she is intrigued to discover 'names without places attached to them, impossible to pronounce, but hinting of stories' (p. 67).

The numerous acts of storytelling which the novel comprises illustrate the fact that culture is in a continual state of evolution and flux. They also foreground, in typically postmodern manner, the interrelation existing between the discourses of 'literature' and 'history'.[51] Galford illustrates the process whereby eyewitness accounts of events take on, as a result of repeated telling, a secretion of fantasy, becoming transformed, with the flux of time, into oral fiction. Commenting on the fertility of the eleventh-century imagination, she reminds the reader that 'Even the simplest thread of a mildly interesting rumour can be twisted and knotted by time and distance into an intricate tapestry of heresy and riot' (p. 119).

The Fires of Bride also introduces other ideas relevant to a poststructuralist approach to history. Galford focuses attention on the different methods available to the individual to achieve access to the past and exposes the dubious nature of so-called historical objectivity and 'truth'.[52] She positions the reader into comparing conventional academic methods of historical research, such as taking part in an archæological dig or studying an early manuscript, with strategies dependent on the imagination. The latter include making spectral contact with figures and events from the past, as Maria finds herself doing when tramping round the island's historical sites, and constructing fictional accounts of earlier periods as Galford herself does in the episodes of the novel describing Mhairi's life in an eleventh-century convent. They involve the interrelation of past and present, fantasy and fact – key factors in Galford's wittily inventive fiction of history.

As the works of fiction discussed in this chapter illustrate, the figure of the witch has been an important source of inspiration for writers of lesbian Gothic over the past twenty-five years, giving rise to a varied array of literary and ideological delineations. The motif assumes a number of different manifestations in novels and stories. These include: powerful crone signifying a separate female space where women can pursue their desires unimpeded by male control; fearsome sorceress representing the contradictions of power/powerlessness embodied in the figure of the mother; benevolent wise woman exemplifying woman's creative abilities and her links with the natural world; and, with the advent of postmodernism and queer theory, a construct utilized by masculinist culture to control the female sex that women, in a performative act of self-invention, attempt to manipulate and exploit. These different images, as well as illustrating the versatile manner in which writers handle the motif, give an insight into some of the changes that have occurred since the 1970s in lesbian/feminist theory and politics, as well as in approaches to lesbian fiction.

The style and tone that writers adopt in depicting the witch also differ, revealing an increasing degree of self-consciousness and stylization as we move into the postmodern era of the 1990s. They range from the emotional intensity of Hanrahan's *The Albatross Muff*, which reproduces the traditional Gothic focus on death and the uncanny, along with its conventional evocation of terror and fear, to the self-reflexive humour of Galford's *The Fires of Bride* and the parodic critique of lesbian/feminist values that the novel encodes. As is illustrated both by Galford's novel and by Winterson's and Donoghue's transformations of the fairy-tale, the approach which writers adopt towards the Gothic mode has become increasingly self-conscious over the years. It is as if, having recognized the limitations and misogynistic distortions in the images of femininity it produces, they are now only willing to utilize it parodically or in a tongue-in-cheek fashion.

Spectral visitation, the motif discussed in the following chapter, has inspired a similarly varied assortment of fictional representations and interpretations. However, it furnishes a vehicle for exploring issues of a different kind. Achieving prominence in lesbian theory and fiction in the late 1980s, when reference to psychoanalysis and a focus on sexuality and erotic fantasy had entered the lesbian agenda, it is associated in theoretical and literary discourse with the Freudian concept of 'the return of the repressed'. The mysterious workings of memory, the complexities of lesbian sexuality and desire, and the intense and often contradictory emotions involved in the experience of mourning are some of the topics foregrounded in the texts discussed.

NOTES

1. Mary Daly, *Gyn/Ecology: The Metaethics of Radical Feminism* (first published 1978; Women's Press, 1979), p. 3. Further page references are to this edition and are in the text.

2. Djuna Barnes, *Nightwood* (1937; New Directions, 1961), p. 168.

3. Barnes, *Nightwood*, p. 148.

4. Michèle Roberts, *The Visitation* (Women's Press, 1983), p. 157.

5. Daly, *Gyn/Ecology*, p. 18.

6. For discussion of these conventional features of Gothic narrative see Day, *In the Circles of Fear and Desire*, pp. 42–50; Jackson, *Fantasy*, pp. 103–12; and Punter, *The Literature of Terror*, pp. 76–98.

7. 'The Imaginary [from a Lacanian viewpoint] corresponds to the pre-oedipal period when the child believes herself to be a part of the mother, and perceives no separation between itself and the world. In the Imaginary there is no difference and no absence, only identity and presence' (Toril Moi, *Sexual Textual Politics: Feminist Literary Theory*, Methuen, 1985, p. 99).

8. Catherine Clément, 'The Guilty One', in Catherine Clément and Hélène Cixous, *The Newly Born Woman* (1975), trans. by Betsy Wing (Manchester University Press, 1987), pp. 5–6.

9. Creed, *The Monstrous-Feminine*, p. 83.

10. Clément, 'The Guilty One', p. 9.

11. *Ibid.*, p. 34.

12. See Elizabeth Wright (ed.), *Feminism and Psychoanalysis: A Critical Dictionary* (Blackwell, 1992), pp. 163–5.

13. Day, *In the Circles of Fear and Desire*, pp. 16–23.

14. *Ibid.*, pp. 23-7.

15. Barbara Hanrahan, *The Albatross Muff* (Women's Press, 1978), p. 112. Further page references are to this edition and are in the text.

16. Karl Marx, 'The Manifesto of the Communist Party', in Frederic L. Bender (ed.), *Marx: Essential Writings* (Harper and Row, 1972), p. 240.

17. Mary Shelley, *Frankenstein* (1818; Oxford University Press, 1969), p. 55. Moers discusses 'the drama of guilt, dread and flight surrounding birth and its consequences' in Shelley's novel in *Literary Women*, p. 93.

18. For reference to Plath's 'presentation of babies, traditionally a symbol of woman's fulfilment and new life, as instruments and harbingers of death', see Annette Kolodny, 'Some Notes on Defining a Feminist Literary Criticism', *Critical Inquiry*, 2 (1975), 81.

19. Clément and Cixous, 'Exchange', in *The Newly Born Woman*, p. 150.

20. Jane Gallop, *Feminism and Psychoanalysis: The Daughter's Seduction* (Macmillan, 1982), p. 146.

21. *Ibid.*, p. 145.

22. See J. Laplanche and J.B. Pontalis, 'Fantasy and the Origins of Sexuality', in *Formations of Fantasy*, p. 19.

23. Bakhtin, *Rabelais and His World*, pp. 353–4.

24. Creed, *The Monstrous-Feminine*, pp. 20, 26.

25. Sedgwick discusses Hogg's novel in *Between Men*, pp. 97–117.

26. Emma Tennant, *The Bad Sister* (Picador, 1979), p. 85. Further page references are to this edition and are in the text.

27. Clément, 'The Guilty One', p. 7.

28. See Bram Dikstra, *Idols*, pp. 263–7.

29. For reference to 'the phallic mother' see Creed, *The Monstrous-Feminine*,

pp. 158–63. Creed describes her as 'a terrifying phantasy of sexual difference' (p. 158) and emphasizes her links with the classical image of the Medusa.

30. For reference to the cultural feminist movement and its values see Cheris Kramarae and Paula A. Treichler, *A Feminist Dictionary* (Pandora Press, 1985), p. 112. Zimmerman discusses the 'Green World' fiction, which the movement helped to inspire, in *The Safe Sea of Women*, pp. 79–86.

31. Clément, 'The Guilty One' pp. 54–5.

32. Jeannine Allard, *Légende* (Alyson Press, 1984), p. 13. Further page references are to this edition and are in the text.

33. Christine Bridgwood, 'Family Romances: The Contemporary Popular Family Saga', in Jean Radford (ed.), *The Progress of Romance: The Politics of Popular Fiction* (Routledge and Kegan Paul, 1986), p. 167. Further page references are to this edition and are in the text.

34. Rich, 'Compulsory Heterosexuality and Lesbian Existence', pp. 51–2.

35. Anne Ferguson, 'Patriarchy, Sexual Identity, and the Sexual Revolution', in Nannerl O'Keohane, Michelle Z. Rosaldo and Barbara C. Gelpi (eds), *Feminist Theory: A Critique of Ideology* (Harvester, 1982), p. 149.

36. Julia Kristeva, *Strangers to Ourselves*, trans. Leon S. Roudiez (Harvester Wheatsheaf, 1991), p. 192.

37. For discussion of the concept of 'the feminine text' see Judith Kegan Gardiner, 'Mind Mother: Psychoanalysis and Feminism', in Gayle Greene and Coppelia Kahn (eds), *Making a Difference: Feminist Literary Criticism* (Methuen, 1985), pp. 136–9.

38. Clément, 'The Guilty One', p. 6.

39. Fay Weldon, *The Life and Loves of a She-Devil* (Hodder and Stoughton, 1983), p. 5. Further page references are to this edition and are in the text.

40. Irigaray, *This Sex*, p. 133.

41. *Ibid.*, p. 76.

42. Fuss, *Essentially Speaking: Feminism, Nature and Difference* (Routledge, 1989), pp. 42–3. Zimmerman discusses the debate and proposes her own interpretation and 'solution', in *Lesbians Like This and That*, p. 56.

43. Butler, *Gender Trouble*, pp. 120–8.

44. Fuss, *Essentially Speaking*, p. 43.

45. Jeanette Winterson, *Sexing the Cherry* (Vintage, 1990), p. 40. Further page references are to this edition and are in the text.

46. Emma Donoghue, *Kissing the Witch: Old Tales in New Skins* (HarperCollins, 1997), p. 211. Further page references are to this edition and are in the text.

47. For discussion of comic versions of Female Gothic see Vincent, 'The Mirror and the Cameo', pp. 153–5.

48. For reference to the subversive effects of humour in lesbian fiction see Palmer, *Contemporary Lesbian Writing*, pp. 78–97.

49. Ellen Galford, *The Fires of Bride* (The Women's Press, 1986), p. 5.

50. Creed, *The Monstrous-Feminine*, p. 77.

51. See Hutcheon, *A Poetics of Postmodernism*, pp. 105–9.

52. See *ibid.*, pp. 87–101.

CHAPTER 3

Spectral visitation: the return
of the repressed

'For each act of forgetting, there is something that comes back; for every act of
memory, a loss.'[1]

NEW APPROACHES TO THE SPECTRAL

Haunting and spectral visitation, whether associated with an individual or a
place, are among the most common signifiers of the uncanny in Gothic
fiction. Freud explains the dread of encountering spirits and ghosts by
reference to our repressed fears of death and our anxiety that, on
materializing before us, they may carry us off to their dark domain.[2]
Cixous, paraphrasing his thought, remarks that 'The Ghost is the fiction
of our relationship to death, concretized by the specter in literature'.[3] She
argues that the reason people fear meeting a ghost is not just that the event
acts as the harbinger of death but that it disturbs the borderline between this
world and the next since, in crossing the boundary, 'the dead man returns in
the manner of the repressed'.[4]

Since the nineteenth century the treatment of spectral visitation in works
of fiction has come to be associated with a trio of related topics: sexuality,
memory and childhood. They interact with differing degrees of complexity
in a number of classic texts. In Henry James's 'The Turn of the Screw' the
governess's infatuation with her reclusive employer finds expression, in
displaced form, in a series of encounters with the ghostly figures of Peter
Quint and Miss Jessel, former employees in the house where she resides. She
becomes increasingly obsessed with the corrupting influence which she
believes they exert on her two young charges. The protagonist of Walter de
la Mare's 'Out of the Deep' (1923), on inheriting the mansion where he
experienced unhappiness as a child, finds himself haunted by the ghosts of
family servants, who emerge disconcertingly from below stairs. The latter

have been interpreted as representing emotions relating to his childhood and his feelings of unresolved hatred towards the uncle who bequeathed him the house.[5] M.R. James's collection focusing on the supernatural[6] also includes several stories exploring the relation between psychic events and childhood.

Sexuality, memory and childhood also achieve prominence in works of fiction by women. The appearance of the ghostly nun in Charlotte Brontë's *Villette* (1858), though discovered to have a rational explanation, can be read, from a psychological point of view, as representing Lucy Snow's repressed sexuality.[7] The ghost of the young Cathy in Emily Brontë's *Wuthering Heights* (1847), persistently tapping at the window in an attempt to regain re-entry into the world of the living, also has strongly sexual connotations. That the motif of spectral visitation is by no means out of date but continues to fascinate writers and readers is illustrated by the success which Hill's *The Woman in Black* has enjoyed, initially as a novel and more recently in dramatic form as a West End play. Hill introduces a number of motifs popular in Female Gothic, including the haunted house, maternal bereavement and the death of a child.

As a vehicle for exploring lesbian sexuality and relationships, spectral visitation has had a chequered history and reveals intriguing contradictions. Castle draws attention to the way that, in works of fiction dating from the eighteenth to the twentieth century, the introduction of imagery of ghosts and haunting has had the effect of disembodying the figure of the lesbian and decorporealizing her desire, thus negating physical intimacy between women and 'denying the carnal bravada of lesbian existence'.[8] Imagery of this kind, however, as she goes on to show, though ostensibly introduced to discredit lesbianism and to avert the threat that it poses to the *status quo* by rendering it insubstantial, in actual fact does the reverse. It emphasizes the persistence with which lesbian desire continues to surface, despite the efforts made by hetero-patriarchy to render it invisible and eradicate it, disturbing and destabilizing heterosexual codes and values.

Since the advent of the lesbian movement in the 1970s approaches to spectral visitation, where lesbianism and homosexuality are concerned, have undergone a significant shift of emphasis. As mentioned in the introductory chapter, the motif has been reclaimed by critics and theorists, including White, Fuss and Castle herself, as a vehicle to discuss issues relating to lesbianism and homosexuality. White, drawing on the concept of 'the return of the repressed', utilizes reference to spectral phenomena to discuss the transgressive aspect of lesbian desire and its disruptive effects, both personal and social. The excess which it signifies, she illustrates, is registered in films such as *The Haunting* (1963) by the introduction of imagery of poltergeists and apparitions.[9] Fuss, in contrast, utilizes the motif to investigate the interaction between homosexual and heterosexual economies and perspectives. In exploring the inextricable link between the two, she turns naturally (or rather supernaturally!) to metaphors of ghosts and haunting:

Heterosexuality can never fully ignore the close psychical proximity of its terrifying (homo)sexual other, any more than homosexuality can entirely escape the equally insistent social pressure of (hetero)sexual conformity. Each is haunted by the other, but here again it is the other who comes to stand in metonymically for the very occurrence of haunting and ghostly visitations.[10]

Although the event has gone unnoticed by critics, the motif of spectral visitation has also been reclaimed by writers of lesbian fiction. Haunted, as it were, by the lesbophobic treatment which, as Castle illustrates, the motif received in earlier texts, they utilize it, in a creative act of exorcism, to explore sexual relations between women and their transgressive dimension from a lesbian viewpoint. Instead of employing it to decarnalize lesbian desire, as writers did in the past, they introduce it in contexts foregrounding the physical dimension of lesbian relations and emphasizing the importance of the body. Like theorists, writers of fiction treat the motif in different ways. Zanger and Martinac, adopting an approach similar to Castle and White, employ scenarios centering on ghosts and haunting to explore the transgressive power of lesbian desire and to demonstrate its refusal to be repressed. They illustrate its powerful effect, one which, they emphasize, is pleasurable as well as disturbing to the individual on whose psyche it intrudes. In Zanger's *Gardenias Where There Are None* and Martinac's *Out of Time* the desire that one woman feels for another or the urge she feels to articulate it verbally and express it in writing is depicted as a form of excess which, refusing to be contained within the parameters of fantasy, insists on erupting and overflowing into everyday life. Brown, in contrast, employs the motif more in the manner of Fuss. She utilizes it to investigate the interplay existing between psychological and social lesbian structures and hetero-sexual ones. The majority of women who identify as lesbian are raised in a conventional family context and develop their identities both in relation to and in tension with the heterosexual model furnished by their parents. It is the formation of lesbian subjectivity in this environment, and the problems in which it can result, which Brown explores in *The Haunted House*.

Winterson's work of historiographic metafiction *The Passion* (1987) furnishes us with yet another version of spectral visitation. The two interrelating narratives that the novel inscribes, the one recounted by the French peasant Henri centring on the Napoleonic campaigns and the other told by Villanelle, the daughter of a Venetian boatman, describing lesbian love, both include episodes introducing the uncanny and spectral presences. Henri's narrative foregrounds the pervasive climate of death brought about by Napoleon's obsession with military conquest, while Villanelle's addresses the problematic aspects of lesbian existence and its abject associations.

Donoghue and Schulman, the two most recent contributors to the lesbian treatment of the spectral, both focus, like Winterson, on the topic of death. However, they treat it from a different angle, introducing imagery of ghosts and haunting to explore the experience of lesbian/gay bereavement. The Gothic realm of the uncanny, conventionally exemplified in the ghost story by the spectral visitor who emerges from beyond the grave, is represented in their novels by the event of death itself. Donoghue's treatment of bereavement is personal in emphasis. She portrays her lesbian narrator, grief-stricken by the death of her partner who has been killed in a car crash, haunted by her image and by memories of their life together. Schulman's focus is wider in scope and explicitly political. Locating her narrative in New York, she explores the strategies that AIDS survivors, traumatized by the death of friends and lovers, employ to cope with their loss and to attempt, as it were, to exorcise their ghosts. The characters she portrays are depicted as suffering, in many cases, from a double loss. They are haunted not only by the memory of the people with AIDS but also by thoughts of the families who have ostracized or rejected them. In interweaving references to homosexual bereavement with heterosexual rejection, Schulman combines the focus on the transgressive aspect of homosexuality, which characterizes Castle and White's approach to the spectral, with Fuss's reference to the interaction between homosexual and heterosexual economies.

The writers discussed in this chapter, in reclaiming the motif of ghosts and haunting from a lesbian viewpoint, appropriate and transform images and scenarios from earlier Gothic texts. Topics of sexuality, memory and childhood continue to inform their work but, in being treated in a lesbian context, assume a newly transgressive slant. The image of the haunted house, while maintaining the connotations of 'family' and the female body familiar to the reader from the novels of Radcliffe and Shirley Jackson, likewise undergoes a shift of interpretation. Instead of necessarily serving as the location of the heterosexual family unit, it assumes, on occasion, a queer resonance, becoming the site of the lesbian subject's discovery of her sexuality and the partnerships she forms. Problems relating to woman's quest for origins, which, as we have seen, are addressed in Hanrahan's *The Albatross Muff* and Tennant's *The Bad Sister*, also play a key role in the novels discussed below. Whereas Zanger and Martinac approach the topic indirectly, Brown treats it explicitly. She examines the unstable aspects of her lesbian protagonist's childhood and explores the conflicts she experiences between masculine and feminine identifications and versions of reality.

Another feature of the ghost story that receives a change of emphasis in lesbian Gothic is the relationship between the spectral visitor and the mortal heroine. Zanger and Martinac, while developing the portrayal of the visitor as a signifier of frustrated female passion found in Charlotte Brontë's *Villette* and Hill's *The Woman in Black*, and representing her as assuming the role of the heroine's double as occurs in Radcliffe's *The Mysteries of Udolpho*,[11] considerably modify the portrayal of the heroine. Whereas in mainstream Gothic it is the ghost or the monstrous double who carries homosexual associations,[12] here the heroine too identifies as lesbian. And far from appearing passive and sexually naive, as is conventionally the case,[13] she emerges as experienced. She is portrayed, however, as suffering from problems and insecurities of a sexual or psychological kind. As her involvement with her spectral double develops and she steps deeper into the world of Gothic fantasy, she and the reader become increasingly aware of the pressures they exert on her psyche.

Brown modifies the relationship between the spectral visitor and the object of haunting even more radically. In fact, she inverts it, breaking the conventional mould. In her version of the motif, it is not homosexuality but heterosexuality that occupies the role of 'repressed', emerging at a crucial moment in the heroine's life to haunt her and destabilize her existence. *The Haunted House* concludes with the narrator discovering that the residence where she and her lesbian partner have set up home is structurally unsound. The walls are crumbling and about to cave in. The building and the partnership it metaphorically represents are haunted and rendered unstable by her memories of her childhood relationship with her parents and the unresolved conflicts stemming from it.

Donoghue and Schulman similarly transform the scenarios of bereavement and mourning which they create. The narrator of Donoghue's *Hood* has kept her lesbian relationship with her partner private from colleagues and family. As a result, she feels forced to conceal the intensity of the grief she experiences at her death. On the contrary, in Schulman's *Rat Bohemia*, the funerals of AIDS victims take place in public view and acquire the status of elaborate urban rituals. They enable the mourners to give expression to their grief and are treated as a 'family' event. Generally, however, it is the queer 'family' composed of the deceased's friends and lovers, not the biological one, which escorts the coffin to the crematorium and participates in the funeral wake.

The works of fiction reviewed in this chapter, while differing markedly, are linked in many cases by a focus on sexuality and the body. It is ironic to note that the motif of spectral visitation, which provided writers in earlier periods with imagery to decarnalize lesbian sexuality, has become in the late 1980s and the 1990s a vehicle for foregrounding its physical aspect. Writers benefit, in this respect, from the liberal approach to sex which characterizes present-day lesbian and queer culture. Topics which in the 1970s they would have avoided mentioning, for fear that they would invite the accusation that lesbians are a sick bunch of women unnaturally obsessed with sex and thus play into the hands of homophobes, they now boldly confront and address.[14] The novels discussed here illustrate this trend. As well as celebrating the pleasures of lesbian sex and erotic fantasy, they also explore some of the emotional and psychological problems that the lesbian subject can encounter. Prominent among these are her fear of failing to achieve a voice and have her identity recognized; anxieties relating to personal relationships, such as her apprehensions that she may lose her sense of autonomy and have her ego submerged in her partner's; worries relating to gender identification, including the fear that she will appear 'masculine' or 'a freak'; and problems relating to jealousy and its disruptive effect on both the partnership and the group.

Another topic which, as mentioned above, writers foreground is the individual's relationship with her body and its desires. In addition to describing lesbian sexual encounters, Zanger and Martinac explore themes of erotic fantasy and examine the individual's personal and communal involvement with the past. Donoghue and Schulman, by juxtaposing images of the dead and dying body with the image of the deceased alive and well in the imagination of the bereaved, emphasize the contradiction between the sexual pleasures of the past and the frustration and barrenness of the present, to which the death of a partner gives rise. In treating these topics writers develop the perceptions of earlier contributors to Female Gothic who focus, directly or indirectly, on sexuality and the body, such as Radcliffe,[15] Flannery O'Connor and Carson McCullers.[16] They build on the ideas of their predecessors and introduce new perceptions of their own.

DESIRE, DISTURBANCE AND THE LESBIAN PAST

Zanger's *Gardenias Where There Are None* and Martinac's *Out of Time*, the two novels discussed in this section, while differing in plot and location, reveal thematic and structural similarities. In both, the excess which lesbian desire signifies in phallocentric culture manifests itself in the form of a female figure from an earlier period of time making contact with a woman living in the present and involving her in a brief love affair. The protagonist's encounter with the spectral figure, while involving her on a psychological plane in a confrontation with a ghostly double who reflects aspects of her own personality, also furnishes her, in terms of woman's quest for origins, with an entry into the lesbian past. The encounter, though emotionally disturbing, is nonetheless represented as instructive. From a psychological viewpoint, it enables the protagonist to achieve a greater degree of self-awareness while, in terms of woman's search for origins, it gives her and the reader an insight into constructs of femininity and female sexuality from an earlier era. It also has the effect of enabling the protagonist to make contact with a lesbian community or 'family'. This reflects the fact that the spectral visitor, in addition to assuming the role of her double, plays the role of her ghostly foremother in certain episodes.

Zanger's *Gardenias Where There Are None* centres on the familiar Gothic motif of the haunted house. The motif carries symbolic connotations of the womb and is discussed by Freud in relation to the uncanny. Commenting on the ambiguous significance of the phrase '*das Unheimliche*', he points out that it denotes, on an obvious level of meaning, something which is secret and concealed. However, it also signifies, paradoxically, the homely and the familiar. Both meanings come together in the images of the womb and the female body. These, though striking us as hidden and mysterious, are familiar in the sense that we originate from them. Freud also comments on the associations that the haunted house has with death. Uncanny sensations, he observes, occur particularly in relation to objects related to death, such as corpses and houses allegedly haunted by the spirits of the deceased.[17]

The motif of the haunted house has understandably proved popular with women writers. It is utilized in works of Female Gothic to explore the complexities of female sexuality and, as Claire Kahane comments, to investigate 'the problematics of femininity which the heroine must confront'.[18] The maze of passages and underground vaults in the castle that forms the setting for Radcliffe's *Udolpho* has obvious connotations of sexuality and the body. The attic of Thornfield House in Charlotte Brontë's *Jane Eyre*, where the mad Bertha Mason is incarcerated, exudes an air of frustrated female passion which on occasion breaks free from constraint to pervade the mansion as a whole. Both buildings, as Nina da Vinci Nichols remarks, comprise 'the history of ghostly women and destructive powers, inimical to life and vitality'.[19] The association of the haunted house – whether ancestral mansion or newly built residence – with a ghostly double whose disturbing presence the heroine encounters is developed in twentieth-century fiction in du Maurier's *Rebecca*, Gilman's *The Yellow Wallpaper* (1892) and, with specifically lesbian significance, Shirley Jackson's *The Haunting of Hill House*.

The house that Zanger chooses as the location for her narrative has little in common with the affluent, upper-class dwellings in the novels cited above. On the contrary, it is a ramshackle building on a farming estate which Mel Myer, a graduate student at a college in Michigan, ignoring the advice of her friends who dismiss the place as a dump, agrees to rent for the term. As is generally the case in Gothic fiction, the house is ambiguous in implication, functioning simultaneously as a refuge and a trap. It is a refuge, in the sense that Mel hopes that it will provide her with a peaceful environment where she can pursue undisturbed her ambitions to become a writer. However, its capacity for entrapment becomes apparent when, on moving in, she finds herself unable to settle to the task of writing but instead embarks, as if compelled by some external force, on a ceaseless round of renovation. In a passage resembling Gilman's *The Yellow Wallpaper* the act of stripping away the different layers of paper, in which she obsessively engages, becomes a metaphor for the revelation of the history of the house and the interests of its previous occupants. Like the protagonist of Shirley Jackson's *The Haunting of Hill House*, Mel catches herself regarding her new home not as an inanimate object but as a person. She envisages 'the lath like ribs, the plaster like flesh, the wallpapers like layers of skin'.[20]

The haunted house in fiction and film generally reveals its secrets gradually – and the one where Mel has set up home is no exception. While busy renovating, she comes across a series of clues which shed light on the identities of the previous occupants. On opening a trunk in the barn, she finds a man's suit from an earlier period and, more ominously, a gun. She starts to resent the emotional grasp which the house exerts upon her and admits to wishing that she lived somewhere else, 'where people own houses, not the other way around' (p. 48). She is also puzzled by the presence of a floral scent, the precise nature of which she is unable to identify, that accompanies her from room to room.

It is at this point in the narrative that Camille, the spectral visitor responsible for Mel's entrapment and her compulsive urge to decorate, makes her first appearance in the narrative. Communicating with Mel in typewritten exchanges and telepathic dialogue, she elucidates the mystery of the scent. It is, she explains, gardenia. It was given to her by her lover Sam who, since she was unable to read and had no knowledge of perfume, mistakenly assumed it to be camellia. Sam lived with her in the house while working as a labourer on the estate and, in order to obtain the job, chose to dress as a boy. The details of the two women's unhappy love affair, which, on account of Sam's sexual inhibitions and feelings of guilt, remained unconsummated, are conveyed to Mel by her spectral visitor in a series of fragmented utterances that become increasingly passionate as the narrative progresses. Though sensing the air of menace pervading the house, Mel, like many a Gothic heroine before her, feels incapable of packing her belongings and moving out.

The contrary emotions of attraction/repulsion that Mel feels towards the house reflect, the reader perceives, her ambivalent response towards Camille. As is often the case with fictional representations of encounters with the uncanny, she is simultaneously scared and elated by her confrontation with the spectral world. In the words of Mark S. Madoff, who discusses the role which the dichotomy 'inside/outside' plays in Gothic narrative, she willingly 'transgresses the boundary between outside and inside *because* the outside is open, obvious, familiar and unsatisfying in its simplicity and rationality' and '*because* the inside is closed, obscure, exotic and alluring'.[21] As a result of her act of transgression, she finds herself entering, again to quote Madoff, 'a forbidden, dangerous place whose articulation with the common, outside place is problematical' (p. 51). However, though her involvement with Camille places her 'inside' the Gothic realm, she maintains sufficient links with 'the outside' world of mundane reality to perceive the abnormality of her situation. As she wryly observes, acknowledging the contradictions and absurdity of her predicament, 'I was in love, hopelessly in love with a woman who'd been dead for eighty years and who inhabited my life more fully than I'd ever allowed a living woman to' (p. 146).

In exploring the interplay between the mundane and spectral dimensions of existence, Zanger makes inventive use of the conventional device of 'doubling', representing the subjectivities of the characters interrelating and merging. As Day argues, doubling is employed in Gothic narrative not only to enhance the air of mystery but also to illustrate the disintegration of a stable unified identity in which the protagonist's encounter with the spectral frequently results. His description of the way in which, in Gothic, 'The line between self and the Other begins to waver, and the wholeness and the integrity of the self begins to collapse'[22] is pertinent to Mel's disturbed psychological state.

Zanger introduces two significant examples of doubling in the novel. Both are erotic in nature and give her the opportunity to explore problems relating to lesbian identity and sexuality. The first hinges on the fact that the spectral

Camille recognizes in Mel aspects of her lover Sam. As she admits, it is Mel's resemblance to Sam that initially prompted her to manifest herself to her. The reader likewise recognizes affinities between the two women. Influenced by the repressive attitudes current in the era in which she lived, Sam regarded sexual relations between women as sinful and experienced confusion about her gender identity. She describes herself as a 'worthless freak' (p. 159) and, far from enjoying crossdressing, insists that it made her feel neither masculine nor feminine but, as she bleakly puts it, 'nothing' (p. 104). Mel, like Sam, has been raised in a sexually repressive environment by parents who refused to acknowledge her lesbianism (p. 713). In addition both women have been involved in incidents of domestic violence. Sam's relationship with Camille, as the concluding pages of the novel reveal, terminated tragically in the latter's death when Sam accidentally pressed the trigger of the gun with which she planned to take her own life. Mel, we learn, was previously involved in a relationship with a female alcoholic who humiliated and physically abused her. Sam's circumstances thus mirror aspects of Mel's troubled past. The doubling of the two characters culminates in a powerful seduction scene in which Camille pleads with Mel to give her the physical expression of the love which Sam, on account of her feelings of guilt, denied her. She poignantly demands, 'Be Sam for me' (p. 106). Mel complies – and the relationship between mortal protagonist and spectral visitor culminates in a passionate love scene.

However, it is not only Sam who occupies the role of Mel's double. The ghostly Camille does too. From the moment of her initial appearance in the text the reader has doubts about whether she actually exists or whether she is merely a projection of Mel's imagination, an erotic fantasy she has conjured up to compensate for feelings of loneliness in her new home. Zanger keeps the evidence for and against these alternatives nicely balanced, maintaining a note of mystery. In the love scene between the two women with which the novel concludes, Camille's status continues to remain ambiguous. The episode is written in such a way that, while it is possible to read it as a sexual encounter between two autonomous female figures, it can alternatively be interpreted as a fantasy on Mel's part accompanying a solitary act of masturbation.

A feature of Zanger's narrative that sets it apart from the conventional ghost story is the affirmative viewpoint it adopts towards lesbianism and the positive note on which it terminates. The sexual encounter between mortal protagonist and spectral visitor, instead of concluding with the death of the former and with the stigmatizing of lesbianism as a symptom of female immaturity, as is the case in Shirley Jackson's The Haunting of Hill House, is accepted as valid. In fact, it has a positive outcome for both parties. Camille, having succeeded in achieving sexual fulfilment after a sexual drought of eighty-odd years (!), ceases to haunt Mel, while Mel herself returns to everyday life, eager to form a stable, non-violent relationship. Her decision to treat her encounter with the uncanny as the theme for a novel indicates her mature ability to distance herself emotionally from the event while exploring it intellectually. Having recovered from the experience of psychic enthralment that her encounter with the spectral Camille involved she returns, apparently none the worse for wear, to her former life as student and writer.

Martinac's *Out of Time* resembles Zanger's novel in more ways than one. Like Zanger, Martinac brings together the conventions of the ghost story and the historical romance to recreate an episode from the lesbian past. She also portrays a female figure from an earlier era materializing in spectral form and involving a woman living in the present in a brief love affair. The incident of spectral visitation in Zanger's novel is motivated, as we have seen, by frustrated desire. Camille, having been prevented from consummating her relationship with Sam by the latter's feelings of guilt, projects her feelings of unrequited passion on to Mel and persuades her to become her lover. In Martinac's novel the materialization of the female spectre reflects frustrations of a different kind. It is prompted by the lesbian's unfulfilled ambition to achieve identity and recognition by publishing a work of autobiographical fiction. Woman's aspiration to create an image of herself for posterity by producing a work of this kind is regarded by Barbara Johnson as a motivating impulse in works of Female Gothic, and she cites Shelley's *Frankenstein* as a key example.[23] Martinac develops this idea, with reference to lesbian subjectivity. As she illustrates, writing and publishing are particularly important to the woman who identifies as lesbian since, as a result of external censorship or feelings of personal insecurity, she is frequently denied an identity and a voice. *Out of Time* portrays a lesbian living in the 1980s assisting a predecessor from the 1920s to overcome these problems by retrieving the manuscript that she has produced, editing it and seeing it into print.

Out of Time opens in the manner of the classic ghost story with the narrator Susan, who is herself a writer, coming across a photograph album from the 1920s in an antique shop while searching for a birthday present for her lover Catherine. The album contains a collection of snapshots recording the friendships between four women whom she comes to term colloquially 'the Gang'.[24] It creates, in this respect, a link between the present and the past.

Susan's initial encounter with the album is pervaded by a strong sense of the uncanny. In fact, reference to two of the experiences cited by Freud as exemplifying the sensation are mentioned in the text: the contradictory feeling that something is familiar but at the same time unfamiliar, and losing one's way.[25] Despite the fact that Susan has never before set eyes on the album, on opening it and contemplating the pictures which it contains, she experiences an immediate sense of recognition. And, on attempting to return to the shop on a later occasion, she finds herself unable to locate its whereabouts.

The narrative that develops from Susan's purchase of the album traces her growing involvement with 'the Gang'. It centres on the attempt made by two of its members, both deceased, to make contact with her. Harriet, who was an actress by profession, and her lover Lucy, who wrote novels and plays, pay Susan a series of spectral visits. Lucy engages her in conversation while Harriet initiates a flirtation with her. In the romantic relationship that develops between Susan and Harriet, the uncanny is very much in evidence. Idly wondering what a kiss was like in the 1920s, Susan finds her question unexpectedly answered. She feels lips brush her cheek: ' "That's what a kiss was like in 1926", someone said, and the honeyed tone told me that it was Harriet' (p. 49). As this passage illustrates, the sexual encounters between mortal protagonist and spectral visitor are lighthearted in nature and delightfully sensuous. Responding to Harriet's kisses, Susan describes her mouth as tasting lusciously of 'melted chocolate and brandy' (p. 55). Harriet, intent on taking the relationship further and involving Susan in a full-scale love affair, dismisses her anxieties about infidelity to her partner with the frivolously witty remark, 'It's for your education. Tell yourself it's for history!' (p. 55). The comment is, of course, self-reflexive in significance. It alerts attention to the novel's engagement with lesbian history and to Martinac's reworking, from a lesbian viewpoint, of the conventions of historical narrative.

Determined to discover the motive of Harriet's and Lucy's visits, Susan gives up the course of graduate study in which she has enrolled and devotes her time to investigating the lives of her two spectral visitors. She is assisted in this by a series of apparent coincidences in which, she surmises, the members of 'the Gang' play an instrumental part. Objects relating to them, such as an onyx and marcasite pin belonging to Lucy, unexpectedly come to light. Theatre reviews, letters and diaries also emerge, furnishing her with further information about their identities and lifestyle. On learning, to her delight, that one member of 'the Gang' is still alive, Susan seeks her out and persuades her to agree to an interview. On discovering that Lucy, immediately prior to her death, was engaged in writing a novel, Susan initially assumes that she wishes her to act as her amanuensis. However, when the completed manuscript unexpectedly comes to light, she suddenly perceives the truth: Lucy intends her not to write the novel but to arrange for its publication. Out of Time concludes on a positive note, with Susan making plans to edit the manuscript and locate a prospective publisher.

In recounting the story of Susan's involvement with her spectral visitors, Martinac recasts from a lesbian viewpoint a number of themes and motifs, including voyeurism and doubling, which are conventional to Gothic. The roles that Susan plays in relation to the spectral world alternate, as is often the case in the ghost story, between participant and voyeur.[26] The role of voyeur has a protective influence, enabling her to maintain a degree of distance from the process of enthralment in which contact with her ghostly visitors threatens to engulf her. It also illuminates the shifts of power operating between mortal protagonist and spectral visitor. On first coming across the photograph album in the antique shop and contemplating the pictures of her four 1920s friends Susan has the eerie feeling that, rather than being passive objects of her scrutiny, they boldly return her gaze. Ambiguity, in fact, exists about who controls the relationship – Susan or her spectral visitors. Whereas Susan assumes that it was she who located 'the Gang', its members take a different view: ' "Silly girl," said Harriet, with a smile that melted butter, "we found you" ' (p. 55).

This reference to voyeurism, as well as being a strategy to illustrate the shifting power relations existing between present-day protagonist and 1920s phantoms, also carries sexual connotations. In bed with Catherine one night, Susan glances at the picture of Harriet and Lucy on the nightstand – and is disconcerted to perceive that 'They were watching us, with the faintly amused and intrigued smiles of a voyeur' (p. 28). The situation of the couples is subsequently reversed when the two phantoms become the object of Susan's fascinated gaze. She describes how,

> ... in my dreams I thought I saw Lucy and Harriet having sex. Two figures were tucked away under an enormous quilt in a massive rosewood sleigh bed that dwarfed both of them. Every now and then I spied a bare arm or leg or buttock and heard a satisfied moan. (p. 28)

This episode, as well as foregrounding the pleasures of sexual fantasy, also introduces the theme of the lesbian's quest for origins. Harriet and Lucy, while functioning on a personal level as Susan's friends, also play the role of her foremothers since they originate from an earlier era. In depicting Susan watching the spectral couple making love in a dream scenario, Martinac playfully creates, with an appropriately all-female cast, a lesbian version of the Freudian primal fantasy in which the child watches her parents engage in sexual intercourse.[27]

Martinac resembles Zanger in making significant use of the Gothic device of doubling. On achieving contact with Harriet and Lucy and entering the spectral world which they inhabit, Susan, like heroines in earlier Gothic texts, experiences an uncanny sense of familiarity since she recognizes in her ghostly visitors aspects of her own identity and circumstances. Lucy, like her, is a writer. In addition, the problems that vex Lucy and Harriet's relationship, though differing from those that trouble Susan's partnership with Catherine, reflect a similarly contradictory interplay of 'pain and pleasure' (p. 114). Whereas Harriet and Lucy's partnership is destabilized by the former's infidelities and flirtations, Susan and Catherine's is impaired by conflicts of opinion and lack of trust. Nervous that Catherine, who is a graduate student working in the field of Women's History and exemplifies a scholarly approach to the past, will dismiss her story of an encounter with two ghosts from the 1920s as rubbish, Susan initially refrains from divulging the event to her. She also lies about her lifestyle, pretending that she is continuing to attend graduate classes when, in actual fact, she has given up her academic studies to investigate 'the Gang'. However, despite their flaws and imperfections, both mortal and spectral partnerships somehow manage to survive. When Susan, puzzled by the tolerance which Lucy shows towards Harriet's infidelities, curiously enquires why she puts up with such behaviour, she is met with the prompt question, ' "Why does Catherine stand for your antics? ... Because she loves you, I dare say" ' (p. 181). An attractive feature of *Out of Time*, as this exchange illustrates, is Martinac's acceptance of the contradictions and irrationalities of personal relationships. Susan's involvement with 'the Gang' proves in the long run beneficial, since it encourages her to accept the limitations of her own partnership.

Like Galford's *The Fires of Bride, Out of Time*, in recreating an episode from the lesbian past, deals with issues that are pertinent to the study of lesbian/feminist history. Susan's involvement with 'the Gang' and the attempt she makes to explore the lives of its members raise questions about the methods that researchers employ to investigate the past. Martinac prompts the reader to compare and contrast the strategies of intuition and imagination that Susan utilizes with the conventional academic methods favoured by her partner Catherine. When Susan shows Catherine the album with the photos of 'the Gang' and expresses a desire to investigate it further, the latter sensibly suggests that they approach the local Women's Archives and make use of its resources. In contrast to Susan who is primarily interested in the personal dimension of her spectral visitors' lives, such as their characters and relationships, Catherine is concerned with its public aspect, exemplified by their careers and their participation in feminist activities. She regards the photograph album not as a personal memento but as an historical document and, eager to make the pictures that it contains accessible to the lesbian/feminist community, urges Susan to organize an exhibition. Susan, however, views her proposal with suspicion. She is by no means sure that she wants to share her new friends with strangers. In fact, she is secretly pleased that Harriet and Lucy show no sign of manifesting themselves to Catherine. As she smugly tells herself, 'The women didn't live for Catherine the way they did for me' (p. 17).

Whereas the first half of the novel represents the conflict between the imaginative and the scholarly methods of investigating the past, which Susan and Catherine respectively employ, the second depicts them as complementary. Room exists, Martinac implies, for different methods of historical research, ones dependent on imagination and intuition, as well as ones involving the use of archives. The eclectic approach to the study of history that the novel champions is reflected in its style and structure, which become increasingly fractured and polyphonic as the narrative progresses. In the opening chapters Susan herself acts as narrator and dominates the text but in subsequent ones other voices and viewpoints intervene, complicating and enriching her account. Elinor, the only surviving member of 'the Gang', gives her individual version of events, while reviews of the plays in which Harriet acted and entries from Lucy's journal furnish alternative perspectives.

As well as comparing the different strategies available to the researcher to gain access to earlier periods of history, the novel also comments on the tendency of lesbians and feminists, in their quest for roots and identity, to idealize the past – particularly those facets of it that reflect their personal needs and desires. On account of the strongly visual and emotional appeal that they exert, snapshots act as a catalyst for this. Susan, who is prone to romanticizing lesbian feminist sisterhood, finds herself weaving fantasies around the photos of 'the Gang' and the images of women's community that they evoke. In the photos its members project a harmonious image to the world, which conceals any sign of the discord and friction existing between them. As a result Susan sees only the faces of 'four amazing women' (p. 5). Although intrigued by Harriet's flirtatiously beckoning look, she fails to perceive the capriciousness and potential for disruption which it reflects. Her desire to be incorporated into the enclave of sisterhood and 'family' that 'the Gang' represents is illustrated in the episode when, contemplating the pictures of Harriet and Lucy, she wistfully confesses, 'With their two best friends, their gang, they made a quartet I envied. I wanted such a group' (p. 149). However, as she later discovers, the image of harmony that the photos project is illusory. In real life relations between the four women were by no means tranquil but fraught with discord. Harriet's infidelities, in addition to upsetting her partner Lucy, had a destabilizing effect upon the group as a whole, threatening to shatter its unity. Lesbian/feminist community, Susan is forced to recognize, far from being a stable entity impervious to change, is precarious and ephemeral. The temptation to idealize the past, attractive though it is to the present-day lesbian engaged in a quest for roots and identity, has to be rejected.

HAUNTED HOUSES

Commenting on the effect that the appropriation of psychoanalytic theory has had on the interpretation of Gothic fiction, Kahane draws attention to the way that reference to relations between father and daughter is being increasingly supplanted in critical studies by an emphasis on the pre-oedipal theme of the mother/daughter bond.[28] Kahane illustrates that certain texts such Radcliffe's *The Mysteries of Udolpho* and Shelley's *Frankenstein* lend themselves to analysis from both oedipal and pre-oedipal points of view. This is also the case with Brown's *The Haunted House*. In contrast to Zanger and Martinac, Brown utilizes the topos of spectral visitation and the concept of 'the return of the repressed' associated with it not to explore the protagonist's relationship with a female figure from the past but to investigate the formation of lesbian identity in the context of the heterosexual family unit. Brown's portrayal of her narrator Robin's psychological development and the unresolved conflicts relating to it, along with her analysis of the part that fantasy and repression play in the formation of lesbian subjectivity, foregrounds both oedipal and pre-oedipal themes. The progression of the narrative from the representation of Robin's identificatory relationship with her father, to the description of the unstable, though equally intense, bond which she forms with her mother, resembles, in fact, the trajectory of Freud's 'excavation' of the female psyche. In his essay on 'Female Sexuality' (1931) he describes the pre-oedipal stage of female development as corresponding to the Minoan civilization with its allegedly matriarchal structures, predating the civilization of classical Greece, which he equated with the oedipal.[29] The sequential arrangement and meandering structure of Brown's narrative enact a similar process of psychological excavation.

The importance that the family unit assumes in *The Haunted House* is signalled by the novel's title in which, as is the case in Poe's 'The Fall of the House of Usher' (1839), the word 'house' refers not only to the actual building but also to the family who own it and the relationship between its members. Brown's narrative also resembles Poe's in concluding with the collapse of the house and in emphasizing the devastating effects of 'the return of the repressed' that it signifies. Whereas Poe's story concludes with the ruins of the House of Usher engulfing the ill-fated brother and sister who live there, along with their guilty secrets, Brown's novel terminates with a fissure appearing in the house where Robin and her partner Carrie have set up home, and the masonry and beams, like the lesbian partnership they have painstakingly forged, disintegrating around them. And, just as the fabric of the House of Usher is symbolically undermined by an incestuous involvement between brother and sister, so the house in Brown's novel is destabilized by an over-intense relationship between father and daughter.

Brown's treatment of the haunted house, though indebted to Poe and to writers of Female Gothic such as Shirley Jackson, brings the motif up to date by situating it in the America of the 1980s. In Brown's version the house is exemplified not by an ancestral mansion overlooking a romantic tarn, as in Poe's narrative, or by an ornate nineteenth-century edifice with turrets and buttresses, as in Jackson's, but by a series of downmarket urban lodgings and apartments. Dwellings mentioned in the novel include the series of drab suburban residences where Robin spends her childhood, the magnificent Hollywood apartment purchased by her mother when, her marriage having disintegrated, she achieves fame as a film star, and the house where Robin lives as an adult with her partner Carrie. The rootless nature of contemporary existence, Brown implies, results in the individual no longer passing her/his life in a single location but being constantly on the move. Since her father works for the American military, Robin's life is particularly rootless. She is constantly in transit as, accompanied by her mother and younger brother, she follows him from base to base.

Sexuality, memory and childhood, the trio of topics conventionally informing the classic ghost story, appear in Brown's narrative in a particularly complex configuration. The ritual of moving house which

Robin regularly enacts as a child and the sorting of personal possessions it involves are represented as prefiguring the psychological problems that will trouble her in adult life. On accompanying her mother through the empty rooms of their former home prior to leaving for their new abode, she hears her 'feet echo in the hollow house' and comes across certain trivial objects such as 'crusty pens, a ping-pong ball, a lucky coin'[30] which she had mislaid. Her account of their retrieval foregrounds the themes of memory and 'the return of the repressed' on which the narrative subsequently hinges. Voicing a perception which is ironically prophetic, she remarks,

> It's the first time I've ever found things I'd lost and finally let myself forget. They're unexpected, precious. They're surprises. I feel, almost, like I've been given something. But it's more important than that; I now have proof that things don't get lost, they all come back. (p. 13)

Robin is aware from an early age of the emotional pain that memory can cause and the refuge furnished by amnesia. As an adult she remembers how, on leaving for their new home, she and her mother, in an unspoken attempt to survive the instability of their lifestyle, deliberately avoided speaking about the past and made a silent pact to blot it out. As a result, 'The very shape of the house seemed changed, square and sharp and hollow. We walked together, silently, without a word of memory' (p. 15).

Brown's treatment of the motif of the house, as the passage cited above illustrates, is multifaceted, with new significances accruing and accumulating as the narrative develops. One of the meanings that it acquires, as is often the case in Gothic fiction and film, is 'the place of beginnings, the womb' where the three primal dramas of 'conception, sexual difference, desire – are played out'.[31] It becomes, in this respect, an image of Robin's personal quest for origins.

The house also functions as the site where the conflict of parental loyalties and identifications that Robin experiences as a child is enacted. It becomes an arena of parental discord as she watches her parents fight about her father's bouts of drinking and erratic behaviour. An alcoholic and inveterate fantasist, he is incapable of accommodating the routine of family life and, in order to escape its claustrophobic confines, takes Robin on wild drives round the countryside. During these escapades he shares with her his macho dreams of 'freedom' and daredevil exploits, centring on images of planes and fast cars. Unlike his wife and children, who yearn for a settled existence, he feels an urge to be continually on the move. The house signifies to him not stability and security but the entrapment represented by domesticity and the female body. With a guilty sigh he tells Robin, 'Home is someplace to go back to when you're tired of being out living' (p. 12). In the fantasy scenarios she invents of accompanying him on flying expeditions, he shouts above the roar of the propeller, 'Up here, baby doll, you feel like you're almost goddamn free!' (p. 31) Enthralled by his passion for adventure, she recklessly echoes his words, 'Up here we're over everything. Up here we're big as clouds. Up here we're far from everything, we're far from home, we're free!' (p. 31). It is during this period of her life that her personal mythology takes shape. It revolves around the twin poles of the house as a hub of stability, a concept which she inherits from her mother, and the sky and the open road as signifiers of freedom, derived from her father.

Robin soon discovers, however, the illusory nature of the concept of the house as a place of stability. When the inevitable occurs and, bored with the restrictions of marriage and family life, her father walks out on the family, it is transformed overnight into a place of instability and loss. His departure marks a turning point in her life and she temporarily loses her bearings. The concept of the sky as a signifier of freedom is undermined; it takes on, instead, associations of catastrophe. Looking back on her father's departure, she recalls, 'That very night, the stars all moved. The constellations lurched' (p. 22). From then on her fantasies of flying with him alter in meaning. Scenes of terror, terminating in catastrophe, are juxtaposed with images of erotic transcendence. With a mixture of horror and delight, she pictures the two of them, united at last, falling to earth in a final fatal embrace amid the wreckage of the plane:

> His body will spin. From the earth he'll look like an angel, a bright blue angel falling from sky.
> He'll struggle with his parachute and not be able to open it.
> Because I'm in his arms. He's holding me.
> We fall. (p. 43)

This passage vividly epitomizes the contradictions of idealism/disillusion, pleasure/fear which characterize Robin's relationship with her father. Despite her intense emotional involvement with him, she recognizes from an early age that, like the 'freedom' he claims to achieve in the air, the heroic exploits of which he boasts are fantasies. She is unwillingly forced to admit that 'My father was an ordinary failure, and so he told us ordinary lies' (p. 18). Emulating his example, she too learns to lie, entertaining her classmates with stories of his achievements and enjoying basking in his reflected glory: 'I said you were a hero, Dad. And in my grade school world, that made me something of a hero too' (p. 17). The habit she adopts of taking refuge in lies and half-truths persists into adulthood. She admits that, like him, she prefers fantasy to truth and 'feels more comfortable with shadowy grey, with implication, myth' (p. 11). Acknowledging the problematic effects of his influence, she wryly observes, 'To drink, to leave, to not look back, Dad, this is what you taught me' (p. 45).

The focus of the novel shifts in the second half from the fantasy life of Robin's father, and the formative effect which it has on her, to the dreams and illusions experienced by her mother. Robin, now an adult with a degree in architecture, visits her at her Hollywood apartment and is disturbed to discover the new persona that she has created for herself on achieving stardom. Obsessed with her recently acquired role of celebrity, her mother represses all memory of her earlier life. She suffers from spells of amnesia in which she disavows her marriage, even denying the fact that Robin is her daughter. The fraught relationship existing between the two women is illuminated by reference to Irigaray's analysis of the problematic aspects of mother/daughter relations in phallocentric culture. Irigaray exposes the way that society operates by separating mother and daughter, thus preventing the emergence of a maternal genealogy. She argues that, as a result, women exist in a state of *déréliction* 'never in touch with each other, exiled in a masculine, paternal world'.[32] The state of misunderstanding and non-communication which Robin and her mother experience resembles an extreme version of the Irigarayan state of *déréliction*.

In this section of the novel Brown further develops the motif of the house, transforming it into an image of the female psyche. The restructuring of the Hollywood apartment into a new, exotic environment, which Robin, following her mother's instructions, carries out, becomes a metaphor for the latter's attempt to rearrange her life to erase all forms of experience, such as motherhood and her failed marriage, which conflict with her image as a star. The feelings of disorientation and confusion that Robin suffers as a result are likewise represented by reference to the house and its features. She describes how, losing contact with the present, she regresses in memory to the various houses and apartments where she lived as a child.

> Like a blind woman I stumble, trying to remember where our furniture used to be
> ... I run my shaking hands along the rough painted wall, and take the three steps
> I remember to the big old couch in Monterey. I walk along behind it, rubbing my
> hand along the stiff thread that springs out of it. I turn to find, behind me, almost
> eye level now, the door knobs to the liquor cabinet in Kansas City ... (p. 87)

However, the bond between mother and daughter and the pre-oedipal realm that forms its matrix refuse to be repressed. Catching sight of her mother naked one night, Robin suddenly perceives how small and fragile she looks. Here the representation of the house as the location of the individual's psychological and family life, which has been the focus of the novel up to now, is replaced by the depiction of the body as the location of subjectivity. In a personal meditation that explores woman's search for origins, Robin pictures her mother's relationship with her in infancy and ponders the intimate knowledge of her body which it must have involved (p. 95). The episode heralds the return of the mother's memory. She acknowledges Robin as her daughter and, unlocking the door to the library, reveals the stash of photos and mementoes of marriage and motherhood which, up to now, she has kept hidden. Robin interprets the hoarding of these items of memorabilia as reflecting her mother's desire to halt the flux of time and to relive the past. However, as her mother perceptively insists, 'There's no again, no going back. You learn to live with what you have. You learn how to forget' (p. 102). Here, as in earlier episodes, both memory and its repression emerge as key themes.

The third section of the novel opens on an optimistic note. Robin has formed a partnership with her college friend Carrie and the two are working together on a property they have jointly purchased, in an attempt to transform it into a 'good, solid home' (p. 122). Here the motif of the house acquires yet another meaning, the renovating of the property serving as a metaphor for the building of their relationship. The image of the grotesque body, frequently employed in Gothic fiction and film to foreground themes of monstrosity and horror, is utilized in a playfully celebratory manner. The pleasure that the couple take in each other's company is represented by the surreal transformations which occur to their bodies in the process of decorating:

> Sometimes our whole bodies drip with color, paint spots, lines of stain. In the shower, we rub colours on and off each other, watch the pretty streams of green and blue, the thread of black that swirls down the drain, the faint cool rose that leaves a tint. (p. 117)

Although Robin appears to have recovered from the instabilities and conflicts of her early years, the past and its effects are too deeply entrenched to be erased. Neighbours start to comment on her physical resemblance to her father, observing, 'She's got his angel eyes' (p. 117). Joking with Carrie, she finds herself involuntarily repeating the snatches of jargon that he used to employ; she concludes her remarks with the phrase 'Over and Out', reminiscent of the fantasies of flying she shared with him. She feels increasingly isolated as Carrie, alienated by her brusque manner of speech and masculinist behaviour, turns away from her. Stripping the wallpaper, instead of being fun, becomes an activity fraught with danger. It represents an excavation of the past that Robin is afraid to undertake, conjuring up fears relating to 'the return of the repressed'. In a fantasy episode that, while recalling the fairy-tale 'Blue Beard's Castle', also resembles passages from Doris Lessing's *The Summer Before the Dark* (1973), she discovers, concealed beneath the wallpaper, a claustrophobic secret world of 'sealed passages and locked doors ... windows that look out themselves to – nothing' (p. 120). This subterranean domain carries connotations of the unconscious and the mysteries and terrors which it harbours. It takes on the intricate womb-like/tomb-like appearance of the haunted castle or mansion that features in the narratives of Radcliffe and Poe. As Robin remarks, utilizing a simile that advertises the Gothic tenor of the novel by ominously relating the house to death, 'We peel back this home's skin gingerly, as if we are disturbing, interrupting, dusting off the cover of a grave' (p. 118).

It is at this point in the narrative that the house begins to exhibit the first signs of psychic disturbance and physical disintegration. Robin senses the existence of a needy, frustrated presence lurking within it, registering its proximity in 'a tentative insistent sound, of something that is trying to get through' (p. 127): she herself as an emotionally disturbed child, perhaps, suffering from the effects of her parents' separation? As is the case in the concluding episode of Poe's 'The Fall of the House of Usher', a mysterious noise is audible under the floorboards and a crack appears in the fabric of the wall. Robin and Carrie try to deceive themselves into believing that this is merely a symptom of the foundations settling but, when further fault lines appear, they finally admit that the place is haunted and on the verge of collapse. A fissure appears in the floor of the bedroom, fracturing the bed. Water pours from the ceiling and Carrie, echoing the phrase that recurs in Robin's fantasies of the plane crash, shouts, 'Get out – the whole thing's going down!' (p. 138). The last objects that Robin sets eyes on as the flood engulfs her are, very appropriately, an assortment of mementoes carrying associations of her parents: a leather jacket and a toy propeller, signifying her identification with her father and his dreams of flying, and photographs and movie magazines belonging to her mother. The novel concludes with an ironic allusion to repression and memory as, drowning, she incoherently stutters, 'I forget – no – I remember, just who haunts this house' (p. 138).

Brown's exploration of the way that lesbian relationships reflect and reproduce, in displaced form, aspects of the individual's parental background and her utilization of the motif of the haunted house to explore the destructive effect on the psyche of unresolved parental conflict introduce a cluster of new perceptions into lesbian fiction. Her novel defamiliarizes the familiar, developing the tradition of Female Gothic in a disturbingly original manner.

SPECTRAL DOUBLES

A feature of the conventional ghost story that writers of lesbian fiction frequently exploit is the portrayal of the spectral visitor as reflecting aspects of the heroine's identity and circumstances and representing, in this respect, her ghostly double. Winterson makes effective use of this device in *The Passion*, utilizing it very differently from Martinac and Zanger. Instead of centring her text on the protagonist's encounter with a spectral visitor, she introduces the motif intermittently throughout, employing it to underpin the themes of love and war that the novel treats and to accentuate their emotional resonance. In addition to making innovative use of the concept of the double, she also introduces other themes and ideas that characterize works of lesbian Gothic. Lesbian sexuality and desire, society's tendency to relegate the lesbian to the realm of the abject and the image of the grotesque body, all achieve prominence.

The critical commentary which *The Passion* has inspired[33] reveals it to be one of the most frequently discussed of Winterson's novels. As is often the case with works of postmodern fiction,[34] it achieves much of the fascination it holds for the reader from the inventive manipulation of tension and contradiction. Although creating an intense evocation of lesbian desire, it utilizes a male narrator and focuses, in the first half, on the masculinist arena of war. While foregrounding ideas associated with lesbian feminism such as lesbian agency and the pressures exerted by compulsory heterosexuality it also introduces themes carrying queer associations, such as the interplay between heterosexual/homosexual dimensions of experience and the creation of alternative familial structures. The exuberant atmosphere of carnivalesque festivity and misrule that pervades many of the episodes is undercut in others by reference to the spectral and the emphasis on the abject realms of death and *déréliction* which Winterson utilizes it to evoke.

To clarify the first aspect of *The Passion* mentioned above, the interaction between masculinist and lesbian elements that the novel displays, Winterson cleverly links the two, resolving the apparent contradiction between them by means of her radical treatment of her male narrator Henri. It is Henri, the French peasant who works as Napoleon's cook during his military campaigns, who first introduces themes of sexual politics and love between women, thus paving the way for the transformation of the text from a study of relations between men in the camp and on the battlefield to an analysis of lesbian love. Winterson's portrayal of Henri, in deconstructing conventions of sexual difference, bridges the gap between these two different worlds. Henri displays traits conventionally regarded as feminine, such as sensitivity and a distaste for killing. In addition to sympathizing with the oppressed position of women and commenting on the way that men marginalize and neglect them, he introduces the topics of compulsory heterosexuality and lesbian relations, both of which assume a significant place in the text. The account he gives of his mother's enforced marriage – she agrees to marry only because her parents prevent her from fulfilling her religious vocation and entering a convent – and his description of the brutal treatment to which the cook subjects a prostitute in the local brothel, slapping her face and forcing her to perform fellatio, illustrate the pressures, social and physical, which coerce women into engaging in sexual relations with men. In recounting the incident in the brothel, Henri also focuses attention on the attempt the two prostitutes make to protect each other from male assault and describes the tender kiss which the one bestows on the other. This marks the first reference to love between women in the novel. As these incidents indicate, Henri is instrumental in establishing the novel's lesbian perspective. As Lisa Moore observes, not only does he respect lesbian relationships but he also regards them as exemplifying the intensity of passion which he himself seeks.[35]

In introducing themes of sexual politics and lesbian relations, Henri prepares the way for the entry of Villanelle, the Venetian woman who loses her heart to the mysterious Queen of Spades and acts as the signifier of lesbian love. From the moment of her first appearance, Villanelle appropriates the role of narrator and becomes the focus of narrative interest. Henri falls in love with her, thus attempting to relegate her to woman's conventional role of object of desire, but she successfully subverts this role. Though sleeping with him occasionally, she refuses his offer of marriage and resists his attempt to objectify her by recounting the story of her love affair with the Queen of Spades. By portraying herself not as the object of Henri's passion but as the lover of the Queen of Spades, she successfully positions herself in the text in the role of active agent. Role reversal and the deconstruction of conventions of sexual difference, as the active part she plays in the narrative illustrates, are as important a feature of Villanelle's portrayal as they are of Henri's. Whereas Henri exemplifies attributes conventionally regarded as feminine, Villanelle displays qualities typecast as masculine, such as daring and initiative. In pursing her love affair with the Queen of Spades, she even dresses as a boy, making the most of the opportunity to engage in crossdressing which the Carnival festivities furnish. The topic of compulsory heterosexuality, introduced by Henri in the account he gives of his mother's enforced marriage and his description of his visit to the brothel, is developed in the portrayal of Villanelle and her adventures. Though engaging in sexual relations with men, she seldom does so from choice, but, like Henri's mother and the prostitute whom he encounters, is motivated by social and economic pressures. Her marriage to the physically repulsive 'rich man with fat fingers'[36] whose hands, she recollects with disgust, 'crept over her body like crabs' (p. 98) is an act of pragmatism she performs in order to escape from Venice, an environment that has become intolerable to her on account of the termination of her love affair with the Queen of Spades. The role of *vivandière* in Napoleon's army, which she subsequently adopts, occurs as the result of a wager in which she unwillingly features as object of exchange. Her sexual encounters with Henri, though voluntary, are infrequent. She cares for him, she admits, not as a lover 'but in a brotherly incestuous way' (p. 146). Winterson depicts the two characters forming a bond which, in its emphasis on role reversal and its subtle blend of the 'brotherly' (on Villanelle's part) and the erotic (on Henri's), challenges the orthodox division between homosexual/heterosexual dimensions of experience and, in conflicting with conventional familial formations, emerges as distinctly queer. In transgressing the limits of their respective gender roles, both characters are stigmatized by society as freakish and odd. Henri's lack of aggression and his expressions of disgust at the brutal way in which the army treats women elicit derisive comments from his comrades, while Villanelle's independent attitude arouses puzzlement and indignation in many of the men whom she meets. The lesbian passion that dominates her life also leads her to overstep social convention. The Queen of Spades is married and, in forming a relationship with her, Villanelle comes into conflict with family values. As she herself sardonically admits, a lesbian love affair 'is not the usual thing' (p. 94) in eighteenth-century patriarchal society.

Winterson's portrayal of Villanelle, while notably original, reveals ideological and cultural links with the other works of lesbian Gothic discussed in this study in that, instead of seeking to normalize the image of the lesbian, it foregrounds lesbian specificity and 'difference'. It agrees, in this respect, with the recommendations for lesbian representation put forward by de Lauretis. As mentioned in the introductory chapter, de Lauretis argues that the writer who engages in lesbian representation, in order to subvert the conventional depiction of woman as wife, mistress and mother, has to reject normalizing images of womanhood and portray the lesbian in terms of 'excess'. To achieve this goal, she must utilize metaphors that 'recreate the body otherwise' and introduce 'provocative counterimages' representing the lesbian as 'monstrous or grotesque'.[37] These comments are applicable to Winterson's portrayal of Villanelle. The first facet of her identity that Villanelle reveals to the reader is the secret of her webbed feet. This grotesque feature, as well as acting as a signifier of her sexual difference, parodically reworks the representation of the lesbian as animalistic which, as Creed[38] and other critics[39] illustrate, frequently occurs in homophobic culture. It also relates her to the Bakhtinian image of the grotesque body and to the connotations of social transgression and carnivalesque misrule that it carries. Bakhtin describes the grotesque body as a body in 'the act of becoming', in the process of being 'continually built and created'.[40] It thus comes as no surprise to the reader to find that, in portraying Villanelle, Winterson associates the morphology of the lesbian body, both literally and symbolically, with movement – frequently of a vertiginous kind. In addition to depicting Villanelle admiring the dexterity of the trapeze artists who visit the city of Venice during the Carnival festivities and climbing the railings to catch a glimpse of the Queen of Spades, she also represents her defying the laws of gravity. Emulating Wittig, who, in *The Lesbian Body* (1973), represents the beloved gliding and hovering above the sea, she portrays her performing the miraculous feat of walking on the water of the canal.

In connecting the lesbian with the acrobat and the trapeze performer, Winterson develops the relationship of the latter two figures with the alternative culture of social outcasts and subversives. Clément, developing Bakhtin's association of them with the realm of the carnivalesque, interprets them in a specifically feminine light. In 'The Guilty One' she describes 'deviants, neurotics, women, drifters, jugglers, tumblers' [41] as members of a marginal repressed group with bisexual tendencies, related to the realm of the Imaginary. The patriarchal establishment, she remarks, regards such people with a degree of ambivalence; while relegating them to the realm of entertainment, it simultaneously recognizes their potential for disruption and perceives the threat they pose to social order. Winterson is, of course, by no means the first writer to introduce the acrobat and the trapeze artiste in a specifically lesbian context. Barnes in *Nightwood* portrays the equivocally named Frau Mann as entertaining the circus audiences of Berlin with her displays of agility on the trapeze, while Wittig in *Lesbian Peoples: Materials for a Dictionary* (1976) describes 'groups of wandering companion lovers' entertaining 'the lesbian communities ... with mime, acrobatics, juggling'.[42]

Rather than carrying straightforward connotations of woman as the object of the male gaze, as Mary Russo argues they do when specularized by the male viewer,[43] the acrobat and the trapeze performer evoke, in the fiction of both Wittig and Winterson, an image of vitality and transgressive *jouissance*. They can be interpreted, I suggest, as representing a form of Irigarayan mimesis in which the lesbian or woman-identified woman parodies the role of spectacle and entertainer that phallocentric culture assigns to her, exploiting it for her own particular ends. They also signify the precarious nature of lesbian existence and the dangers, both literal and symbolic, which the woman who oversteps convention by forming primary relationships with members of her own sex encounters in hetero-patriarchal society. She risks not only the obvious danger of social stigma but also the less obvious one of being reabsorbed into the phallic, specular economy as the object of male titillation and voyeurism. In order to survive the homophobic climate in which she lives and avoid falling into the abyss of shame, she has to strive to keep her balance and maintain a sure footing on the high wire. This is precisely the role which Villanelle plays in *The Passion*.

Winterson brings together a reference to the carnivalesque body with an allusion to the precarious nature of lesbian existence when, treating the mouth as a signifier of lesbian love, she portrays Villanelle envying the acrobats who visit the city during Carnival the kisses which, while suspended from the trapeze, they snatch from the lips of the passers-by. Villanelle approvingly remarks, 'I like such kisses. They fill the mouth and leave the body free. To kiss well one must kiss solely. No groping hands or stammering hearts. The lips and the lips alone are the pleasure' (p. 59). Her words, it is interesting to note, anticipate her love affair with the Queen of Spades, which commences shortly afterwards. The love affair resembles the acrobats' kisses in that it is illicit, short-lived and sexually intoxicating. It transgresses convention and has to be concealed from the Queen of Spades's husband. In addition, the stylized positions that Villanelle and her lover adopt while making love and the exclusive focus that they place on the mouth recall the postures and movements of the acrobats. Emphasizing the intensity of the oral pleasures they enjoy, Villanelle describes how,

> She [the Queen of Spades] lay on the rug and I lay at right angles to her so that only our lips might meet. Kissing in this way is the strangest of distractions. The greedy body that clamours for satisfaction is forced to content itself with a single sensation and, just as the blind hear more acutely and the deaf can feel the grass grow, so the mouth becomes the focus of love and all things pass through it and are re-defined. It is a sweet and precise torture. (p. 67)

In portraying Villanelle and the Queen of Spades mimicking the postures of the acrobats in their lovemaking, Winterson, in typically poststructuralist/ queer manner, associates lesbianism with artifice and stylization. The emphasis she places on its cultural and performative dimension is illuminated by a comment voiced by Danae Clark which relates sexual artifice of this kind to the oppressed nature of lesbian existence. Clark perceptively observes that 'Lesbians are accustomed to playing out multiple styles and sexual roles as a tactic of survival and have learned the artifice of invention in defeating heterosexual codes of naturalism'.[44]

Carnivalesque festivity and the transgressive sexual pleasures associated with it represent, however, only one strand in Winterson's emotionally complex novel. They are frequently disrupted and undercut by references to the motif of the spectral and to the abject connotations of death and dereliction which it evokes. Henri and Villanelle, as well as being connected by their experience of the Napoleonic Wars and their involvement in the realm of passion, are also linked by their mutual preoccupation with darkness. Henri comments eloquently on the paradoxical emotions of pleasure/fear which walking in the dark inspires in him. Foregrounding the sensation of suffocation to which it gives rise, he remarks, 'Walking in the dark is like swimming underwater, except you can't come up for air' (p. 33). Villanelle spells out even more explicitly the relation between darkness and death. She describes how, as a child, she envisaged death as a form of dark 'shadow-land where people bought and sold and loved as usual but with less conviction' (p. 57). However, the scenes of bloodshed that she witnesses during the Napoleonic campaigns teach her to perceive that 'darkness and death are not the same: the one is temporary. The other is not' (p. 58). The meditations on darkness voiced by the two characters prepare the reader for their subsequent encounters with the spectral. Henri is haunted by memories of the victims of Napoleon's thirst for military conquest and by the contributory part which, as a member of his army, he himself played in their slaughter. After experiencing a series of bloody battles, he suffers fantasies of the mutilated corpses returning to the land of the living in quest of retribution. He describes himself grotesquely as 'covered in dead men' and comments hysterically on 'the madness of arms and legs that pushed in at my ears and mouth' (p. 25). The spectral corpses that invade Henri's fantasies, as well as being a device to impress the horror of war upon the reader, give us an insight into his psyche; they evoke both his feelings of guilt at participating in the bloodshed and his fear of death. They also serve to relate him to the abject. Kristeva describes the corpse as 'the utmost of abjection'.[45] She points out that it lacks a soul and is, in biblical terms, a signifier of pollution. Existing at the edge of life, it threatens to destabilize the borders between life and death and to infect the world of the living. The image of the corpse has a similarly destabilizing effect on Henri's sanity. When, in the concluding section of the novel, he is incarcerated in the island fortress of San Servelo, he loses contact with the present and descends into a private world of mental disturbance. The ghost of the deceased Napoleon visits him in his cell, pathetically inquiring if he still loves him. As the object of Henri's former hero worship, the idol who turned out to have feet of clay, Napoleon, like Henri's other ghosts, represents an aspect of his own psyche. Unimpressed by Villanelle's assertions that these spectres are figments of his imagination and that 'There are no voices, no shapes' (p. 142), Henri persists in his morbid fantasies; he continues, as he grimly puts it, to encounter 'the dead walking the halls and watching me with their hollow eyes' (p. 142).

Villanelle's encounters with the world of the spectral, in contrast to Henri's and in keeping with her role as the signifier of lesbian passion, centre on the domain of love rather than war. Images of the abject pervade her consciousness, reflecting her anxieties about the realm of *déréliction* and loneliness to which, as a social misfit who enjoys crossdressing and loses her heart to a member of her own sex, she risks being relegated. Winterson utilizes topographical imagery to represent this realm. While describing Venice as the focus of carnival festivity, she also ascribes a darker side to the city which the visitor, involved in a hedonistic quest for pleasure and entertainment, seldom glimpses.[46] She describes the cortège of gondolas with their load of coffins setting out for the funeral isle of San Michele and refers to the ghosts of family ancestors who haunt the alleys and waterways 'seeing to their own' (p. 62). Even more mysteriously, she describes Venice as harbouring 'a city within a city which is the knowledge of the few' (p. 53). This inner city, she observes, takes the form of a labyrinthian domain of canals and alleyways, 'littered with ghosts' (p. 61) and peopled by outcasts and slant-eyed children who 'roam in packs like the cats and the rats' (p. 53). Judging from the uncanny terms she employs to depict it, it is as much a state of mind as an actual place. On entering its precincts, Villanelle encounters, as is usual with the entry of the heroine into the realm of Gothic fantasy, a mirror image of herself. Catching sight of her reflection in the water of the canal, she sees 'in the distortions of my face what I might become' (p. 62). She also encounters a more disturbing *doppelgänger*. This is the unnamed woman with 'ghoulish green hair' ornamented with a crown of rats' tails who has made her home in a nook in the wall of one of the canals. Despite the derelict circumstances to which she is reduced, she boasts a set of ornate goblets, interpreted by Villanelle as a relic of her former aristocratic lifestyle, and entertains a group of invisible guests to supper with strips of rancid meat. She has an uncanny habit of materializing at crisis points in Villanelle's life and uttering warnings couched in riddlingly sibylline phrases. As a result, Villanelle regards her as a spectral messenger with access to occult powers. She associates her with ' the spirits of the dead' who haunt the city, 'speaking in tongues' (p. 75).

This unnamed woman, distinguished by the crown of rats' tails she wears and the imaginary supper parties she hosts, can be read as representing a grimly parodic image of Carnival festivity – one that, on account of its associations with water and performativity, has connections with Villanelle herself. She prefigures Villanelle's derelict situation in the concluding episode of the novel when, having relinquished Henri to madness and the island fortress of San Servelo and refused the Queen of Spades' invitation to renew the love affair, she rows alone on the waters of the lagoon, listening to the cry of the gulls. Alternatively, we can interpret the woman's grotesque appearance and weird behaviour as representing the monstrous image that patriarchal society assigns to woman/lesbian. She haunts the city of Venice in a manner similar to that in which, as Fuss and Castle comment, the presence of the lesbian haunts hetero-patriarchal culture. Whichever interpretation the reader chooses, the woman's appearance in the narrative and the sense of mystery she evokes contribute to the novel's uncanny atmosphere. They transform it from a picaresque tale predominantly carnivalesque in mood to an experiment in mixing genres, the glittering fabric of which is shot through with strands of a darker hue.

THE WORK OF MOURNING

Death and the fears and anxieties relating to it, exemplified in Winterson's *The Passion* by Henri's spectral encounters with the victims of the Napoleonic wars and Villanelle's references to the ghosts haunting the city of Venice, also assume centrality in Donoghue's *Hood* and Schulman's *Rat Bohemia*. Here, however, it is the experience of mourning and bereavement that is the focus of analysis. This is a topic which, though occupying a central place in texts by gay men, such as the stories and novels of Adam Mars-Jones and Edmund White, has up to now received little attention in lesbian fiction. Donoghue and Schulman approach it in notably different ways. *Hood* is set in the rural outskirts of Dublin. It portrays Pen, a teacher at a Roman Catholic convent school, who has deliberately kept her sexual orientation secret from the local community, struggling to cope and come to terms with the sudden death of her lover Cara. In keeping with the intimate mood of the novel and the solitariness of Pen's predicament, Donoghue employs a single narrator throughout, filtering all the events recounted through the consciousness of Pen herself. *Hood* emits a distinct air of claustrophobia. Far from being inappropriate, this suits the focus that the novel places on the isolated situation of the closet lesbian living in a homophobic society. The sense of psychological and social entrapment that pervades the narrative is accentuated by the fact that Donoghue encapsulates Pen's experience of bereavement into a brief seven days and introduces few changes of setting.

Rat Bohemia, on the contrary, is urban in location, set in a rodent-infested, slum district of New York. Instead of concentrating on the individual's encounter with death as Donoghue does, Schulman focuses on the American gay community, exploring its members' attempts to cope emotionally with the numerous deaths resulting from the AIDS crisis. In order to register this communal emphasis, she employs three different narrators: two lesbians and a gay man. The latter is HIV-positive and, as if to impress upon the reader the immediacy of the threat which death presents, is portrayed dying in the course of the narrative. The novel concludes with an account of his funeral and with an episode juxtaposing the contrary responses which his gay friends and his heterosexual family adopt to his demise.

However, despite these obvious differences, the two novels display significant points of affinity. Although many of the aspects of bereavement to which they refer are of general relevance, both writers understandably concentrate on those features that are especially pertinent to lesbians and gay men. Donoghue explores Pen's feelings of loneliness and traces her growing feelings of guilt and anger at the pressure which she feels the local community exerts on her to conceal her sexual identity. Schulman contrasts the supportive approach that gay friends and lovers adopt towards people with AIDS with the ignorant and insensitive attitude of their heterosexual families. She also focuses attention on the problematic position that lesbians occupy in relation to the AIDS crisis. She illustrates their distress at the frequent loss of male friends and examines their ambivalent response to the role of carer and mourner which, whether they choose it or not, the gay community expects them to perform.

Resemblances are also apparent between the two writers' treatment of the motif of the spectral. By introducing spectral imagery and, more especially, by structuring the narratives they create around the concept of haunting, both Donoghue and Schulman foreground the impact that death has on the subjectivities of the living, illustrating the way it extends into life through acts of memory and imagination. Central to their treatment of death is the ironic perception that, the more the living try to dispose of the dead and strive to exorcize their memory by means of ritual visits to the mortuary and the performance of elaborate funeral ceremonies and wakes, the more psychically alive the dead, in fact, become. The 'return of the repressed' is, in this sense, as important a theme in these two novels as it is in the other texts discussed in this chapter. The utilization of spectral imagery in contemporary lesbian Gothic, as mentioned in the introductory section, instead of serving to disembody the figure of lesbian and decarnalize her/his desire, foregrounds the importance of the body, its passions and vulnerability. The novels of Donoghue and Schulman furnish further evidence of this. Both hinge on the contradiction between the representation of the dead or dying body, lying emaciated in bed or decaying in the earth, and the fantasy image of it, alive and sexually active, in the memory of the bereaved. In addition to emphasizing the precariousness of life and sexual pleasure, this has the effect of highlighting the poignant contrast between the vivid mental image of the deceased and her/his physical inaccessibility.

In utilizing spectral imagery to explore the lesbian experience of bereavement, Donoghue and Schulman both become involved in scrutinizing and evaluating the conventions of the Gothic mode in which they write. They indirectly critique certain features, in particular the clichés and superficially scary effects of the popular ghost story. The fears aroused by the appearance of a spooky-looking figure robed in white or the occurrence of mysterious supernatural events are, the two writers imply, trivial and insignificant in comparison with those stemming from the first-hand encounter with death to which the demise of a loved one gives rise.

The part that actual reference to the spectral plays in *Hood* is relatively minor, though Donoghue introduces the motif with sufficient frequency to establish it as a metaphor for the assault on Pen's consciousness of a cluster of images which serve to evoke the memory of her deceased lover Cara. She employs it in a tone of self-conscious wit, as if attempting to distance herself from it and to critique the clichéd use which it frequently receives in popular fiction and film. After experiencing a dream of making love with Cara, Pen remarks, 'I woke wet, my body straining to her ghostly wrist'[47] – to have her desire abruptly quenched by the sudden recognition of her lover's death (p. 35). Illustrative of the use of word-play and punning that characterizes the novel's narrative style, creating an element of macabre wit which prevents Donoghue's treatment of death from lapsing into sentimentality, is the question that unexpectedly strikes Pen when composing a notice of Cara's death for the local newspaper: 'Was I her ghost writer now, putting words in her mouth?' (p. 8). Donoghue's use of word-play in relation to death gives the novel a distinctly metaphysical slant – 'metaphysical' both in the philosophical sense of the term and as it is utilized to describe the style of writing employed by seventeenth-century poets such as John Donne. As is the case in metaphysical poetry, word-play and punning, instead of being devices to provoke laughter or an eerie shudder, act as a strategy to explore the tension and interaction between life and death. They also inform the title of the novel and the multiple meanings that it carries. *Hood*, in denoting as it does sisterhood, maidenhood and the hood of the clitoris, brings together the social dimension of femininity with the sexual (pp. 113, 257).

More important than actual references to the spectral in evoking the conflict that Pen experiences between her rational recognition of her lover's death and her desire to keep her image alive by clinging to her memory is the way that Donoghue builds the concept of haunting into the structure of the narrative. Whatever Pen does and wherever she goes in the days following Cara's death, events conspire to trigger tantalizing images of her lover in her mind. Watching a red-haired girl crossing the school car park, she is momentarily tricked into thinking that it is the teenage Cara, while the arrival of Cara's clothes from the hospital, where her body was taken after the accident, arouses in her an unexpectedly erotic response:

> Under a layer of cotton I found a cream satin camisole. I fingered its milky folds; for a moment I imagined its pencil straps on Cara's freckled shoulders, and smiled in anticipation, my mouth watering. Then I remembered, like a great hand closing around my throat. How many times would I have to remember and make myself believe it, before I remembered once and for all? (p. 74)

The disturbing effect of this passage stems from the way in which the fantasy image of Cara alive and physically accessible, which the sight of her camisole evokes in Pen, is abruptly and cruelly shattered by the recognition of the inexorable fact of her death.

In 'Mourning and Melancholia' Freud describes the mourning of the death of a loved one as characterized by the bereaved's lack of interest in the external world and by the difficulty s/he experiences in detaching her/his affections from the deceased and transferring them to an alternative object. He portrays the bereaved as involved in a painful conflict between, on the one hand, accepting the fact that the loved one no longer exists and, on the other hand, seeking to keep her/him alive through the operations of memory and fantasy. Freud sees the function of 'the work of mourning' as the resolution of this conflict by reconciling the bereaved to the fact of death and enabling her/him to gradually withdraw feelings of libidinal attachment from the deceased. This process, Freud emphasizes, can be extremely painful and may take some time. Discussing the bereaved's state of mind, he remarks:

> In the meantime the existence of the lost object is psychically prolonged. Each single one of the memories and expectations in which the libido is bound to the object is brought up and hypercathected, and the detachment of the libido is accomplished in respect of it.[48]

Freud's observations shed light on the difficulty that Pen encounters in relinquishing her attachment to Cara. They help to explain the conflict she experiences between her recognition, on a rational plane, of the fact of Cara's death and the intense need she feels to keep her image alive through acts of memory and imagination.

A strategy Donoghue employs to represent this conflict is to juxtapose representations of the two physical states which, according to Bakhtin, most clearly exemplify the grotesque body: the body in a state of sexual excitement and the corpse.[49] Both, Bakhtin emphasizes, involve transformation, presenting the body not as static but in a condition of process and flux. The dream Pen experiences of making love with Cara, in which, as she sensuously comments, she feels once again 'the white of her skin rushing through my fingers', is brutally disrupted by the image of her rotting body 'in a box underground' (p. 153). In an attempt to gain relief by masturbating, she creates a fantasy image of 'Cara's pale, elongated hand with the freckles on the back of the knuckles and its long fingers' – only to have her feelings of desire quickly stopped by the 'thought of those fingers beginning to putrefy in the cemetery' (p. 163).

The disturbing contrast between the image of Cara alive and sexually active and the image of her corpse rotting in the grave, which Pen obsessively conjures up, has the effect of relating her, in her state of bereavement and *déréliction*, to the realm of the abject. As mentioned in connection with Winterson's *The Passion*, the corpse has traditionally been regarded as exemplifying the extreme of abjection. Pen's fixation with the contrary images of her lover, alive and dead, may also be read as implying that 'the work of mourning' is not progressing as it should. In 'Mourning and Melancholia' Freud distinguishes between what he sees as the normal response to death, characterized by the successful operation of the work of mourning, and the condition of melancholia in which the individual is unable to move beyond an unhealthy attachment to the deceased. Pen's state of mind suggests that, in her isolated situation as a closet lesbian, unable to share the intensity of her grief with friends and relatives and racked by feelings of anger and guilt at the burden of secrecy which she feels society imposes upon her, she clings particularly intensely to Cara's image and its sexual associations. Her grief, in consequence, becomes tinged with melancholia.

In addition to causing Pen intense distress, Cara's death also has a politicizing effect on her. Her feelings of anger at the bigotry and blindness of the heterosexual community prompt her to make an effort to 'come out' and, in the days following the funeral, she manages to make a few chinks in the wall of the closet. She divulges her lesbian identification to Robbie, a colleague at the school where she teaches, and, in the concluding pages, is on the verge of broaching the topic of her lesbian identification to her mother.

Yet, while interrogating the position of the closet lesbian and foregrounding its psychological and moral difficulties, Donoghue also problematizes the act of 'coming out'. Pen's revelation of her lesbianism to Robbie, though successful in the long run in that he responds supportively, commences on a note of farce. So unaccustomed is he to the idea of women forming primary relationships with one another that he initially misinterprets Pen's words, mistakenly assuming that she is confessing to having an affair not with Cara but with Cara's father. The advice on homosexual bereavement, inscribed in the book which he purchases as a gift for her in a well-meaning if clumsy gesture of consolation, strikes both her and the reader as inadequate and platitudinous.

Donoghue utilizes the motif of haunting, it is interesting to note, not only in relation to Cara's death but also to describe the effect of her absences during her lifetime when, we learn, she used sometimes to desert Pen to pursue affairs with other lovers, male as well as female. Looking back on these desolate occasions, Pen describes herself, in her uncertainty as to if or when Cara would return, as feeling 'haunted' by her image (p. 100). Cara herself also employs spectral terminology. In one of the retrospective episodes with which the text abounds, she informs Pen that she dislikes living at home after her parents' divorce because, with her mother and sister in New York, the place feels like 'a ghost house' (p. 43). The introduction of spectral imagery to evoke other forms of absence besides those relating to death extends the novel's scope beyond the topic of bereavement, prompting the reader to compare and contrast different forms of absence. It raises the question, how do the feelings of loss which we experience when a loved one is living abroad or involved in a relationship with someone else differ from those resulting from the permanent absence which death creates?

Cara's death and the difficulty that Pen experiences in relinquishing her passionate attachment to her, in addition to motivating her to reconsider her closeted lifestyle, also prompt her to re-evaluate her lover's personality.

The novel concludes with her deciding that any attempt to discover Cara's 'true self' is, in fact, pointless, since her identity was not single but multifaceted. Defending Cara against her sister's accusation that she was merely a heartless flirt who enjoyed exercising power by cultivating numerous lovers, Pen fiercely insists that 'She wasn't someone you'd want to restrict to just one of their selves' (p. 201). Attendant on this perception is the recognition that Cara's infidelities were motivated by a desire less for sexual pleasure than for 'the freedom of unconstrained possibilities' (p. 214). As is the case in Kate Millet's *Sita* (1977), another novel that focuses on the narrator's infatuation with a charismatic bisexual with which *Hood* reveals pronounced affinities, Cara's attraction stems, paradoxically, from the very thirst for experience which was the source of her infidelities.

In turning from Donoghue's *Hood* to Schulman's *Rat Bohemia*, we move from the intimate representation of individual mourning to the focus on the expressions of communal grief generated by the AIDS crisis.[50] Schulman's treatment of AIDS and its psychological and social repercussions differs radically from that of her male contemporaries White and Mars-Jones. The lesbian viewpoint which she inscribes enables her to approach the topic with a degree of distance and, while treating the male gay community's experience of sickness and death compassionately, criticize some of its attitudes. In evoking the feelings of distress, anger and emotional numbness experienced by the female characters as they see their male friends fall sick and die, Schulman makes major use of Gothic structures and imagery. In fact, her novel relates to Gothic in more ways than one since, in addition to drawing on the conventions of the ghost story, it appropriates from horror film and fiction, as the title signals, the motif of the rat. The creature is a well-known signifier of decay and abjection, including among its credentials connections with Dracula and a walk-on (or, rather, creep-on!) part in a number of horror films. Werner Herzog exploits these associations to good effect in *Nosferatu* (1979), his postmodern reworking of F.W. Murnau's expressionist classic. By interweaving the rat motif with imagery relating to the spectral, Schulman creates a highly distinctive Gothic brew. She also extends the critique of the ghost story, which Donoghue introduces in *Hood*, to encompass the popular genre of horror. The sensationalistic depiction of events in horror fiction and film geared to arouse feelings of terror in reader and audience are, she sardonically implies, outdated, since they have been superseded by the actual physical and psychological suffering of AIDS victims and their survivors.

The phrase 'Rat Bohemia', as Schulman employs it, denotes in literal terms the rat-infested, slum area of New York which, as well as being frequented by the homeless and drug addicts, is one of the main centres of the American AIDS crisis. However, it quickly becomes apparent from the surreal tone of her description that 'Rat Bohemia', in addition to denoting a geographical area and the alternative social groups who live there, signifies a state of mind. It represents, on a symbolic plane, a Gothic realm of *déréliction* and death in which the individual, having once entered, is entrapped for good. The rat, with its connotations of disease and abjection, acts as a signifier of this realm. Despite the efforts of the New Yorkers to exterminate the rodents by means of traps, poison or shooting, they continue to breed, 'swarming', as the narrator Rita May Weems observes in a simile notable for its vivacity as well as its nastiness, 'like larvae on old cat food'.[51] They emerge unexpectedly from their nests and hiding places, startling the unsuspecting pedestrian and invading her/his thoughts with pallor-inducing fantasies of the monstrous. The fear they arouse is apparent from the fact that Rita describes the visit which she makes to the rat-infested tenement where her female friend Killer lives in terms of a military offensive:

> When I approach that corner I get really tense, like a foot soldier on the banks of the Mekong Delta. I scan the sidewalk thoroughly and then try to race past as quickly as possible. If a piece of paper or a plastic bag should suddenly blow out of the sea of rats, I'll jump ten feet and scream. Later on, I'll be clammy and pale, as though the actual monster ran across my bedsheets. And when the real ones do surface, they are huge and deformed with tumors and other disfigurations. (pp. 41–2)

While the image of 'a sea of rats' which Rita introduces in this passage depicts the creatures as a seething mass threatening, like a flood of water, to engulf the world, her reference to 'the monster' running across the bedsheets relates them to the fantasy world of nightmare and the horror film. Her reference to the rats' physical deformities also links them to people with AIDS, whose abject social situation the novel powerfully evokes.

The motif of the rat, in addition to being related to the male gay community, also reveals connections with the lesbian. Though loathing rats and enjoying shooting them, Rita confesses to regarding them as an image of her own condition. Rendered homeless in her teens as a result of being thrown out of the family home for having an affair with a girl friend, and denied an education on account of her poverty, she identifies with the abject realm which the rats inhabit. Her experience of watching a female friend die from drug-related diseases and her male friends die of AIDS, while she herself continues to survive, accentuates, in her view, her affinity with the creature. She describes herself, with grim irony, as resembling a new breed of super rat which, immune to poison and traps, continues to flourish while its weaker brethren crawl away to die.

A disturbing claim the novel makes, one which, in my view, Schulman fails convincingly to substantiate, is that, just as human beings strive to exterminate rats because they are carriers of disease, so parents seek, on a subliminal plane, to expel and destroy their lesbian and gay offspring on account of the embarrassment and disappointment they cause by failing to conform to accepted norms. This experience of parental rejection and cruelty, Rita maintains, constitutes a significant point of connection between the members of the lesbian/gay community; it is, she claims, a 'truth' which they discuss among themselves but keep secret from the world at large:

> The most common link between all gay people is that at some time in our lives, often extended, our families have treated us shabbily because of our homosexuality. They punish us, but we did not do anything wrong. We tell each other about this all the time but we never tell the big world. It is the one secret which is not for public consumption. (p. 163)

Schulman's aim in the novel, as the polemical tone of this and other similar passages illustrates, is to publicize this 'truth'. However, her treatment of it is one-sided and ageist. A contradiction exists between her sensitive and complex representation of gay men and lesbians, which, inscribing a queer viewpoint, introduces a range of transgressive sexualities and attitudes, and the unitary and flatly stereotypical image she creates of their parents. The latter are chiefly second-generation immigrants. Schulman treats them unsympathetically, making little attempt to explore their subjectivities or viewpoint. As a result, she not only gives a one-sided image of familial conflict but also sacrifices a productive source of narrative tension.

In contrast to her superficial treatment of the breakdown in relations between children and parents, Schulman's representation of the AIDS crisis and her utilization of spectral imagery to illustrate its traumatic effect on both victims and survivors is intelligently handled. 'The work of mourning'[52] is rendered problematic in this case not, as in Donoghue's novel, by the fact that the bereaved is unable to withdraw her libidinal attachment from the deceased but because of the numbing effect which the widescale occurrence of death has on the emotions of the survivors. Freud, commenting on the deaths that occurred in the First World War, remarks 'A number of simultaneous deaths strikes us as something extremely terrible'.[53] He points out that an event of this kind has the effect of bewildering and disorientating the survivors. Schulman describes a similar situation. As Rita despondently comments, 'These days everybody is dying. There's no illusion left to let a person feel immune' (p. 4). In keeping with the numerousness of the deaths, the word 'ghost' is, more often than not, employed in the plural. Rita remarks on the fact that the leather queens whom she used to know in her teens are now 'ghosts', while Killer's lover Troy, in a sudden outburst of apocalyptic prophesy, foretells that, with the spread of AIDS, 'Memorial services will be held at every hour of the day and night' and 'the ghosts will have to compete wildly for remembrance' (p. 127).

Other differences also exist between Schulman's treatment of spectral imagery and Donoghue's. Not all the personal losses to which Schulman refers are caused by death. On the contrary, some of the most poignant, as mentioned above, stem not from the AIDS virus but from parental rejection. Rita, David and the other characters whom Schulman introduces are portrayed as haunted not only by memories of deceased lovers and friends but also by the image of the parents who rejected them and by the fantasies of the love and support which, on account of their bigoted attitudes, they failed to provide.

Memory and its contradictions play as important a part in Schulman's novel as they do in Donoghue's. The characters whom she portrays, intelligent and articulate New Yorkers who enjoy analysing their own feelings and emotional responses, contemplate and discuss them in painful and, in Rita's opinion, tedious detail. Her friend David who is dying of AIDS makes a deliberate effort to achieve what he terms 'remembrance'; he self-consciously utilizes strategies, such as writing and building friendships, which he hopes will serve to preserve him from oblivion and keep his memory alive. However, Rita, who views events with the cynical gaze of one who has witnessed numerous deaths, expresses doubt about the immortalizing power of memory. Death, she insists, has become so commonplace that it no longer has the ability to move or shock: 'Let's face it, this death, itself, is no longer extraordinary, emotionally, to me' (pp. 50–1). While promising David to his face that she will remember him, she privately admits that she does not know how long she will do so or in what way.

Memory, as well as being represented as a means of consolation, is also recognized to be a source of pain. David is distressed to find that his memories of his boyfriend Don in the early days of their relationship, when he was healthy and physically attractive, have been erased by the image of him on his deathbed, emaciated and hollow-eyed, 'with silvery worms of plastic coming out of his nose' (p. 72). Rita, thinking about her mother who died of cancer when she was a child, acknowledges the way that, with the passing of the years, the boundary between memory and fantasy becomes blurred. Dismissing her memory of her mother as 'an inventory of voids', she bitterly observes, 'I wish I could dispose of memories. What good are they? Just a yearning for something that didn't happen, something sweet that was never said' (p. 49).

Another point of connection between *Rat Bohemia* and *Hood* is the allusions the two novels make to the realm of the abject. Schulman treats the concept in a multifaceted manner, dextrously juxtaposing and interweaving three different examples: rats, homosexuals and people with AIDS. All three, despite society's attempt to exterminate/reject/ignore them, refuse to be disposed of/obliterated/repressed. Like the rats which, surviving the attempts of the New Yorkers to exterminate them, continue to swarm and the lesbians and gay men who, ignoring their parents' disapproval and rejection, persist in leading a homosexual lifestyle, the dead and the dying, despite the efforts made by the living to exorcize their memory, continue to invade their minds and memories. They taint and disorientate their thoughts, destabilizing the demarcation line between life and death. Rita, trying to concentrate on the piece of his writing that David is reading her, finds herself distracted by feelings of disgust at his physical appearance; she watches him read with sweat cascading from his face, literally pouring all over himself and the paper. I watched it dripping and was utterly repulsed. I didn't want to be, but honestly, I was. I felt like I was going to throw up – the way you vomit at the smell of homeless people while having nothing against them and a great deal of pity. (p. 107)

Rita's reference to the homeless in this passage is ironic, since it anticipates the way that some months later, on the occasion of David's own funeral, a crowd of homeless people enter the square and swarm around his coffin. They get mixed up with the mourners, confusing the distinction between friends and strangers and generally undermining the dignity of the ceremony.

The destabilizing of the border between life and death, in which the AIDS crisis and its association with the abject domain of the corpse results, receives frequent illustration in the novel. The dead and the dying continually obtrude themselves into the conversation of the living, threatening to become the sole talking point. People who are not HIV-positive are in the minority and, as a consequence, feel excluded. The sick David, instead of envying his friend Manuel who is HIV-negative, admits to feeling sorry for him, since he recognizes that he is 'surrounded by the faces of his future ghosts' (p. 91). Rita herself internalizes the community's obsession with death. Instead of expressing relief at her survivor status, she experiences feelings of isolation and guilt, describing it in the negative phrase of 'being left behind'.

Images relating to the grotesque body, utilized by Donoghue to illustrate the way that the impact of death destabilizes order and identity and distorts the perspectives of the living, are employed by Schulman to depict the physical transformations which AIDS effects, and to highlight people's fear of contracting the disease. David, who prides himself on his intellect and hopes to be remembered for his literary achievements, is ironically spoken of by his friends in terms of his deteriorating physical condition – his diminishing number of T-cells and his resultant decline in health. In the months prior to his death he too starts to take on the appearance of a ghost. Killer, who has watched other men decline in a similar manner, remarks on 'How skinny he'd gotten. To that point where all their clothes are falling off but have to be loose to avoid swelling. It just hangs on their bodies kind of shapeless and you could tell he'd had hours of diarrhea' (p. 106).

The bodies and sexual practices of the lesbian population, rather than being unaffected by the impact of AIDS, are indirectly influenced by it. The atmosphere of candlelight and romance conjured up by the Cuban girl, with whom Rita has a brief affair, is abruptly shattered when she insists on putting on a pair of latex gloves to make love. Even though, as Rita tells her, no evidence exists that lesbians can contract the disease from one another, the atmosphere of panic pervading the city scares her into taking protective measures.

Like Donoghue, Schulman juxtaposes representations of the healthy, sexually active body with images of physical decay. David contrasts the touch of his lover Don's chest beneath his hands, firm and hunky 'like the side of a mountain', when the two first met, with the image of him 'toothpick thin and covered with KS' on his deathbed (p. 75). Gay icons of health and beauty, such as the handsome Kurt who, in his sparkling white jeans and shirt, is satirically described by David as 'a goddess of masculine beauty, Sir Venus', appear doubly attractive and desirable when contrasted with men in the latter stages of AIDS. Schulman astutely exposes the way that, as the gay community's fear of death escalates, so, paradoxically, does its obsession with physical cleanliness and good looks, along with its superstitious belief in the myth of immunity which the visual image of purity promotes. David cynically comments on the way that 'on Tenth street boys flirt with clean-cut scrub-brushed clones of themselves. Everyone looks clean. Short hair, white T-shirt, clean jeans, pierced ear, collegiate. We're trying out for the Varsity Squad because clean boys don't have it. Only the dirty ones have it' (p. 60). Even he, who prides himself on his intelligence and rationality, indulges in the consolatory fantasy that, 'If one night I can meet the right Mr Clean and we can keep our minds AIDS free ... maybe it will neutralize my infection and I'll never have to worry again' (p. 61). The horror of AIDS, Schulman illustrates, instead of encouraging people to accept the limitations and imperfections of the body as one might optimistically hope, makes them increasingly intolerant and fearful of them. They respond by taking refuge in compensatory fantasies of physical perfection and becoming fixated with superficialities of image and appearance.

The treatment of spectral visitation and the imagery relating to the motif in contemporary lesbian fiction is characterized both by its diversity and its innovative reworking of the conventions of the past. While all the novels discussed in this chapter create variations on the format of the ghost story, they differ considerably in perspective and style. They include the utilization of scenarios of ghosts and haunting by Zanger and Martinac to recreate episodes from the lesbian past and to explore the transgressive effects of lesbian desire; Brown's reworking of the image of the haunted house as a vehicle for delineating the traumatic effect that parental conflict and familial breakdown have on the lesbian subject; Winterson's focus on ghostly doubles to express the emotional resonances of love and war; and the introduction of spectral imagery in the fiction of Donoghue and Schulman to impress upon the reader the anguish of lesbian/gay bereavement. However, different though these versions of spectral visitation are, they reveal significant connections and correspondences. In addition to hinging on the concept of 'the return of the repressed', they all illustrate, in different ways, the preoccupation on the part of writers, in the period of the late 1980s and the 1990s, with the complexities of lesbian subjectivity and sexuality.

Sexuality also plays a prominent role in the novels and stories discussed in the following chapter. These centre on a motif that is explicitly sexual in significance and, partly as a result of the emphasis on sex and erotic fantasy promoted by the sexual radicals and the queer movement, has recently achieved a marked degree of popularity in lesbian culture – the vampire.

NOTES

1. Rebecca Brown, *The Haunted House* (Picador, 1987), p. 134.

2. Sigmund Freud, 'The "Uncanny"', in *Freud: Complete Psychological Works*, vol. 17, p. 242.

3. Hélène Cixous, 'Fiction and Its Phantoms: A Reading of Freud's *Das Unheimliche* (The "Uncanny")', *New Literary History: A Journal of Theory and Interpretation* 7:3 (1973), 542.

4. Cixous, 'Fiction and Its Phantoms', p. 543.

5. Punter, *The Literature of Terror*, p. 302.

6. M.R. James, *Ghost Stories* (Penguin, 1986).

7. See Mary Jacobus, 'The Buried Letter: *Villette*', in *Reading Woman: Essays in Feminist Criticism* (Methuen, 1986), pp. 44–56.

8. Castle, *The Apparitional Lesbian*, p. 30.

9. White, 'Female Spectator, Lesbian Specter', pp. 142–72.

10. Fuss, *Inside/Out*, p. 3.

11. For reference to the double, see Day, *In the Circles of Fear*, p. 78; and Kahane, 'The Gothic Mirror', p. 337. Kahane remarks, ' The ongoing battle with a mirror image who is both self and other is what I find at the center of the Gothic structure' (p. 117).

12. Illustrations are to be found in du Maurier's *Rebecca*, James's 'The Turn of the Screw' and Stevenson's *Dr. Jekyll and Mr. Hyde*.

13. Day, *In the Circles of Fear and Desire*, pp. 78, 103–7.

14. Zimmerman writes perceptively about the pressures on writers to avoid writing too explicitly about sex in *The Safe Sea of Women*, p. 96.

15. See Cynthia Griffin Wolff, 'The Radcliffean Gothic Model: A Form for Feminine Sexuality', in Fleenor (ed.), *The Female Gothic*, pp. 207–23.

16. See Kahane, 'The Gothic Mirror', pp. 347–8.

17. See Freud, 'The "Uncanny"', p. 245.

18. Kahane, 'The Gothic Mirror', p. 336. See also Creed's discussion of the cinematic treatment of the motif in *The Monstrous-Feminine*, pp. 54–8.

19. Nina da Vinci Nichols, 'Place and Eros in Radcliffe, Lewis and Brontë', in Fleenor (ed.), *The Female Gothic*, p. 190.

20. Molleen Zanger, *Gardenias Where There Are None* (Naiad Press, 1994), p. 50. Further page references are to this edition and are in the text.

21. Mark S. Madoff, 'Inside, Outside, and the Gothic Locked-Room Mystery', in Kenneth W. Graham (ed.), *Gothic Fictions: Prohibition/Transgression* (AMS Press, 1989), p. 61. Further page references are to this edition and are in the text.

22. Day, *In the Circles of Fear*, pp. 21–2.

23. Barbara Johnson, 'My Monster/My Self', *Diacritics*, 12 (Summer 1992), 1–5.

24. Paula Martinac, *Out of Time* (Seal Press, 1990), p. 17. Further page references are to this edition and are in the text.

25. Freud, 'The "Uncanny"', pp. 220–6, 236–7.

26. See Day, *In the Circles of Fear*, pp. 63–8.

27. See Freud, 'Infantile Sexuality', in *Complete Psychological Works*, vol. 7, pp. 194–7; and Laplanche and Pontalis, 'Fantasy and the Origins of Sexuality', p. 19.

28. Kahane, 'The Gothic Mirror', pp. 334–8.

29. Freud, *Complete Psychological Works*, vol. 21, p. 226.

30. Rebecca Brown, *The Haunted House* (Picador, 1987), p. 13. Further page references are to this edition and are in the text.

31. Creed, *The Monstrous Feminine*, p. 55.

32. *The Irigaray Reader*, p. 91. For reference to the theory of *déréliction*, see 'The Bodily Encounter with the Mother', in Margaret Whitford (ed.), *The Irigaray Reader*, pp. 35–46; and Margaret Whitford, *Luce Irigaray: Philosophy in the Feminine* (Routledge, 1991), pp. 77–8, 81–9.

33. Critical discussions of *The Passion* include Lisa Moore, 'Teledildonics: Virtual Lesbians in the Fiction of Jeanette Winterson', in Elizabeth Grosz and Elspeth Probyn (eds), *Sexy Bodies: The Strange Carnalities of Feminism* (Routledge, 1995), pp. 104–27; Paulina Palmer, '*The Passion*: Storytelling, Fantasy, Desire', in Helena Grice and Tim Woods (eds), *'I'm Telling You Stories': Jeanette Winterson and the Politics of Reading* (Rodopi, 1998), pp. 103–17; and Scott Wilson, 'Passion at the End of History', in Grice and Woods, *'I'm Telling You Stories'*, pp. 61–74.

34. See Patricia Waugh, *Feminine Fictions: Revisiting the Postmodern* (Routledge, 1989), pp. 7–16.

35. Moore, 'Teledildonics', p. 112.

36. Jeanette Winterson, *The Passion* (Penguin, 1988), p. 96. Further page references are to this edition and are in the text.

37. De Lauretis, 'Sexual Indifference and Lesbian Representation', p. 150.

38. Creed, 'Lesbian Bodies: Tribades, Tomboys and Tarts', in Grosz and Probyn (eds), *Sexy Bodies*, pp. 96–9.

39. Dikstra, *Idols*, pp. 296–313.

40. Bakhtin, *Rabelais and His World*, p. 317.

41. Clément, 'The Guilty One', p. 9.

42. Monique Wittig and Sande Zeig, *Lesbian Peoples* (Virago, 1980), p. 31.

43. Mary Russo, *The Female Grotesque: Risk, Excess and Modernity* (Routledge, 1984), pp. 41–51.

44. Clark, 'Commodity Lesbianism', in Abelove *et al.* (eds), *The Lesbian and Gay Studies Reader*, p. 194.

45. Kristeva, *Powers of Horror*, p. 4. See also Creed, *The Monstrous-Feminine*, p. 10.

46. For reference to Winterson's representation of Venice in terms of a feminine sexual economy and a discussion of her lesbian/feminist reworking of episodes from Italo Calvino's *Le città invisibili*, see Palmer, '*The Passion*: Storytelling, Fantasy, Desire', pp. 112–16.

47. Emma Donoghue, *Hood* (Hamish Hamilton, 1995), p. 35. Further page references are to this edition and are in the text.

48. Freud, 'Mourning and Melancholia', *Complete Psychological Works*, vol. 14, p. 245.

49. Bakhtin, *Rabelais and His World*, pp. 353–4.

50. Studies of AIDS include Simon Watney, 'The Spectacle of AIDS', and D.A. Miller, 'Sontag's Urbanity', in *The Lesbian and Gay Studies Reader*, pp. 202–11, 212–20.

51. Sarah Schulman, *Rat Bohemia* (Plume, 1997), p. 42. Further page references are to this edition and are in the text.

52. Freud, 'Mourning and Melancholia', p. 244.

53. Freud, 'Thoughts on War and Death', in *Complete Psychological Works*, vol. 14, p. 290.

CHAPTER 4 The vampire: transgressive
sexuality

'The vampire is the queer in its lesbian mode.'[1]

DRACULA'S DAUGHTERS

The image of the vampire has been frequently in the public eye in the 1990s.
In addition to inspiring numerous novels and stories, it has generated two
major critical studies. Ken Gelder, in tracing the creature's shifting fortunes
in literature and myth from the eighteenth century to the present day,
explores the varied and at times bizarre assortment of interpretations that
theorists and writers assign to it. Meanings that he discusses include the
foreigner, such as the Jew or black, contact with whom imperialist nations
fear will contaminate their blood; communist tyranny in Eastern Europe;
queer relationships; and (unlikely though it sounds) the Lacanian concept of
'the Real'.[2] Nina Auerbach, adopting a more populist approach, focuses on
the vampire's links with contemporary politics and culture; she examines,
among other things, the significance it assumes in relation to the fears of
communism and nuclear war that haunted the American imagination in the
1950s and 1960s.[3] However, there is one topic which both writers, different
though their perspectives are, prioritize. This is the vampire's homoerotic
associations. They concentrate attention on the character who, they agree,
furnished the model for the representation of the vampire as we are familiar
with it today in fiction and film: Stoker's Count Dracula. Whereas Gelder
teases out the homoerotic nuances in the Count's relationship with Jonathan
Harker,[4] Auerbach makes the interesting suggestion that his main
progenitor, rather than being John Polidori's Lord Ruthven or James
Rymer's Varney, as critics generally assume, was the ill-fated figure of 'Oscar
Wilde in the dock'.[5] Dracula's solitariness, the intense opprobrium which he
arouses and the stance of silence he assumes in contrast to the loquaciousness

of Van Helsing and his Crew of Light who hold forth volubly about their moral rectitude – all these features, she observes, correspond to the circumstances of Wilde during his trial.

The vampires that dominate the story lines of film and fiction, whether their sexual preferences are heterosexual or gay, are generally represented as male. However, female vampires have also achieved a degree of notoriety – frequently of a misogynistic kind. Nineteenth-century artists and writers utilized the motif as a vehicle to delineate the woman who takes excessive pleasure in sex and to illustrate the destructive effect her inordinate sexual demands have upon men. Philip Burne-Jones portrays her gloating over the limp body of her unconscious lover, while Franz Flaum, in a powerful sculptural representation, depicts her in the act of stalking her prey.[6] It is interesting to note that Stoker, although centring his novel on the activities of Count Dracula, also introduces a clutch of female vampires. Lucy Westenra who, on becoming Dracula's victim, is herself transformed into a member of the undead reveals, prior to her metamorphosis, symptoms of the sexual promiscuity associated in nineteenth-century *fin-de-siècle* culture with the figure of 'the New Woman'. This is signalled by her inability to choose between the three suitors who compete for her love and by her playfully voiced remark that she wishes that society would allow her to marry all three.[7]

Appearing less frequently in nineteenth-century literature, though representing an even greater threat to marriage and the fabric of society, is the lesbian vampire. Zimmerman traces her origins to the Countess Elizabeth Bathory, a sixteenth-century Hungarian aristocrat who allegedly engaged in the gruesome practice of bathing in the blood of local virgins to preserve her youth, and to the Countess Millarca Karnstein, the eponymous heroine of Joseph Sheridan LeFanu's *Carmilla* (1872).[8] LeFanu, although depicting Carmilla's transgressive behaviour as being punished with death, portrays her with unexpected sensitivity. Her unconventional sexual attentions, though producing the usual symptoms of pallor and lethargy in her victims, elicit a response of pleasure from Laura, the young woman whom she loves. Carmilla, as Auerbach points out, is, in fact, 'one of the few self-accepting homosexual vampires in Victorian literature'.[9] Instead of resting content with homosocial bonding, as is the case with her male counterparts Byron's Augustus Darvell[10] and Polidori's Lord Ruthven,[11] she has the courage to act on her desires and form a relationship that is overtly sexual.

In contrast to LeFanu's liberal approach, other nineteenth-century writers treat the lesbian vampire in a homophobic manner, associating her with evil and sexual depravity. Coleridge portrays her in his unfinished poem *Christabel* (1816) seducing her victim and winning her trust with a display of insidious charm, while Charles Baudelaire[12] and Algernon Charles Swinburne utilize vampiric imagery to typecast the lesbian as decadent and morally corrupt. Swinburne describes in vampiric terms the 'shameless, nameless love' in which the Roman empress Faustine, inspired by 'the stray breaths of Sapphic song that blew through Mityline', supposedly indulged.[13] As Clemence Dane's *The Regiment of Women* (1917) and Francis Brett Young's *White Ladies* (1935) illustrate, the introduction of vampiric imagery to stigmatize the figure of the lesbian continued in the twentieth century. D. H. Lawrence's *The Rainbow* (1915) contains a particularly vicious example in the portrayal of Winifred Inger, the school teacher who becomes the lover of the heroine Ursula. Having transformed Winifred into a kind of predatory lamia by comparing her to 'a prehistoric lizard', Lawrence emphasizes the vampirish nature of her lovemaking by describing it depleting Ursula's vitality and leaving her with a 'heavy, clogged sense of deadness'.[14]

With the advent of the horror film, directors have tended to exploit the image of the lesbian vampire for sensationalistic, pornographic ends, taking advantage of the appeal of the motif to male fantasy. *The Vampire Lovers* (1970) and *Twins of Evil* (1971) illustrate this trend, associating lesbian love with violence and narcissism.[15] Nonetheless cinematic representations, despite their misogynistic resonances, frequently display an element of ambiguity. As Zimmerman's reading of the *Daughters of Darkness* (1970)[16] and Creed's discussion of *The Hunger* (1983)[17] illustrate, the lesbian vampire, though ostensibly portrayed as monstrous and unnatural, simultaneously emerges as a signifier of female power. Like the other Gothic motifs discussed in this study, she displays a potential for lesbian/ feminist revision. Her shape-changing abilities can be read as denoting her refusal to become entrapped in the conventional domestic role, while her erotic relations with women represent a challenge to the institution of marriage and the control men seek to exert on female sexuality.

Transgressive sexuality is a key feature of the lesbian vampire's representation, differentiating her from the other mythic images of womanhood that feature in lesbian Gothic. Whereas the witch is utilized by Hanrahan and Tennant to explore the disruptive effects of female eroticism, and the spectral visitor, as illustrated by the novels of Martinac and Zanger, acts as a signifier of repressed desire, the vampire, on account of her connections with blood and oral sex, is explicitly sexual in significance, carrying associations of a perverse eroticism that violates accepted taboos.[18] The vampire's reputation for transgressive sexuality explains, of course, the popularity that the motif is currently enjoying in lesbian and queer culture. Although the reclamation of the lesbian vampire commenced in 1984 with the publication of Scott's *I, Vampire*, only recently, in the late 1980s and the 1990s, has it captured the imagination of writers and readers, and texts centring on the motif have proliferated.[19] The lesbian vampire's rise to fame has coincided with the emphasis on the sexual dimension of lesbianism promoted by the sexual radicals and the queer movement. Three of the texts discussed in this chapter, Gomez' novel and the stories of Forrest and Califia, reveal the influence of these movements and can be read, in certain cases, as manifestos for them. The three writers portray the lesbian vampire as a signifier of an alternative economy of sexual pleasure which is more emotionally intense and fulfilling than its heterosexual counterpart. The descriptions of lesbian sex that they create, in some cases successfully and in others less so, function as a fantasy space of transgressive eroticism which exists beyond the limits of mundane reality and the confines of patriarchy. These passages foreground the relationship between sexuality and the body, exploring its boundaries, flows, ruptures and exchanges.[20]

In challenging the homophobic associations of the lesbian vampire and transforming the motif into a signifier of lesbian sexual pleasure, the writers discussed in this chapter appropriate ideas from both classic vampire narratives and feminist/queer readings and critiques. Instead of portraying her as the epitome of the monstrous Other, as is the case with texts reproducing a hetero-patriarchal viewpoint, they position her as narrator or protagonist and allow her to address the reader directly. They also tease out the metaphorical connections between 'lesbian' and 'vampire'. These, as illustrated below, are both numerous and complex.

A key point of affinity between the lesbian and the vampire, which writers frequently exploit, is their dual existence both as independent loners and members of a loosely knit network or group. Both figures experience a tension between the need for privacy and anonymity on the one hand and interaction with members of 'their own kind' on the other. While concealing their lesbianism/vampirism from the prying eyes of the world, they seek to recognize and be recognized by a group of like-minded sisters. The association of the vampire with the period of twilight, since the sunset is supposed to liberate her from her coffin and permit her to venture abroad to stalk her prey, is pertinent in metaphoric terms to the closeted lesbian who, having concealed her sexual orientation during the day, emerges at night to seek romance in the half-lit world of clubs and bars. The popularity that lesbian vampire fiction is currently enjoying, in addition to reflecting the interest in the sexual dimension of lesbianism which characterizes present-day lesbian/queer culture, also mirrors the re-evaluation, frequently nostalgic in tone, of the lesbian social life of the 1950s with its emphasis on a furtively illicit lifestyle centring on the night-time scene.[21] The reason the lesbian and the vampire feel forced to conceal their identities and lead a double life is because they are targets of persecution. Terms of abuse such as 'unnatural', 'perverse' and 'monstrous' are directed at both. As Case observes in her essay 'Tracking the Vampire', where she discusses the potential the motif displays for lesbian and queer appropriation, 'the identification with the insult, the taking on of the transgressive, and the consequent flight into invisibility' traditionally typifying lesbian existence 'are inscribed in the figure of the vampire'.[22]

The association of the vampire with sterility and death is also, sad to say, applicable from a homophobic point of view to the figure of the lesbian. Although many lesbians and gay men do raise children, homosexuality tends to be linked in the mind of the general public with barrenness and sterility. Gillian Hanscombe and Jackie Forster in their study of lesbian motherhood comment on the fact that, on account of the confusion existing between female sexual pleasure and reproductive sex and the notion that lesbians are psychologically or physiologically 'masculine', many people assume that they are incapable of bearing children. Alternatively, if by some quirk of fate they do bear them, they are deemed unfit to care for them.[23] The connection existing between homosexuality and death is illustrated by Jonathan Dollimore; he points out that the linking of the two in homophobic studies of AIDS is by no means new since reference to death is, in fact, common in discussions of same-sex desire throughout history.[24] Yet despite the fact that particularly in the present era of AIDS, male homosexuality and lesbianism, like vampirism, tend to be associated with sterility and death, they also paradoxically carry connotations of immortality. Though frequently experiencing intense pressure to submit to heterosexual norms, lesbians and gay men refuse to do so. Resisting harassment and persecution, they continue, like the vampire, to pursue an alternative lifestyle and survive.

The lesbian and the vampire also reveal links in terms of sex and sexual politics. Livia foregrounds three significant points of affinity when in *Minimax*, a novel discussed in this chapter, she commands the reader with evident relish to 'think of all those beautiful female heads rising superbly from between their lovers' thighs, mouths dripping with menstrual blood. Triple taboo: no oral sex, no sex during periods, no female to female sex ...'.[25] And while, as Livia humorously emphasizes, the lesbian, like the vampire, breaks the 'triple taboo' of sexual relations with women, oral sex and sex during menstruation, she also challenges the institution of marriage by forming primary attachments with women. Whereas the vampire unsettles our assumption of clearly defined categories by traversing the borderline between the living and the dead, the lesbian destabilizes conventional gender roles by usurping the male prerogative of choosing a woman as love-object. In addition, both display perverse connections with the maternal. The lesbian vampire, Creed argues, is a particularly terrifying creature since, in causing woman's blood to flow while also initiating her into eternal life, she reworks, with perverse displacements, the primal scene of birth. The lesbian, by taking a woman as her lover, indirectly embarks on a taboo return to the pleasures of the mother/daughter relationship.[26]

The connections between the vampire and the lesbian furnish the frame for the novels and stories discussed in this chapter. Writers treat them inventively, developing different aspects of vampire lore and utilizing them for a variety of intellectual and ideological ends. Scott and Livia, concentrating on the vampire's relation to the abject, humorously problematize the concepts of the monstrous and the abnormal which she conventionally embodies, exposing them as relative and arbitrary. They utilize the vampire's shape-changing abilities as a vehicle for addressing issues relating to the construction of role and identity. The excess which in hetero-patriarchal culture lesbian sexuality signifies is mirrored in the style the two writers employ. It finds expression in an unconventional mingling of genres, unexpected flights of humour and a witty utilization of parody and pastiche.

In the fiction of Forrest, Califia and Gomez the transgressive dimension of lesbianism and the excess that it signifies are expressed primarily by reference to sex and the body. The physical transformations the vampire enacts and the exchange of blood in which s/he engages inspire the three writers to create representations of the body in its grotesque form, foregrounding its orifices, protuberances, fluids and sexual rhythms. Experimental forms of sexual practice such as oral sex, S&M, and butch-femme role-play also assume prominence. Califia and Gomez juxtapose, in a manner deliberately intended to disturb the reader, images of maternal nurture with depictions of lesbian/vampiric sexual encounters. The latter are emphatically violent, involving reference to blood and wounds.

A focus on the grotesque, as well as being reflected in the three writers' representations of the body and sex, is also apparent in their treatment of the family. The vampire network or 'family', they illustrate, does not depend on the Law of the Father[27] but, on the contrary, reflects a genealogy based on the direct exchange of body fluids. It resembles queer relationships and groups in furnishing a transgressive alternative to the patriarchal familial formation and the values which it encodes.[28] In her essay theorizing the vampire as a signifier of queer politics, Case makes the point that the queer movement, like the vampire, seeks to deconstruct the binaries of normal/abnormal, nature/culture, fertility/infertility by untying the knot that traditionally links sex to procreation and by foregrounding other forms of creativity besides child-bearing. The novels and stories discussed in this chapter, in exploring alternative familial formations and reproductive technologies and centring attention on examples of vampiric/gay creativity, furnish fictional illustrations of these ideas.

The texts which are the focus of this chapter, while differing in style and ideological viewpoint, share a similarly transgressive perspective. Lesbian Gothic, as we have seen, evinces little interest in normalizing lesbian relations and highlights their socially disruptive aspect and foregrounds lesbian difference. As the grotesque nature of the vampire motif and its explicitly sexual character lead us to expect, a focus on lesbian 'otherness' and the problematizing of hetero-patriarchal norms and structures are particularly to the fore in the narratives which it inspires. Case's theorization of the vampire again endorses this point. She jubilantly affirms the fact that the queer movement is uninterested in normalizing or sanitizing homosexuality but, as she luridly puts it, 'revels in the discourse of the loathsome, the outcast, the idiomatically proscribed position of same-sex desire' (p. 3). A similarly celebratory emphasis on 'difference' and 'otherness' is apparent in the texts discussed below.

HUMOUR, GENRE AND LESBIAN HISTORY

The period of the mid-1980s marked a decided upturn in the fortunes of the vampire. It witnessed its reclamation from monstrous Other to a creature which, if not exactly cuddly, is capable of enlisting the understanding and sympathy of the reader and audience. Three texts focusing on the vampire and, more significantly, assigning to her/him a subjectivity and a voice appeared around this time: Tony Scott's art film *The Hunger* (1983), focusing on the glamorously bisexual Miriam Blaylock (Catherine Deneuve) and her love affairs with mortals; Anne Rice's *The Vampire Lestat* (1986), the second volume of her *Vampire Chronicles*, which explores the history and growth of a vampire network; and Jody Scott's *I, Vampire* (1986), which utilizes the vampire as a mouthpiece for the pleasures and problems of lesbian existence. The comic dimension of Scott's novel challenges the stereotypical image of lesbian feminists as a dreary puritanical bunch who lack a sense of fun. Scott utilizes humour both to entertain the reader and as a strategy to address and popularize ideas relating to sexual politics.

The idea of treating the vampire in a comic light, which furnishes the germ of Scott's novel, has precedent in film. Roman Polanski's *The Fearless Vampire Killers* (1967) introduces a gay vampire and employs in the scenes in which he appears a brand of humour that is playfully camp. Stan Dragoti's *Love at First Bite* (1979), in portraying the vampire hero emigrating from Eastern Europe to New York when his castle is commandeered by the communist government, also exploits the vampire narrative's comic potential. Whereas film furnished Scott with an example of the humorous treatment of the vampire and the creature's homosexual associations, feminist science fiction provided her with a model for utilizing fantasy as a vehicle for sexual politics. *I, Vampire* is a work of lesbian feminist political fiction[29] in the tradition of Joanna Russ's *The Female Man* (1975). Scott emulates Russ in employing science fiction conventions to investigate the construction of gender and, by parodically manipulating stereotypes, interrogate hetero-patriarchal norms and values. Like Russ, she also advertises the fictionality of her narrative and alerts attention to its ideological import by punctuating it with jokes, intertextual allusions and passages of authorial comment. In contrast to her predecessor, however, Scott chooses to rework not one popular genre but two. She inserts into a typical science fiction scenario of interplanetary travel the Gothic motif of the vampire, exploiting the explosion of wit in which the clash between the two genres results for ideological ends. By humorously interrogating the conventional notion of the vampire's monstrous nature, she problematizes not only the idea of lesbianism as monstrous and abnormal but also the concepts of monstrosity and abnormality *per se*, exposing them as inauthentic and arbitrary.

Scott structures her novel on a series of encounters between her vampire protagonist Sterling O'Blivion and Benaroya, a visitor from outer space, and the meeting of 'the grotesque' and 'the alien' which it exemplifies. Benaroya and her fellow Rysemians are light-years ahead of the human race in intelligence. They number among their numerous talents the art of self-transformation, the enjoyment of immortality and the ability to manufacture their own physical forms and 'realities'. Benaroya has learnt everything she knows about life on earth from the novels and films she has studied on her native planet while preparing for her trip abroad. She is used to adopting different personae and, in order to win Sterling's trust, chooses to materialize before her in the guise of Virginia Woolf, signifier of female creativity and lesbian love. The aim of her visit to earth is to prevent the human race from destroying the universe, a course on which, she angrily observes, it appears to be hellbent. As she informs the astonished Sterling, she has chosen her as mediator in the mission to save the earth because, as a vampire, she represents a link between the human and the immortal. Sterling, Benaroya flatteringly observes, in addition to being 'the most advanced, and by far the oldest bat on the planet', is 'very wise, and not only a damned good theoretical physicist but a square shooter'! (pp. 51, 54). Though flattered by Benaroya's good opinion of her and quickly falling for her extraterrestrial charms, Sterling finds the encounter with her disconcerting and, in certain respects, humiliating. Up to now she has always regarded herself as the epitome of the weird and the perverse. She prides herself on the fact that in the sixteenth century she 'vampirized a famous Shakespearean actor whose name was a household word' (p. 31), grabbing the crucifix he was holding for self-protection and adding it to her collection of 947 similar items. Now, however, confronted by Benaroya in the unlikely guise of Virginia Woolf, she has to admit that there are creatures in the universe who are even more alien and weird than she herself. Her response to the image of the abject which, in her eyes, Benaroya represents is typically ambiguous. While she finds the image of 'a sea pig or fat dolphin, all flippers and bloated neck' (p. 59), the form that Benaroya adopts on her native planet, utterly repulsive, she regards the Virginia Woolf persona she assumes during her visit to earth as enthralling and delightful. Benaroya signifies, Sterling nervously admits, 'the edge of something'. Her description of Benaroya as combining both 'the charm of the unhuman – and the *fear*' (p. 59) agrees with Kristeva's description of the contradictions of fascination and disquiet which the abject generally evokes.

Sterling's unexpected encounter with this highly intelligent visitor from outer space, as well as undermining her pride in her own 'otherness' and monstrosity, also proves to be educational. She is astonished when, in response to her sarcastic quip 'You're the superior alien who knows it all!', Benaroya promptly retorts, 'There are no aliens' (p. 61). The inauthenticity and arbitrariness of the concept 'alien' is the novel's key theme. Its importance is illustrated by the way that, while Sterling projects the category 'alien' on to Benaroya, Benaroya and her Rysemian colleagues, despite recognizing its inauthenticity, instinctively project it on to the human race.

As they pointedly remark, parodically mimicking the expressions of bigotry and aggression which human beings habitually utter, 'What I am is *right*, and if you're different, you're on an infantile level, so I have the right and duty to bully you until you act like *me*' (p. 153). In problematizing the concepts of the alien and the Other and exposing them as oppressive constructs, Scott anticipates Case's queer approach to the vampire. Case, as mentioned above, associates the creature, on account of its unconventional sexual practice and its ability to generate a discourse which celebrates proscribed desires, with the deconstruction of the binaries normal/abnormal, nature/culture.

In problematizing the concepts of the alien and the monstrous and exposing them as inauthentic, *I, Vampire* also foregrounds the constructed aspect of culture and identity. Sterling acts as a mouthpiece for this by expressing irritation with the popular image of the vampire which people habitually project upon her. In a passage parodying lesbian/feminist complaints about the oppressive and degrading scripts which women are forced to enact, she mournfully laments the fact that she is merely 'a semi-mythological creature ... expected to act out a script written by others; one that ignores my true nature' (p. 22). Relaxing in bed, flicking through the pages of the latest vampire novel, she denounces it for producing 'boring characters, wooden writing, and no ideas' (p. 22) – and, in consequence, failing to register the fact that, as she paradoxically states, 'Vampires are as human as anyone; in fact, more so' (p. 15). Disenchanted with the tacky culture of twentieth-century America, she reminiscences nostalgically about her youthful years in Renaissance Spain when, as she proudly puts it, 'I was inventing, and I mean *personally creating*, that baroque dramatization known as the classic [vampire] style' (p. 18). She is by no means pleased when Benaroya, instead of sympathizing with her stories of the disrespect she meets with in present-day New York, accuses her of wallowing in self-pity and manifesting symptoms of self-oppression – 'Revelling', as she puts it, 'in all the bad things that have been done to you' (p. 62). Benaroya callously concludes, adding insult to injury by questioning her identity, 'This vampire thing; what is a vampire? Who projected this image onto you?' (p. 201).

Scott's humorous analysis of the vampire image and the changes it has undergone furnishes her with a vehicle to interrogate essentialist concepts of identity and, by introducing allusions to classic works such as Stoker's *Dracula*, highlight the fictionality of her own text. It also enables her to parody the syndromes of self-oppression in which women who identify as lesbian can become entrapped. Sterling's attitude towards her vampire/lesbian identity fluctuates wildly according to her mood. The exaggerated sense of pride she feels when in a positive frame of mind resembles the politically right-on views expressed by the 1970s Gay Liberation Movement; she enthusiastically proclaims, 'I adore being a vampire, I love the lore, history, rich tradition and sense of fabulous majesty it confers' (p. 5). On other occasions, however, she experiences bouts of severe self-doubt, pathetically confessing that she is tired of the stigma and would 'love to be "cured"'' (p. 5). While taking refuge in the essentialist cliché 'I was born this way' (p. 13), she expresses resentment at the prejudice that vampires frequently encounter and determines, as a result, to keep her identity secret. In her case, however, concealment is by no means easy. As she ruefully comments, alluding to the longevity that vampires allegedly enjoy, 'It's tough to keep a secret for seven hundred years' (p. 12). The stresses and strains of a lesbian lifestyle are amusingly parodied in her admission that vampiric immortality is a mixed blessing, since 'It's demonic to outlive fifty-two lovers!' (p. 33).

Further reference to the construction of lesbian identity, this time on a literary plane, is provided by Scott's intertextual allusions to Radcliffe Hall's *The Well of Loneliness* (1928). Echoing the self-justificatory assertions voiced by Hall's protagonist Stephen, Sterling insists that she 'is not a bit guilty' about her lesbian orientation since 'God has made me this way' (p. 3). Like Stephen, she finds religion a comfort in times of crisis; she nostalgically recalls that, on being thrown out of home by her outraged parents, 'I bowed my head and commended my soul to Saint Jude, the patron saint of vampires' (p. 3). She also emulates Stephen's warm response to the animal world. Whereas Hall portrays her upper-class protagonist communing with her horse in moments of depression, the socially inferior Sterling admits, on a humbler level, to 'crying myself to sleep between two warm, friendly cows' (p. 3). These references to shifting constructs of vampirism/lesbianism, combined with the critical asides Sterling makes when she steps beyond the parameters of the conventional vampire role to ridicule hetero-patriarchal values and attack the oppressive nature of the scripts assigned to women through the ages, foreground the artifice of the vampire narrative itself. They also highlight its problematic aspects. They draw attention to its intellectual and ideological limitations – in particular, the prejudiced and deficient images of femininity and homosexuality that it has produced.

Scott's humorous treatment of the vampire motif as a strategy to problematize concepts of the alien and the monstrous and to discuss constructs of lesbian identity created a blueprint for later writers. Livia's *Minimax*, published in 1991, seven years after Scott's novel, develops many of its key features. The similarities between the two texts are in some cases so close as to suggest that Livia is deliberately reworking Scott's narrative with the aim of creating a postmodern version relevant to the lesbian culture of the 1990s. Both writers structure their novels on an encounter between the present-day protagonist and a lesbian icon from the past. Whereas in Scott's novel the figure with iconic status is Virginia Woolf, the persona which the extra-terrestrial Benaroya adopts on her visit to earth, in Livia's it is Renée Vivien and her ex-lover Natalie Barney who unexpectedly materialize in 1990s Perth as members of the living dead. While Scott assigns the role of vampire to her protagonist Sterling, Livia ascribes it to Vivien and Barney.

The two novels also reveal stylistic and intellectual similarities. In addition to creating humorous versions of the vampire narrative, both utilize fantasy for anti-essentialist ends. Whereas Scott, as we have seen, problematizes concepts of the alien and the monstrous, exposing them as ideological constructs, Livia investigates changing fashions in lesbian role and identity. The representation of Vivien and Barney in vampiric form enables her to resurrect the two women from the grave and bring them face to face with her present-day protagonist Minnie. The clash of attitudes and styles which the encounter generates is a source of lively humour throughout the text. It also gives Livia the opportunity to compare and contrast the 'decadent' image of lesbianism which flourished in early twentieth-century Paris with the constructs of lesbian identity produced in the 1970s and 1980s.

Minimax opens with a parodic description of the lesbian feminism of the 1980s, emphasizing the rigidity and narrowness which, after the heady radicalism of the 1970s, tended to descend upon the lesbian community. Livia playfully illustrates that the adoption of a lesbian identification, far from being a passport to behaviour that is transgressive and individualistic, often brings with it a new set of rules – sexual, social and sartorial – which can be every bit as stifling as their heterosexual counterparts. Minnie, unemployed and living in London, is portrayed donning her lesbian feminist 'uniform' of dark jeans and sweater, purchased from the local jumble sale, and sallying forth on a shopping spree to Marks and Spencer. Here she intends to purchase a new outfit to wear to a job interview which, by dint of much effort, she has succeeded in achieving. She is delighted when the arrival of two letters, both by the same post, relieves her from the dual responsibilities of deciding what to wear and finding herself a job. One is from her mother Beryl, who has recently emigrated to Australia, inviting her to pay a visit and offering to pay her air fare to Perth. The other is a mysterious missive with a New York postmark containing the succinctly worded summons, 'Come. I must meet you' (p. 15). It bears the signature of Natalie Barney. This understandably puzzles Minnie since, as an admirer of Barney's writing, she knows that she died in 1972. Minnie, however, has had enough of life in Thatcher's Britain and is in the mood for adventure. Enthusiastically taking advantage of both invitations, she contacts a travel agency and books a flight round the world, with stops off in Perth and New York.

On meeting up with her relatives in Perth, Minnie is astonished to see the improvement that has occurred in their material circumstances. Whereas when last she heard from them they were homeless and on the breadline, now they are living in relative affluence. As she subsequently discovers, it is her mother Beryl who is responsible for this unexpected upturn in the family fortunes. Beryl is also responsible for the transformation of Livia's narrative, which up to now has been feminist realist in style, to a version of comic Gothic, complete with the standard components of vampires, coffins and incidents of shape-changing. Beryl, we discover, has entered into a business agreement with Renée Vivien who, accompanied by crateloads of Parisian furniture and memorabilia, has set up home in Perth in vampiric guise. In return for agreeing to clean her decadent mansion with its black marble staircase and chandeliers and tend her conservatory of exotically funereal plants including 'black orchids and Lethean lotuses' (p. 71), Beryl can rely on Vivien's uncanny powers to ensure her family's health and financial security.

Livia's representation of Vivien and her ex-lover Barney as members of the living dead creates a comic pastiche of the decadent construct of lesbianism that Vivien herself cultivated in her lifetime,[30] humorously ridiculing the Gothic aspects of her image. It also develops and parodies the vampiric allusions that characterize the treatment of lesbianism in nineteenth-century *fin-de-siècle* culture. Baudelaire and Swinburne portray the lesbian as a vampiric figure whose unnatural desires, though fascinating to the male voyeur, are morally corrupt and threaten to undermine the fabric of society.[31] Vivien herself was strongly influenced by this cult of decadence and reworks in her writing the sadistic image of the lesbian popularized by the male writers of the period. Critics disagree about the precise significance of her appropriation of it. Lillian Faderman disapproves, regarding it as oppressive,[32] while Susan Gubar interprets it in a more sympathetic light. She argues that Vivien, in reworking decadent aesthetic conventions, reclaimed them for women, transforming the lesbian into the prototype of the artist.[33] Livia's portrayal of Vivien interrelates these contrary viewpoints. Minnie is irritated rather than impressed by Vivien's anorexic appearance and pose of world-weary sullenness; she privately refers to her by the unflattering epithet of 'the thin pout'. However, her friend Nea, who hails from California, finds Vivien immensely attractive. In fact, she is so captivated that she accepts her invitation to embark on a love affair. The New Age construct of lesbianism, Livia mischievously implies, is not only compatible with the *fin-de-siècle* decadent image but also reveals affinities with it. Nea and Vivien discover to their surprise that, despite the significant age gap between them, they have interests in common. Both enjoy enacting models of femininity from earlier periods and revel in displays of role play and pseudo-religious ritual. Nea, who regards herself as 'a reincarnation of an Inca priestess' (p. 152), is delighted by Vivien's description of herself as 'an altar maid of an Eastern temple' (p. 153).

The decadent model of lesbianism that Vivien, with her anorexic looks and conservatory of funereal plants, epitomizes acts as a foil to the romantic Sapphic image exemplified by Barney. Conquered by the latter's seductive rhetoric, Minnie throws caution to the winds and, forgetting Barney's reputation for capriciousness and infidelity, accepts her invitation to become her lover. However, after a few weeks of happiness Barney, true to the belief in sexual freedom and experimentation which she championed during her life, tires of her new conquest and abandons her. She sails away on her yacht accompanied by Vivien and Nea to savour the Sapphic pleasures of California, leaving lesbian feminist Minnie standing forlornly on the quayside in the classic pose of jilted womanhood.

A feature of Livia's novel that differentiates it from Scott's is the focus it places on historical constructs of lesbianism. Unlike Scott who, writing in the early 1980s, makes only passing reference to the topic in her intertextual allusions to Woolf and Hall, Livia, influenced by the interest in lesbian history that emerged towards the end of the decade, gives it pride of place. *Minimax* can be read as a playfully inventive fiction of history which endorses the postmodern view that the investigation of the past involves the use of imagination as well as the documentation of facts. However, even regarded in postmodern terms, the methods of research that Livia assigns to her protagonist Minnie strike the reader as unorthodox and eccentric. Minnie achieves information about two famous lesbian writers from the past not by reading the texts they produced or perusing their biographies but by conversing with them and embarking on a love affair with one of them. Ironically, rather than valuing the opportunity which the encounter offers for gaining an insight into an important episode of lesbian history, Minnie treats it very casually. She is more interested in flaunting what she regards as her own superior knowledge and in slotting Vivien and Barney into present-day cultural paradigms than in listening to their views and ideas. Livia cynically suggests that, when the present-day lesbian actually does have the chance to investigate lesbian history at first hand, her egocentricity and obsession with political correctness act as a barrier to communication and blinker her vision.

Another issue of topical interest in the late 1980s and early 1990s that *Minimax* explores is role-play, lesbian as well as Gothic. As the relationships between the two couples around whom the narrative revolves develop, the novel becomes a veritable masquerade of shifting roles and identities. In a Gothic context, the reader is treated to the ludicrous picture of Barney entertaining Minnie in her cabin by offering her a glass of the freshly squeezed orange juice, while she herself enjoys a glass of rhesus positive from the icebox. From a lesbian point of view, the novel addresses the topic of butch-femme role-play. This was of particular interest to readers at the time of the novel's publication, since the late 1980s and the 1990s saw the attempt on the part of the lesbian sexual radicals to re-evaluate the practice and, in some cases, revive it. The controversy that this provoked was, of course, a contributory factor in the lesbian 'Sex Wars'.[34] Livia treats the debate about role-play in an irreverently frivolous manner. The emphasis she places on the performative aspect of identity looks forward to the concept of 'gender as performance' promoted by Judith Butler. Gender, Butler maintains, rather than reflecting an essence, is constituted through a set of 'discursively constrained acts that produce the body through and within the categories of sex'.[35] She argues that butch-femme and gay roles do not, as people generally assume, mirror original heterosexual identities. Instead, they have the effect of exposing and 'bringing into relief the utterly constructed status of the so-called heterosexual original' (p. 31). *Minimax* similarly foregrounds the constructed aspect of role and identity, heterosexual as well as gay. A significant source of humour in the novel is the arbitrary nature of role, along with the social and sexual confusions that can occur if the semiotics of behaviour and dress are misread. Californian Nea, who identifies as femme and favours brightly coloured clothes, mistakenly assumes that Minnie, who wears dark sweaters and jeans, identifies as butch. In actual fact, Minnie identifies as lesbian feminist and has no use for role-play. Episodes of this kind illustrate the novel's satirical scope. In addition to commenting on the current vogue for investigating and reconstructing the lesbian past, *Minimax* also critiques present-day images of lesbianism, exposing their contradictions and absurdities.

SEX AND EROTIC FANTASY

The sexual connotations of the vampire, which are instrumental in accounting for the popularity the motif is currently enjoying, make it an appropriate vehicle for discussing other aspects of lesbian sex besides the topic of butch-femme role-play which Livia addresses in *Minimax*. Oral sex, S&M partnerships and different forms of erotic fantasy are all topics that achieve representation and analysis in the lesbian vampire narrative. The two stories by Forrest and Califia discussed in this section exemplify this focus. They are influenced by and contribute to the debates about sexuality which, surfacing in the 1980s, continue to provoke discussion and controversy among women who identify as lesbian or bisexual.[36] The sexual encounters on which the stories centre are introduced not merely for purposes of characterization or to stimulate the reader erotically – though they certainly are erotic. They are ideological in emphasis, contributing to a deliberately worked out political agenda. Aligning themselves with the lesbian sexual radicals,[37] Forrest and Califia seek to affirm the importance of the sexual dimension of lesbianism and to expand the reader's appreciation of sexual pleasure. The image of sex they create differs from the lesbian feminist model in prioritizing experimentation and role-play. In foregrounding the interaction between dominant/submissive positions in butch-femme relationships or S&M encounters, it also represents lesbian partnerships as involving the negotiation of power. In contrast to the lesbian feminists who associated power and violence with heterosexual relations, the lesbian sexual radicals regarded them as intrinsic features of sex in general. They promoted butch-femme role-play and S&M scenarios as a vehicle for channelling and controlling these tendencies. In consonance with their belief in sexual experimentation, they also advocated an interest in erotic fantasy. These ideas, in addition to informing collections of essays and stories such as the groundbreaking volume *Desire: The Politics of Sexuality* (1984),[38] are also reflected in the lesbian magazines of the 1980s, such as the American publication *On Our Backs* and the British *Quim*. *Serious Pleasure* (1989), a collection of erotic stories produced by Sheba Feminist Publishers, likewise aims to stimulate the readers' enjoyment of the erotic. It contains, it is interesting to note, a story by Gomez,[39] whose contribution to the lesbian reclamation of the vampire motif is discussed below.

The vampire, with its associations of power struggle, transgressive eroticism and the image of sex as paradoxically pleasurable and dangerous, makes a suitable vehicle for the radical image of lesbian sexuality which Forrest, Califia and Gomez seek to convey. As we shall see, the three writers treat the motif from notably different angles – and with varying degrees of success.

Forrest's 'O Captain, My Captain', interpreted in terms of the debates about lesbian sexuality and sexual practice which dominated lesbian politics in the 1980s and the early 1990s, creates a bridge between the approach promoted by the lesbian sexual radicals and the lesbian/feminist model. On the one hand, Forrest celebrates sexual pleasure, represents lesbian sex as involving the negotiation of power and introduces episodes that are explicitly erotic. On the other hand, however, by revising the traditional image of the vampire and repudiating the thirst for blood traditionally attributed to the creature, she rejects the focus on pain associated with S&M.

In addition to mediating between these contrary approaches to sex, Forrest also brings together two different styles of vampire narrative. She combines the focus on humour and the interplay of genres which Scott employs with the emphasis on the erotic reflected in the texts of Califia and Gomez. Like Scott, she utilizes the simple but effective device of inserting the Gothic motif of the lesbian vampire into a science fiction frame, thus subverting the latter's masculinist associations. Captains of space ships are generally portrayed as male and heterosexual. They are certainly not depicted as lesbian vampires who engage in love affairs with female members of the crew and perform the uncanny trick of transforming themselves into bats – as is the case with Drake, the Captain of *Scorpio IV*, the spacecraft that is the setting for Forrest's story.

Connections are also apparent between Forrest's and Scott's two vampire protagonists. Captain Drake resembles Scott's Sterling O'Blivion in both her intelligence and her articulateness. Like Sterling, she utilizes these attributes to interrogate the myths and fallacies of male-supremacist culture. Whereas Sterling ridicules contemporary vampire romances, dismissing them as mindless rubbish which fail to do justice to the complexities of vampire existence, Drake – ironically, considering the fact that her name is indebted to its protagonist – comments disparagingly on Stoker's *Dracula* (1897). In fact, she regards Stoker not as a writer of fiction at all but, as she scornfully remarks, 'a historian – and a most limited one at that' (p. 215). Other features of classic vampire lore also provoke Drake's contempt. She demolishes the idea that vampire sexual practice is necessarily injurious to human beings and explodes the myth that vampires always sleep in coffins. In exposing the popular image of the vampire as inaccurate and prejudiced and correcting misconceptions about it by reference to personal experience, both Sterling and Drake advertise the deconstructive aims of the texts in which they appear. They also emulate the role of the writers who created them, acting in this respect as their doubles. They dismantle outdated myths about vampires just as Scott and Forrest dismantle erroneous images of lesbianism.

Here, however, the similarities between the two writers end. In contrast to Scott, who concentrates on interrogating and problematizing the concepts of the alien and the monstrous, Forrest aims to affirm and celebrate lesbian sexuality. Her story hinges on a topic which, as we saw in the introductory section to this chapter, creates a link between vampirism and lesbianism. This is oral sex and the breaking of the taboo relating to it in which both the vampire and the lesbian engage.

Captain Drake is accompanied on her voyage in space by her second-in-command Lieutenant Harper, a re-creation of Stoker's Harker. Harper is positioned in the text as a naïve persona. Her initial inability to perceive the fact that Drake is a vampire, a discovery which the reader, alerted by the tell-tale signs of Eastern European origins, unnatural pallor and unusual sleeping habits, makes early on, is a source of humour that Forrest effectively exploits. Harper interprets Drake's reclusive habits and lack of interest in socializing as eccentricities stemming from long spells of duty away from home. When, spying on Drake in her cabin, she unexpectedly sees her transform herself into a bat, she refuses to credit the evidence of her own eyes and thinks that she must be hallucinating. Even when, succumbing to Drake's androgynous beauty and flattered by her expressions of sexual interest, she finds her hostility giving way to a feelings of attraction and, forgetting her lover Niklaus who patiently awaits her return on earth, embarks on a love affair with her, she still fails to perceive the truth. Drake's lovemaking, though assertive, does not involve the infliction of pain. On the contrary, it is the height of sensual pleasure. It consists of her employing her supple fingers and tongue to caress Harper's body. As Harper pleasurably observes, commenting approvingly on her lover's sexual skills, 'The velvet tongue stroked, and stroked and stroked her to an incandescence of orgasm' (p. 200).

In the complex mingling of infatuation and disquiet, which they reflect, Harper's feelings for Drake resemble the response of LeFanu's Laura towards her vampire lover Carmilla. When in the latter stages of the story Harper suddenly perceives Drake's vampire identity, she panics. Her fears centre, of course, on the dreaded vampire bite which, now she knows the truth about her lover's identity, she assumes she must inadvertently have suffered. Humour escalates as, rushing into her cabin, she positions herself in front of the mirror and scrutinises every inch of her skin for tell-tale fang marks. Her failure to find any puzzles her. How, she wonders, does Captain Drake acquire nourishment?

The answer to this question, which Forrest, intent on keeping the reader in suspense, delays revealing, hinges on the topic of oral sex. Drake, we learn, is not the standard predatory vampire, familiar from film and fiction. She is a vampire with a conscience who seeks to pleasure her partners, not hurt them. In order to do so, she has succeeded in renouncing the vampire bite. As she explains to the astonished Harper, blood is unnecessary to her survival since she acquires nourishment just as good from imbibing female sexual juices. When Harper, angry at the act of deception which her lover has perpetrated on her, sarcastically enquires, 'You mean you diet between women?' (p. 223) and accuses her of exploiting her physically, Drake rejects the charge. She pointedly replies, 'Your body is not my food.... Your pleasure is' (p. 225).

The modifications that Forrest introduces in the vampire narrative transmute it from the conventional tale of horror to a playful celebration of the pleasures of lesbian sex. She transforms the lesbian vampire from a predatory monster who lives on human blood to the signifier of a feminine erotic economy. In describing Harper's initiation into vampirism as a result of her sexual encounter with Captain Drake, she also investigates the growth of the vampire network or 'family'. This, she illustrates, is not patrilineal in origin but, like the lesbian community which it symbolically represents, develops and expands by means of female contact and the sharing of erotic pleasure.

Forrest neatly concludes her story by bringing together the two themes of sexual pleasure and 'family' around which it revolves. She portrays Lieutenant Harper, now safely returned to earth, sitting in her study absentmindedly erasing the welcome home message that the ever-faithful Niklaus has inscribed on her computer screen. She is preparing to reply to another message which she has just received from a mysterious Colonel Westra. Colonel Westra introduces herself, very appropriately since her name resembles Count Dracula's conquest Lucy Westenra, as a former shipmate of Captain Drake. She invites Harper to meet her in order, as she euphemistically puts it, to 'share a beverage' (p. 226). The fact that Harper intends to accept her invitation indicates that she does not regard her love affair with Drake as a 'one-off' but intends to pursue further vampiric/lesbian encounters. Forrest's story, it emerges, differs from the usual vampire narrative in that, as well as focusing on the production of vampires, it explores – more interestingly from the viewpoint of the lesbian readership to whom it is addressed – the *production* of lesbians. Harper's enthusiastic response to Captain Drake's lovemaking and her readiness to embark on a lesbian lifestyle enables us to read it as a Gothic variation on that perennially popular fictional form, the 'coming out' story.

In celebrating sexual pleasure and treating, albeit humorously, power relations between lovers, Forrest's version of the vampire narrative corresponds, in general terms, to the viewpoint of the lesbian sexual radicals. However, in revising the traditional image of the vampire, she goes out of her way to reject the emphasis on pain associated with S&M sex.

Califia's version, on the contrary, as her reputation as a leading advocate of S&M who has published a study of the topic[40] leads us to expect, concentrates attention on it. Her story 'The Vampire' takes the form of an S&M manifesto. Concepts relating to S&M such as the interplay of 'power and trust' between the two partners, the consensual nature of the S&M relationship and the view of S&M sex promoted by its practitioners as exceptionally transgressive, are all interwoven in the narrative. So too are references to practices conventionally associated with it, such as role-play, whipping and cutting. The vampire motif makes, in many ways, an effective vehicle for S&M fantasy. Conventional features of the motif such as the power relationship between the vampire and her/his prey, the piercing of the skin in which the vampire bite results, the interplay between pleasure and pain which the victim experiences and the initiation of her/him into the vampire cult or 'family' can, with a degree of imagination on the writer's part, find equivalents in S&M practice and theory.[41] Nonetheless, as we shall see, Califia's utilization of it, though inventive in many respects, reveals limitations and flaws.

An important aspect of lesbian S&M sex, according to its advocates, is the physical and emotional intensity that the experience offers. A contributor to *Coming to Power*, a collection of essays and stories focusing on the practice, observes that, 'In S&M sex each seeks to open as much as possible, to push past the limits, to turn each on so intensely that there is no possibility but full satisfaction, not just physically but emotionally and psychically as well'.[42] 'This is yet another feature of S&M sex that finds an equivalent in the vampiric encounter. Commenting on LeFanu's *Carmilla*, Williams argues that the eponymous protagonist's emotional commitment to the realm of the undead 'does something other than simply assert the possibility to vampiric immortality', since it 'suggests that women's fulfilment is to be had through a developmental route which is projected towards the liminal'.[43] The sense of moving 'towards the liminal', which S&M sex shares with the vampiric encounter, is central to Califia's story. To impress its significance upon the reader, she centres her narrative on two S&M scenarios of escalating intensity and power. The first takes place in the sex club, aptly named 'Purgatory', which furnishes the setting for the opening episode. It is here that the butch Kerry and the femme Iduna, the two characters around whom the story revolves, initially meet.

A tenet of S&M theory is the belief that, since power and violence are intrinsic features of sexual relations, they are best channelled into forms of play and theatre, as this will have the effect of rerouting them away from uncontrolled outbreaks of cruelty and abuse. In keeping with this, an emphasis on stylized forms of role play is strongly to the fore in Califia's description of the club. She builds into the scene the concept of 'gender as performance'.[44] An air of theatricality is reflected not only in her description of role and costume but also in the reference she makes to voyeurism and spectacle. The club, as well as being the haunt of S&M practitioners, is frequented by a group of tourists who, intrigued by its notoriety, achieve a thrill from playing the spectator. Their presence introduces a note of self-reflexivity into the story since, like us the readers, they furnish an audience for the activities taking place.

Califia intersperses reference to S&M and butch-femme roles, covertly at first and later in a more explicit manner, with allusions to the role of vampire. Iduna, dressed in the femme costume of low-cut black dress with a red stone shaped like a skull between her breasts, initially mistakes the butch Kerry for a young boy. Kerry wears leather, tellingly described as 'the color of dried blood' (p. 245). Kerry's taste for blood becomes even more apparent when, reacting to the taunts of a male client who claims that she is too physically feeble to dominate him, she invites him to position himself on the bondage frame, which forms the club's centrepiece, and proceeds to whip him until his back bleeds. This incident exemplifies the first S&M scenario. Iduna watches the event with interest. Her attention, however, is focused not on the pain the man is suffering but on a feature of Kerry's performance which furnishes a clue to her vampire identity: while inflicting the whipping, she concentrates her gaze not on her victim's face but on the stream of blood trickling from his back.

Having enacted this display of dominance, Kerry abruptly drops her whip and stalks out of the club. Iduna, eager to discover if her suspicions are correct and that she is, in fact, a vampire, follows her. The sexual encounter between the two women which ensues commences on a note of antagonism. Kerry, aware that she has inadvertently revealed the secret of her identity, is on the defensive. Angered by Iduna's persistent questioning, she draws a knife and threatens to stab her. Iduna, however, manages to reassure her. Taking Kerry's hand, still clasping the knife, she guides it to her own cleavage, makes a cut in the skin, and offers Kerry her breast to suck. The act of vampiric intercourse, to which this forms a prelude, represents the second, climactic S&M episode. It differs from the first, both in its intensity and in the fact that it involves two women. Advocates of S&M sex sometimes maintain that one of the ways in which lesbian S&M differs from its heterosexual counterpart is that the pleasure it offers the participants, as well as being more intense, is reciprocal, frequently involving an element of role exchange.[45] Califia's description of the encounter between Iduna and Kerry makes precisely this point. Although in the initial stages Kerry is the aggressor, the roles which the two women play are subsequently reversed. The episode concludes, in fact, with Kerry relinquishing the role of dominant and making herself vulnerable to Iduna who, in the concluding sentence of the story, is also unexpectedly revealed to be a vampire.

In describing the encounter between the two lesbian vampires – for so, with hindsight, we perceive them both to be – Califia foregrounds certain key features of lesbian S&M. These include the contradictions of pleasure/pain and liberation/discipline and, as mentioned above, a focus on role exchange. However, the most striking feature of her representation is the comparison of the S&M partnership, and the vampiric encounter which metaphorically represents it, to the relationship between mother and infant. Iduna describes Kerry's hand 'clasping the small of her back, holding her the way a mother holds an infant' and depicts herself as 'being picked up, cradled' (p. 259). She admits to finding the sensation pleasurable since, as she acknowledges, it enables her to enjoy access to 'infantile pleasure' which 'adults are usually not lucky enough to re-experience' (p. 259). Her remarks recall the observations voiced by the theorist Tania Modleski. Modleski, perceiving the relevance of the terms 'discipline', 'trust' and 'submission' utilized in S&M discourse to the mother/infant relationship, argues that the dominant partner in the S&M partnership represents 'the symbolic mother', a figure who in Lacanian theory signifies female power, while the submissive partner enacts the role of 'daughter'. The dominant partner performs, according to Modleski, 'an almost archetypal function, initiating symbolic order, but transferring and transforming a patriarchal system of gender inequalities into a realm of difference presided over by women'.[46] This analysis is applicable to the sexual encounter between Kerry and Iduna. Califia's description of the encounter similarly transfers concepts of power relations and 'difference' to a world where women reign supreme.

Califia's 'The Vampire' successfully illustrates the tension that exists between pleasure and danger in sexual relations. It also furnishes the reader with an insight into the distinctive facets of lesbian S&M practice and the theoretical ideas underpinning it. The story nonetheless reveals problematic features. The most obvious hinges on its uniformity of mood. It is a truism of Gothic criticism that the most thrilling and disturbing examples of the genre create a tension or interplay between the familiar and the unfamiliar, the mundane and the surreal.[47] Califia appears to have this in mind when, in preparation for depicting the encounter between the two vampires, she shifts the location of the narrative from the indoor space of the club to the mysterious outdoor world of the nocturnal city streets. However, this is insufficient to achieve the necessary contrast in mood. In fact, both her description of the S&M club and her representation of the vampiric encounter strike the reader, despite the change of location and the escalating degrees of intensity in the S&M scenarios she describes, as similarly melodramatic. By the time we reach the concluding paragraph of the story we have become so accustomed to the highly charged emotional mode in which she writes that her final fantastic revelation – the fact that Iduna too is a vampire – fails to impress or interest us.

Another problem with Califia's story is her failure to critique or transform the stereotypical image of the lesbian vampire, which she appropriates from popular fiction and film, and the phallocentric image of woman that it encodes. In fact, she uncritically reproduces the very attributes that masculinist culture conventionally assigns to woman/lesbian. Kerry and Iduna, in addition to being related to darkness and the night, are portrayed as excessively sensual and are associated, in a displaced form, with the maternal. Kerry in addition, as is illustrated by the attempt she makes to stab Iduna, is prone to fits of irrationality and violence. The two figures emerge despite their superficial vestiges of radicalism and their ostensibly transgressive behaviour as very conventional members of the living dead!

QUEER ENCOUNTERS

The criticism of failing to transform the image of the lesbian vampire, which Califia's treatment of the motif invites, cannot be levelled at Gomez' *The Gilda Stories*. A distinctive feature of Gomez' version of the motif is the interplay that it establishes between tradition and innovation. In contrast to Scott and Livia, who employ strategies of humour to discuss issues relating to role and identity and to explore historical constructs of lesbianism, and Forrest and Califia who focus on sex and erotic fantasy, Gomez creates a narrative which, in appealing to the reader's enjoyment of mystery and the uncanny, reproduces the traditional aspects of the genre exemplified by Stoker's *Dracula*. Gomez is also influenced by the updated version of the vampire narrative, which transfers the creature to an urban location and portrays him frequenting bars and rock concerts, achieved by Rice in her *Vampire Chronicles*. Like Rice, she traces the growth of a vampire network and develops the concept of the vampire as a traveller in both time and geographical terrain. She further emulates Rice in portraying her vampire protagonist mixing with mortals in clubs and bars and, by joining a theatre troupe and singing in nightclubs, participating in the entertainment scene.

However, Gomez' treatment of the vampire narrative, though undoubtedly indebted to Rice, reveals significant differences. Whereas Rice, while introducing a mixture of different races and ethnicities, focuses chiefly on characters who are white, Gomez prioritizes the experience of blacks and coloureds. The characters whom she portrays include among their ranks, in addition to the African-American Gilda, a Creole and an American-Indian. And, in contrast to Rice, who, while exploring queer and homosexual lifestyles, reveals notably little interest in lesbianism, Gomez, though referring to bisexuality and male homosexuality, foregrounds lesbian experience and perspectives. It is the interaction she creates between the discourses of race, sexual orientation and gender which serves to distinguish her treatment of the vampire narrative from other versions and makes it imaginatively vital. It also gives it a politically subversive edge which the fiction of Rice lacks.

The Gilda Stories, as the title signals, takes the form of a series of loosely knit episodes, each of which, as the title indicates, forms a separate story. As Gilda discovers in the course of her travels, vampires, since they enshrine in their memories images of the distant past, represent a form of 'living history' (p. 177). As a result the novel displays links with the historical romance. In the unusually lengthy lifespan that vampires enjoy (in Gomez' version of the myth, vampires, though long-lived, are not necessarily immortal and can choose, if they wish, to terminate their life), Gilda experiences, in a variety of roles and guises, a number of different moments of American history. Having escaped in the 1850s from an American slave plantation at the age of fourteen, she is given refuge by the female owner of Woodards, a Louisiana brothel, and her partner Bird, who initiate her into the vampire cult. When the brothel owner, weary of longevity and disillusioned with hopes of political progress, moves away to seek solace in 'the true death', Gilda appropriates her name and forms a partnership with Bird. In the 1890s she participates in the sophisticated *fin-de-siècle* world of Yerba Buena, drinking champagne and attending the opera as the guest of Sorel and Anthony, two homosexual vampires who run a fashionable nightclub. Other personae she adopts in the course of the novel include manager of a 1950s Boston beauty parlour, lighting technician to an alternative theatre company in New York (1971) and performer in a chain of New Jersey nightclubs (1981). As this summary of her trajectory illustrates, the society she frequents tends to be alternative and bohemian. The novel offers an illuminating insight into the changing lifestyle of African-American women and the black community. While all the works of fiction discussed in this chapter make inventive use of genre, Gomez' treatment is particularly imaginative. She interweaves the conventions of the travelogue and the historical romance with the family saga and the 'coming out' narrative. The concluding episode, which represents Gilda and her companions struggling to escape the clutches of the vampire hunters and to survive the pollution which is speedily engulfing the planet, addresses, in futuristic style, two political issues that achieved prominence in the 1980s: the backlash against homosexuality and the recognition of the fragile state of the ecology. The pessimistic viewpoint that Gomez adopts towards these topics has the effect of moving the novel into the realm of dystopian fiction.

Another feature of *The Gilda Stories*, besides the interplay of different genres it creates, which contributes to the novel's success, is Gomez' radical remodelling of the image of the vampire. She replaces the bloodthirsty monster, familiar from popular fiction and film, with a portrayal which, as well as being sympathetic, is psychologically complex. Vampire existence, instead of being represented as a sadistic round of violence, takes the form of a process of education and learning. Bird and Sorel, who act as Gilda's mentors, believe that vampires, rather than wantonly destroying life, have a duty to enhance it. In accord with this, the acts of vampirism depicted in the novel take two different forms. There are 'primary' acts involving a mutual exchange of blood which serve to initiate a new member into the vampire family. These take place relatively infrequently and are performed only after a period of careful consideration on the vampire's part. In addition, there are 'secondary' acts which the vampire performs regularly, in order to survive. Having hypnotized the victim, s/he takes from her/him a small amount of blood, heals the wound and, in return for this 'gift', implants in her/his consciousness a dream or an idea. One of the first lessons that Gilda learns after her initiation into the vampire family is that 'We draw life into ourselves, yet we give life as well. We give what's needed – energy, dreams, ideas. It's a fair exchange in a life full of cheaters' (p. 45). The contribution Gilda herself makes to theatre and literature exemplifies this creativity.

The emphasis that Gomez places on gay creativity is self-reflexive, commenting by implication on her own narrative and on the relationship that it establishes with the reader. In exchange for winning the reader's attention and enticing her into the Gothic realm of fear and suspense, Gomez plants in her/his mind a series of ideas and fantasies. Writer and reader thus mingle fluids, in a manner similar to the vampire and her/his prey.

Auerbach, reviewing Gomez' novel, complains that it lacks tension and excitement since, in her opinion, 'Gilda exists entirely apart from antagonism'.[48] This critique is unjust since Gilda is portrayed in terms of conflict, both external and internal. She and her companions are represented in several episodes combating those vampires who, rejecting the moral idealism of Sorel and Bird, take delight in bloodshed and behave with conventional cruelty. In addition, she also experiences conflict of an emotional kind. Feelings of loneliness or desire tempt her, on occasion, to renounce the principles of the vampire code and to initiate into the vampire family someone whom she knows rationally to be incapable of maintaining the high standards of secrecy and self-control on which, in Gomez' version of the myth, its survival depends.

Gilda's characterization, as well as revealing elements of conflict, is enriched by her ethnic identity and the experiences of persecution this involves. Her memories of life on the slave plantation haunt her throughout her life, influencing her response to subsequent events, personal and political. The attempt which the white Eleanor makes to dominate her elicits from her the sarcastic retort, 'I'm no longer a servant. We been freed!' (p. 99). Gomez exploits Gilda's vampiric longevity to allow her firsthand knowledge of certain formative moments in the history of the black community. The exceptionally wide perspective on events to which Gilda has access enables her to make connections between different episodes of ethnic oppression. For example, she relates the newspaper pictures of the murder of the blacks at Attica in the 1970s to the scenes of victimization that she witnessed as a child on the nineteenth-century slave plantation. 'The image', she poignantly remarks, 'was always the same as her memories of the slave quarters: dark men with eyes full of submission and rage. Their bodies plumped with bullets were the same ashen color as those fallen beside the trees to which they had been tied as punishment' (p. 169). In the course of her unusually long life, she encounters a range of relationships between blacks and whites, friendly as well as hostile, and comes to accept the shifts and contradictions which they display. Teasing out the meanings of the term 'queer', Sedgwick observes that 'A lot of the most exciting recent work around "queer" spins the term outward along dimensions that can't be subsumed under gender and sexuality at all'. She draws attention to 'the ways that race, ethnicity, postcolonial nationality crisscross with these and other identity-constituting, identity-fracturing discourses'.[49] *The Gilda Stories*, in interrelating factors of race, gender and sexuality, re-creates this interplay in fictional form.

Another feature of Gomez' novel which carries queer resonances is its treatment of the 'vampire family'.[50] This develops the idea of a vampiric/ lesbian network, the formation of which, as other texts discussed in this chapter also illustrate, depends not on the Law of the Father but on the direct transmission of blood/sexual pleasure. The vampire family, as Gomez describes it, further subverts hetero-patriarchal convention in that the relationships and roles which it comprises reveal, in terms of conventional familial roles, anomalies and contradictions. Roles that are generally regarded as incompatible combine and merge – as in Gilda's description of the way Bird acts as 'mother, father, sister and lover' to her (p. 177). The enfolding of one relationship into another is again exemplified by the way that Bird, in initiating Gilda into the vampire cult, transforms her into her daughter, while simultaneously becoming her lover. It is also reflected in Gilda's comment that Anthony, who gently washes her back while she is having a bath, 'seemed to be brother and sister to her at the same time' (p. 71). A spectrum of transgressive sexualities, including homosexuality, lesbianism and bisexuality, are represented in the novel. While Gilda's primary attachment is to Bird, she also becomes involved with Julius, a young man whom she meets while working in the theatre troupe in New York. Gomez' unorthodox treatment of sexual reproduction and familial relationships is notably queer in emphasis. It agrees with Case's representation of the vampire as a signifier of the queer movement's interest in deconstructing the binaries of nature/culture, fertility/infertility.

Gomez' approach to lesbian/gay political and ideological attitudes is as eclectic and unconventional as her perspective on race and sex. She reconciles and depicts as compatible contrary attitudes and lifestyles which have generated controversy among lesbians. Whereas her reference to a range of transgressive sexualities and her representation of lesbians and gay men living and working together is typically queer, the emphasis she places on the lesbian/feminist community and on acts of female support has more in common with the separatist position associated with the lesbian feminist movement. Examples of the latter abound in the novel. Bird and her partner give refuge to Gilda when she is escaping from the bounty hunters who seek to return her to the slave plantation, while Gilda herself, on reaching adulthood, goes out of her way to help the various women whom she encounters in different periods and social contexts. She treasures the 'womanist atmosphere' of the beauty parlour she establishes in Boston; she describes it as 'a woman's place, open and intimate, utilitarian like a kitchen but so easily transformed by heat and laughter', and delights in the fact that 'Women came here to be massaged by other women, made beautiful by other women' (p. 136).

As mentioned above, a key point of connection between the vampire and the woman who identifies as lesbian is the tension between the role of independent loner and member of a group or community. This tension underpins the design of Gomez' novel since Gilda's lifestyle alternates, like the hero of the traditional quest narrative, between periods of solitude and anonymity in which she travels alone and periods when she enjoys companionship by frequenting centres of vampire community. The brothel where she first encounters Bird, the club run by Sorel and Anthony, and the Boston beauty parlour which she herself sets up exemplify centres of this kind. The security and warmth they represent is reflected in her comment, voiced in relation to the club: 'To those like herself, it was home of sorts' (p. 65).

The longing for 'home', reflected in the emotional significance which Gilda attaches to these communal centres, carries resonances of woman's quest for maternal nurture. This, Gomez illustrates, informs Gilda's trajectory throughout the novel. Like Irigaray[51] and Joanna Ryan,[52] Gomez represents lesbian involvements as reproducing, with complex displacements, aspects of the infant attachment between mother and daughter. Her treatment of the topic, though superficially analogous to Califia's, displays a greater degree of emotional subtlety. At the centre of the novel, and the relationships that Gilda forms with women in the course of her travels, is the figure of the absent mother – the mother from whom, when she escaped from the slave plantation in her teens, she was untimely wrenched. This moment of separation, as well as being, on a literal plane, a specific event in Gilda's life, also signifies in symbolic terms the experience of maternal loss that Lacanian psychoanalysis regards as intrinsic to the human condition; it forms the basis of both desire itself and the subject's entry into language and culture.[53] The interrelation between sexual and maternal impulses is exemplified in the descriptions of primary vampiric encounters which occur throughout the novel, in particular the episode in which Bird initiates Gilda into the vampire cult. Here Gomez folds together, in a manner which is typically queer, allusions to S&M sex with images of the child suckling the mother's breast, the act of birthing and the mother's abject, bleeding body. She describes how Bird, having made an incision in the skin beneath her breast,

> pressed Gilda's mouth to the red slash, letting the blood wash across Gilda's face. Soon Gilda drank eagerly, filling herself, and as she did her hand massaged Bird's breast, first touching the nipple gently with curiosity, then roughly. She wanted to know this body that gave her life. Her heart swelled with their blood, a tide between the two shores. To an outsider the sight may have been one of horror: their faces red and shining, their eyes unfocused and black, the sound of their bodies slick with wetness, tight with life. Yet it was a birth. The mother finally able to bring her child into the world, to look at her. It was not death that claimed Gilda. It was Bird. (p. 140)

This passage is of interest in a number of ways. In addition to highlighting the ambiguous pleasure/violence of the primary vampire act and illustrating the processes involved in the production of vampires, it foregrounds, in symbolic terms, the way sexual relations between women indirectly reproduce features of mother/daughter relations, such as sensuous contact, emotional and physical interdependence and patterns of dominance/ submission. The act of breastfeeding, radically defamiliarized, is transformed here into the source of illicit *jouissance*. The pleasures of oral sex, the S&M partnership and the breaking of the interdiction against the return to the maternal body, all come together in a manner that is both powerful and disturbing.

The passage also alerts us to the ambiguity that the image of blood acquires in the novel and the contradictions it inscribes. Blood is generally associated with death and violence. Simultaneously, however, through its connections with menstruation and childbirth, it has connotations of life and sexual vitality. As Kristeva comments, it represents 'a fascinating semantic crossroads, the propitious place for abjection where *death* and *femininity*, *murder* and *procreation*, *cessation of life* and *vitality* all come together'.[54]

However, while alerting the reader's attention to the connections between lesbian relationships and the mother/daughter bond, Gomez avoids sentimentally advocating a simple 'return to the mother' by positioning her characters in some kind of utopian pre-oedipal realm. Episodes focusing on intimate female encounters of the kind cited above play, in fact, a minor role in the novel. They are juxtaposed with scenes of a very different kind in which Gilda, who is portrayed as essentially solitary, asserts her independence and travels alone. In juxtaposing these contrary images of her protagonist, Gomez combines a recognition of woman's nostalgic desire for the recovery of the maternal presence with a clearsighted recognition of its illusory nature.

The vampire, as is evident from the popularity which the motif is enjoying at the moment and the varied approaches writers adopt towards it, makes an effective vehicle for affirming lesbian difference and exploring the transgressive dimension of lesbianism. However, as Califia's version of the motif illustrates, it is by no means easy to employ successfully. In treating it, writers run the risk of indulging in sensationalism and reproducing the very essentialist stereotypes of woman/lesbian which the writer of lesbian Gothic, in seeking to reclaim the genre, aims to redress. A number of writers, however, succeed in steering clear of these pitfalls. Reclaiming the motif from its lurid and frequently lesbophobic past, they transform it into a vehicle for exploring issues of political and cultural interest. Scott and Livia deliberately exploit the artifice and stylization of the vampire image. They utilize it to humorously problematize concepts of the monstrous and the alien, to explore the construction of role and identity and to recreate and comment on episodes from the lesbian past. With the emergence of the lesbian sexual radicals and the queer movement, the potential which the motif displays for addressing issues relating to sexuality has achieved fruition. The fiction of Forrest, Califia and Gomez furnishes a varied range of illustrations.

Lesbian versions of the vampire narrative, despite the intellectual and ideological differences they display, are, as the texts discussed above illustrate, frequently linked by an experimental use of genre. An emphasis on the interweaving of different generic forms and conventions is also to the fore in the final chapter of this study. This focuses on one of the most idiosyncratic and versatile genres which writers of lesbian fiction are currently utilizing as a frame for their creative skills: the Gothic thriller.

NOTES

1. Case, 'Tracking the Vampire', p. 9.

2. Gelder, Reading the Vampire, pp. 11–23, 48–52, 108–18.

3. Nina Auerbach, Our Vampires Ourselves (University of Chicago Press, 1995), pp. 1–23, 160–73.

4. Gelder, Reading the Vampire, pp. 74–6.

5. Auerbach, Our Vampires, p. 83.

6. See Dikstra, Idols, pp. 350, 346.

7. Dikstra discusses the connection between the vampire and the 'New Woman' in Idols, pp. 345–51.

8. Zimmerman, 'Daughters of Darkness: The Lesbian Vampire on Film', in Barry Keith Grant (ed.), Planks of Reason: Essays on the Horror Film (Scarecrow Press, 1984), pp. 157–62.

9. Auerbach, Our Vampires, p. 41.

10. Lord George Gordon Byron, 'Fragment of a Novel', in Alan Ryan (ed.), The Penguin Book of Vampire Stories (Penguin, 1988), pp. 1–6.

11. John Polidori, 'The Vampyre', in The Penguin Book of Vampire Stories, pp. 7–24.

12. Charles Baudelaire, Les Fleurs du Mal (Harvester, 1982), pp. 126–30.

13. Charles Algernon Swinburne, 'Faustine', in Humphrey Hare (ed.), Selected Poems (William Heinemann, 1950), p. 70.

14. D.H. Lawrence, The Rainbow (Penguin, 1949), p. 344. Faderman discusses the use of vampiric imagery to stigmatize the figure of the lesbian in twentieth-century fiction in Surpassing the Love of Men, pp. 341–5.

15. Weiss, Vampires and Violets, pp. 92–6.

16. Zimmerman, 'Daughters of Darkness'.

17. Creed, The Monstrous-Feminine, pp. 59–72.

18. Christopher Frayling, quoting Ornella Volta, remarks, 'First and foremost the vampire is an erotic creation....The vampire can violate all taboos and achieve what

is most forbidden' (*Vampyres: Lord Byron to Count Dracula*, Faber & Faber, 1991, pp. 387–8).

19. Contemporary lesbian vampire fiction includes Ouida Crozier (ed.), *Shadows after Dark* (Rising Tide Press, 1993); Pam Keesey (ed.), *Daughters of Darkness* (Cleis, 1993); Pam Keesey (ed.), *Dark Angels* (Cleis, 1995). Lesbian vampire stories also appear in Eric Garber (ed.), *Embracing the Dark* (Alyson, 1991) and Victoria A. Brownworth (ed.), *Night Bites: Vampire Stories by Women* (Seal Press, 1996).

20. Passages of this kind occur in Pat Califia, 'The Vampire', in *Macho Sluts*, (Alyson Publications, 1988), pp. 258–61; Katherine V. Forrest, 'O Captain, My Captain', in *Daughters of Darkness*, pp. 208–9; and Jewelle Gomez, *The Gilda Stories* (Sheba Feminist Publishers 1991), p. 140. Further references are to these editions and are in the text.

21. See Sue-Ellen Case, 'Toward a Butch/Femme Aesthetic', in Lynda Hart (ed.), *Making a Spectacle: Feminist Essays on Contemporary Women's Theatre* (University of Michigan Press, 1989), pp. 282–97.

22. Case, 'Tracking the Vampire', p. 2.

23. Gillian H. Hanscombe and Jackie Forster, *Rocking the Cradle – Lesbian Mothers: A Challenge to Family Living* (Peter Owen, 1981), pp. 1–38.

24. Jonathan Dollimore, 'Sex and Death', *Textual Practice*, 9:1 (1995), 27.

25. Anna Livia, *Minimax* (Eighth Mountain Press, 1991), p. 112. Further page references are to this edition and are in the text.

26. See Creed, *The Monstrous-Feminine*, p. 61.

27. For reference to 'the Law of the Father' which dominates the symbolic order, see Toril Moi, *Sexual/Textual Politics*, p. 11.

28. For reference to queer social and sexual formations see Sedgwick, 'Queer and Now', pp. 5–7. Gelder discusses Rice's *Vampire Chronicles* in the light of queer theory in *Reading the Vampire*, pp. 112–19.

29. For a discussion of the lesbian political fiction of the 1970s and early 1980s see Palmer, *Contemporary Lesbian Writing*, pp. 37–62.

30. Shari Benstock discusses Vivien's life and writing in *Women of the Left Bank: Paris 1900–1940* (Virago, 1987), pp. 215–90.

31. Faderman, *Surpassing the Love of Men*, pp. 289, 273–4.

32. *Ibid.*, p. 362.

33. Susan Gubar, 'Sapphistries', *Signs*, 10:1 (1984), 43–62.

34. For reference to butch-femme roles and the controversies the issue has generated see Faderman, *Odd Girls*, pp. 260–70; and Healey, *Lesbian Sex Wars*, pp. 118–55.

35. Butler, *Gender Trouble*, p. x.

36. Faderman, *Odd Girls*, pp. 252–70; Healey, *Lesbian Sex Wars*, pp. 61–155.

37. For reference to the 'lesbian sexual radicals', see Faderman, *Odd Girls*, pp. 253–7; and Palmer, *Contemporary Lesbian Writing*, pp. 22–30.

38. See Jessica Benjamin, 'Master and Slave: The Fantasy of Erotic Domination' and Myra Goldberg, 'Issues and Answers', in Ann Snitow, Christine Stansell and Sharon Thompson (eds), *Desire: The Politics of Sexuality* (Virago, 1984), pp. 292–311, 276–81.

39. Jewelle Gomez, 'White Flowers', in *Serious Pleasure: Lesbian Erotic Stories and Poetry* (Sheba Feminist Publishers, 1989), pp. 49–59.

40. See Pat Califia, *Sapphistry: The Book of Lesbian Sexuality* (Naiad, 1980).

41. For reference to S&M practice and theory, see Healey, *Lesbian Sex Wars*, pp. 89–112; and Palmer, *Contemporary Lesbian Writing*, pp. 26–7.

42. Juicy Lucy, 'If I Ask You to Tie Me up, Will You Still Love Me?' in SAMOIS, *Coming to Power: Writing and Graphics on Lesbian S&M* (Alyson Publications, 1982), p. 31.

43. Linda Ruth Williams, *Critical Desire: Psychoanalysis and the Literary Subject* (Edward Arnold, 1995), p. 163.

44. See Butler, *Gender Trouble*, pp. 7–78.

45. Juicy Lucy, 'If I Ask You to Tie Me up', p. 32.

46. Tania Modleski, *Feminism Without Women: Culture and Criticism in a 'Postfeminist' Age* (Routledge, 1991), pp. 156–7.

47. See Jackson, *Fantasy*, pp. 1–37.

48. Auerbach, *Our Vampires*, p. 185.

49. Kosofsky, 'Queer and Now', pp. 8–9. Case also refers to the queer movement's contribution to the politics of race in 'Tracking the Vampire', pp. 4–5.

50. See note 26.

51. See Christine Holmlund, 'The Lesbian, the Mother and the Heterosexual Lover: Irigaray's Recodings of Difference', *Feminist Studies*, 17:2 (1991), 283–308.

52. Joanna Ryan, 'Psychoanalysis and Women Loving Women', in Sue Cartledge and Joanna Ryan (eds), *Sex and Love: New Thoughts on Old Contradictions* (Women's Press, 1983), pp. 196–209.

53. See Grosz, *Jacques Lacan: A Feminist Introduction*, pp. 82–114.

54. Kristeva, *Powers of Horror*, p. 96. Cited in Creed, *The Monstrous-Feminine*, p. 62.

CHAPTER 5

The Gothic thriller

I walked out into the snow trying to get away from Delores's ghost. It was sitting
back there in the apartment waiting for me.[1]

SLEUTHS, SEX AND SECRETS

The thriller is another fictional form which, like the vampire narrative,
achieved prominence in the mid-1980s, its emergence reflecting the interest
in the appropriation and transformation of popular genres that informed
the lesbian/feminist literary scene around that time.[2] The success which it is
currently enjoying, illustrated by the numerous titles on display in
alternative bookstores and many mainstream ones, can be explained by
the multifaceted nature of its appeal. On the level of light entertainment, the
thriller offers the reader a fast-moving plot which, while focusing on crime
investigation and catering for the reader's enjoyment of suspense, gives
scope for the representation of sexual encounters and episodes of romance
between women. On a more sophisticated plane, its ability to respond
speedily to shifts of perspective in lesbian/feminist culture and politics gives
the texts exemplifying it an attractive air of topicality.[3] Its versatility is
reflected in the range of styles that writers employ and the variety of
different topics they treat. The lesbian thriller includes in its ranks novels in
a feminist realist style focusing on women's community and 'coming out',
such as Barbara Wilson's *Murder in the Collective* (1984); novels treating
the sleuth's encounter with the supernatural and exploring outbreaks of
homophobia in society, represented by McConnell's *The Burnton Widows*
(1984); and examples of postmodern parody such as Mary Wings's *Divine
Victim* which, like du Maurier's *Rebecca* whose storyline it reworks,
portrays the protagonist haunted by disturbing events from the past and
addresses, in relation to this, themes of female subjectivity and memory.

The two novels by McConnell and Wings cited above, though differing
markedly in other ways, have one important feature in common. In
transforming the thriller into a vehicle for lesbian representation, they

interweave crime fiction conventions with structures and motifs appropriated from Gothic. The interplay between the two genres which occurs in
these and other texts discussed in this chapter, while developing a traditional
literary historical trend, also involves issues which are specifically lesbian.

From a historical point of view the thriller, from the time of its inception
in the nineteenth century, has revealed significant links with Gothic and has
frequently introduced Gothic components. The intermingling of the two
genres is visible in early texts such as Wilkie Collins's *The Woman in White*
(1860) and Sir Arthur Conan Doyle's *The Hound of the Baskervilles* (1902).
Both narratives, in addition to unfolding against a Gothic backdrop of
desolate lake or moonlit moor, introduce events which, though discovered to
have a rational explanation, are initially regarded as supernatural. The
phantom-like appearance of Anne Catherick, the eponymous heroine of
Collins's novel, leads people to assume that she is a ghost, while the
monstrous appearance of the hound in Doyle's gives rise to a similarly
paranormal interpretation. Critics approach the connections between the
two genres from different viewpoints. Day concentrates on examining their
causal aspect. Discussing the evolution of the detective narrative in the
fiction of Poe and Collins, he describes it as representing 'a natural response
to the Gothic vision'. He points out that, while the Gothic novel generally
takes the form of a mystery, raising questions about identity, family origins
or supernatural events, it lacks 'an effective hero, a character who through
his own efforts can resolve the mystery and put an end to the horror'.[4] The
detective or sleuth who in the thriller solves the mystery and, as a result,
restores order to a disordered world exemplifies, Day argues, just such a
figure; he is, in fact, 'the hero the Gothic world needs but cannot sustain'
(p. 51).

Maureen T. Reddy, in contrast, examines the connections between the
thriller and the Gothic novel from a feminist perspective and concentrates on
tracing literary influences. Seeking to establish a female genealogy for
women's detective fiction which acknowledges the importance of its 'literary
foremothers',[5] Reddy argues that fiction of this kind has its roots in the
Gothic novels of Mrs Radcliffe and the sensation novels of Mary Elizabeth
Braddon and Mrs Henry Wood. It is these, she maintains, rather than the
detective works of Poe and Doyle, which represent its major influence. The
victimized but triumphant heroine and the preoccupation with secrets and
mysteries which characterizes Female Gothic are developed, Reddy argues, in
the detective novels of Agatha Christie, Dorothy Sayers and Ruth Rendell.

However, in addition to developing the historical connections between the
two genres which Day and Reddy explore, the interaction between thriller
and Gothic conventions in the novels of McConnell, Wings and the other
writers I propose discussing reflects interests that are specifically lesbian in
nature. The feature of the text where the interplay between the two is most
clearly apparent is the portrayal of the sleuth. Her characterization combines
the roles of imposer of justice and restorer of order associated with the

thriller and the victim of spectral visitation, either literal or figurative, appropriated from the Gothic novel. The interaction between these two different roles accentuates the contradictions which, on account of her gender and sexual orientation, the lesbian sleuth embodies.[6] Whereas the portrayal of her in the role of investigator foregrounds her agency, the depiction of her as the focus of spectral events or the victim of disturbing memories, frequently of an erotic kind, undermines her role as agent, relegating her to the position of subject and representing her as vulnerable to forces beyond her control. It also increases her transgressive aspect, transforming her from the politically correct representative of social order, the image assigned to her in the early works of lesbian crime fiction produced by Barbara Wilson and Forrest, to a figure of conflict who, while seeking to achieve justice, is something of an outsider and reveals a potential for disruption. Her portrayal, in this respect, has more in common with the queer image of the lesbian promoted by Case and Sedgwick than with the lesbian feminist image associated with Bunch and Rich. Indicative of this is the fact that the lesbian Gothic thriller, like lesbian Gothic in general, has increased in prominence and popularity with the growth of queer politics, and the transgressive image of the lesbian as outlaw which it promotes.

The novels discussed in this chapter present us with a protagonist of just this kind: a figure of conflict and contradiction who, while seeking to solve the crime on which the narrative centres, becomes in the course of the investigation prey to the darker aspect of spectral influences and/or past events – either her own past or other people's. They establish, in this respect, a tension between the quest for order and justice which informs the thriller and the entry into the fantasy realm of terror and psychic fragmentation which the Gothic novel traditionally inscribes. In investigating the crime, the protagonist feels herself haunted, either literally or emotionally, by characters and events beyond her control. She becomes involved, like the Gothic heroine in whose footsteps she treads, in a process of doubling in which she finds herself confronting, often with traumatic effect, aspects of her own identity and circumstances. How, and to what extent, she manages to liberate herself from this experience of psychic entrapment differs from text to text. Although she generally succeeds in solving the crime and achieving a form of justice, she does not necessarily resolve the psychological mystery from which it stems.

In interrelating the constructs of the sleuth and the Gothic heroine, writers rework the features that the two figures share, transforming them into a vehicle for lesbian representation. The role of spy and voyeur is important in this respect, lending itself particularly well to lesbian appropriation. The sleuth in both the British detective novel and American crime fiction generally centres her/his investigation on the search for clues and the observation of suspects. The lesbian, living as she does on the margins of society and frequently keeping her relationships secret, is similarly adept at playing the spy. Scrutinizing acquaintances and workmates to ascertain whether they have perceived her sexual orientation and, if so, how they react to it, and attempting to decipher theirs, becomes habitual to her. Her powers of observation and her skills in deciphering social and sexual semiotics are utilized to good effect in terms of narrative and characterization in the lesbian Gothic thriller. In some novels, such as those of Wings and Schulman, they take on, in addition, a tinge of sexual voyeurism.

Voyeurism, as well as creating a link between the woman who identifies as lesbian and the crime investigator, is also, of course, pertinent to Gothic.[7] In texts dealing with spectral visitation such as James's 'The Turn of the Screw' and in lesbian versions of the motif such as Martinac's *Out of Time*, it serves, as we have seen, to illuminate and define the relationship between mortal protagonist and spectral visitor. In Martinac's novel it marks the initial stage of the protagonist's involvement with her ghostly double and indicates which particular figure enjoys a position of dominance in the relationship. It performs a similar function in the Gothic thrillers of Wings and Schulman.

Relevant to the role of voyeur, as appropriated and reworked in the lesbian Gothic thriller, is the figure of the *flâneur*. The relationship between the *flâneur*, the male individual who strolls the streets contemplating the dream-like appearance of the urban spectacle, and the detective has been established by Walter Benjamin[8] and elaborated by critics writing subsequently.[9] Benjamin argues that the *flâneur*, since he devotes much of his time to observing the urban masses, is exceptionally well suited to identify criminals and solve crimes. Lesbian studies have produced further developments in the analysis of the figure of the *flâneur*. The concept of 'the lesbian *flâneur*', who self-consciously appropriates the male prerogative of the gaze, has become a fashionable topic in lesbian criticism. Munt, for example, discusses the role she plays in the poetry of Nestle and the fiction of Jane DeLynn.[10] In examples of the lesbian Gothic thriller utilizing an urban backdrop, such as O'Rourke's *Jumping the Cracks* and Schulman's *After Delores*, the sleuth enacts the role of *flâneur* – up to a point. However, in reclaiming the city space for women and controlling the street scene with her gaze, she simultaneously makes herself vulnerable to the gaze of others. As a result, her confident stance risks being undermined and she may encounter harassment and persecution. She is in danger of becoming an abject presence on the city streets, vulnerable to ridicule and assault. The contradiction between controller/object of the gaze is a key tension informing the portrayal of the sleuth in the lesbian Gothic thriller.

Another motif pertinent to the situation of the lesbian in hetero-patriarchal society, which appears in both the thriller and the Gothic novel, is 'secrets'. In Gothic fiction the concept of secrets is particularly rich in implication. Three meanings which it commonly assumes are mysteries relating to identity or family origins, the enigma represented by the locked or concealed chamber, and clandestine sexual relationships, either within the family unit or beyond its bounds. It can also signify the hidden reaches of the unconscious.[11] In the thriller, as Geraldine Pederson-Krag illustrates in an illuminating essay, 'secrets' generally carries a more precise meaning. It signifies a secret crime or, as she puts it, 'some secret wrong-doing between two people, discovered when one of the participants has been murdered'.[12] Pederson-Krag interprets the secret crime and the sleuth's deciphering of the enigma which it represents as corresponding symbolically to the scenario of the Freudian primal scene. She parallels the figure of the sleuth – engaged in investigating the crime and following a trail of clues in order to discover its motive and perpetrator – to the child who, on overhearing or glimpsing its parents engaging in sex, ponders the event in an attempt to make sense of it. Just as the primal scene and the mystery which it signifies evoke feelings of intense curiosity in the child, so the crime and its enigmatic aspect arouse the curiosity of both sleuth and reader. The correspondence existing between the secret nature of the crime and the 'secrets' of the primal scene explains, Pederson-Krag argues, the fascination the thriller holds, helping to account for its perennial popularity.

The motif of 'secrets' understandably occupies a central place in the lesbian thriller. Here, however, its significance is somewhat different. It is, I suggest, *lesbian sexuality itself which constitutes the secret*. In contemporary Western culture sex in general tends to be associated with secrecy. However, there is one particular form of sex that is regarded as more secret than others. This is, of course, homosexuality which, as Sedgwick observes,[13] represents in homophobic society *the* sexual secret. Indicative of this is the fact that it is frequently defined in terms of the binaries of knowledge/ ignorance, innocence/initiation, secrecy/disclosure. In the lesbian Gothic thriller the connection between homosexuality and 'secrets' is particularly pronounced. The search for the motive of the crime often corresponds to the unravelling of the secret of lesbian desire – either the sleuth's desire, as is the case in McConnell's *Mrs Porter's Letter* (1982), which portrays the investigator discovering and coming to terms with her own lesbian identification, or that of the victim or perpetrator of the crime as in Wings's *Divine Victim*. Alternatively, or in addition, it may correspond to the discovery of feelings of homophobia, either in the individual or the community. This is the case in both McConnell's *Mrs Porter's Letter* and *The Burnton Widows*; in the former, the crime is revealed to stem from homophobic prejudice on the part of the individual and, in the latter, the community as a whole. The hostility which the heterosexual community evinces toward the homosexual in *The Burnton Widows* is so intense that it has the effect of hampering the crime investigation. It infects the police force, prompting its members to attempt to close the case and put an end to the investigation before the crime has been satisfactorily solved. It also gives rise to an act of assault on the person of the lesbian sleuth.

While the works of fiction reviewed in this chapter all interweave Gothic and thriller conventions and foreground themes of voyeurism and 'secrets', they differ significantly in other ways. McConnell and O'Rourke, writing in the 1980s, utilize the interplay between the two genres to investigate a topic that has achieved considerable prominence in this study and the discussion of lesbian Gothic it inscribes: society's relegation of the lesbian to the realm of the abject. By exposing the unsettling effect that her presence has on society and exploring the contrary emotions of repulsion/fascination it arouses, they examine the problematic aspects of the lesbian subject's situation and interrogate the boundaries of the abject. In McConnell's *Mrs Porter's Letter* and *The Burnton Widows* the crime on which the narrative focuses stems, as mentioned above, from incidents of homophobia, while in O'Rourke's *Jumping the Cracks* it originates in an act of male violence. O'Rourke explores the oppressive effect of the tentacular web of male power which dominates metropolitan life on people relegated to the social margins such as women, homosexuals and the working class.

Schulman and Wings, writing in the late 1980s and the 1990s, while continuing to refer to the typecasting of the lesbian as abject, move beyond the tensions and antagonisms dividing heterosexual and homosexual communities to focus on lesbian/queer experience. Reacting against the idealized, 'politically correct' image of the lesbian sleuth promoted by Forrest and Barbara Wilson in the crime fiction of the 1980s,[14] they concentrate on exploring the imperative of lesbian desire and on depicting its disruptive effects, psychological and social. *Divine Victim* and *After Delores* both foreground, in different ways, the intensity of lesbian passion, exploring the jealousies and power struggles which it can generate among women. The two writers, as their innovative treatment of sexuality illustrates, bring the lesbian Gothic thriller up to date by introducing postmodern features. Wings, in creating a queer version of *Rebecca*, pays tribute to an earlier work of Female Gothic while parodically reworking du Maurier's story line in the context of present-day lesbian culture. By manipulating stereotypes of femininity and representing her characters becoming entrapped in roles and emotions beyond their control, she also problematizes concepts of individual identity and agency. Schulman's *After Delores* likewise exemplifies the art of postmodern parody. However, it is early versions of the lesbian thriller in general, with their linear narrative structure and politically correct role models, rather than one particular text which Schulman reworks. Like Wings, she interrogates and problematizes conventional concepts of identity and 'character'. The characters who people her novel strike the reader more as figments of the protagonist's imagination than as autonomous individuals, since they appear to exist in terms of the projections she imposes upon them. The novels of the two writers are further linked by an emphasis on the performative aspects of gender and a focus on a spectrum of transgressive sexualities. This gives them a decidedly queer resonance.

HAUNTINGS AND CORPSES

Mrs Porter's Letter and *The Burnton Widows*, McConnell's two contributions to the Gothic thriller, were written in a period when lesbian crime fiction was still in its infancy – a fact that helps to account for their relatively unsophisticated handling of character and narrative. Munt describes them in her study of the feminist thriller as 'in the best tradition of lesbian pulp fiction', offering us 'light duty but pleasurable reading'.[15] The two novels are linked by the figure of Nyla Wade, journalist and amateur sleuth, as well as by the introduction of common themes. Both centre on Nyla's encounter with a lesbian couple from the past who have been victims of bigotry and homophobia. They explore, as mentioned above, the abject role which heterosexual society conventionally assigns to the lesbian and the attempt it sometimes makes to silence or annihilate her. Their interest lies in the fact that they are two of the earliest examples of the lesbian thriller to introduce Gothic motifs and structures and to treat, albeit somewhat clumsily, a topic which features prominently in present-day lesbian studies – the haunting of the heterosexual community by the phantom of its homosexual Other, and the acts of violence to which it frequently resorts in order to exorcize it.[16]

Mrs Porter's Letter, the earlier of McConnell's two novels, creates an intriguing if somewhat schematic interplay between the conventions of the thriller and the Gothic novel. It opens with Nyla discovering a cache of love letters from the 1960s in an antique bureau and traces her efforts to return them to their rightful owners – the mysterious Cybil Porter and her enigmatically named lover W. Stone. In attempting to ascertain the couple's identity and establish their whereabouts, Nyla is assisted by two prostitutes who are involved in a lesbian partnership. Having sought her out with the aim of enlisting her help in composing a pamphlet to publicize an act of crime on the part of a local pimp, they offer to help with the investigation in return.

Although Cybil Porter and W. Stone are not in fact phantoms, Nyla habitually speaks of them as if they were. On first reading the letters recording their love affair, she refers to them as ghosts and remarks mystically, in a phrase redolent of an encounter with the occult, 'I felt as if Cybil had reached out of time and touched me'.[17] The novel concludes with her initial assumptions about the couple undergoing a series of dramatic reversals. Cybil Porter, whose grave in the Rochester cemetery leads both Nyla and the reader to assume that she is dead, is unexpectedly discovered to be alive. She was coerced into feigning death in order to extricate herself from an unhappy marriage and to enable her to set up home with her lover W. Stone. Equally startling, W. Stone, whom Nyla first assumed to be a man, turns out to be a woman. The initial W. stands not for William or Walter, as she had previously surmised, but for Winona. The reader is also treated to a further revelation, one characterizing the preoccupation with 'coming out' which typifies the lesbian fiction of the early 1980s. Nyla's discovery of the couple's lesbianism, combined with her encounter with the two lesbian prostitutes, has the effect of triggering her discovery of her own lesbian orientation. As she wonderingly remarks in the concluding pages, her quest for information about the two lovers can be seen, with hindsight, as a quest for self-knowledge and personal fulfilment.

Cybil Porter, McConnell emphasizes, did not feign death voluntarily. On the contrary, she was coerced into doing so by a male relative who, regarding her lesbian identification as tainting the family name, sought not only to expel her from its enclave but also, in legal terms, to erase her existence. McConnell is, of course, not the first contributor to the Gothic thriller to represent a female character being declared dead and furnished with a counterfeit funeral and tombstone to satisfy the selfish interests of a male relative. Her treatment of the motif echoes that of Collins who in *The Woman in White* portrays Sir Percival Glyde, aided and abetted by the villainous Count Fosco, incarcerating his wife Laura in an asylum for the insane and declaring her dead, in order to gain possession of her fortune. McConnell's debt to Collins is accentuated by the fact that, in her novel as in his, the fake grave of the woman who is supposedly deceased plays a significant part in the narrative; it furnishes an appropriately eerie location for certain key encounters and events.

The abject, according to Kristeva, is characterized by its potential for social disruption[18] and by the fear of pollution it arouses in the individual and the community. This is very much the role that Cybil Porter's relatives assign to her. Regarding her lesbianism as tainting and disruptive, they are highly relieved when she agrees to remove herself from public view by pretending to be dead. Their relegation of her to the realm of death, exemplified by their provision of a mock funeral and grave, further accentuates her abject status. As mentioned in the previous chapter in relation to the fictional treatment of spectral visitation, the corpse, since it destabilizes the border between life and death and threatens to infect the world of the living, has traditionally been regarded as one of the most abject of objects.[19] By failing for the major part of the narrative to perceive the existence of lesbianism, either her own or that of the couple whose identities she investigates, and in accepting society's view of Cybil as dead, Nyla unwittingly colludes in both their abjection and that of lesbians as a group. Cybil emerges, in this respect, as her double. The 'living death' which she experiences can be read, in symbolic terms, as representing Nyla's repressed lesbian orientation; it illustrates the way it has been rendered invisible and, as it were, 'buried alive' by the codes of compulsory heterosexuality operating in society. Nyla's eventual encounter with Cybil, with which the novel appropriately concludes, in addition to marking Cybil's resurrection from the grave and her return to public life, coincides with and signifies the liberation of her own lesbian desires.

McConnell published *The Burnton Widows* two years after *Mrs Porter's Letter*. In contrast to the earlier novel where she takes a figurative approach to the spectral, here she treats the topic literally, taking as her subject an actual occurrence of haunting. She focuses, in fact, on an even grimmer example of society's relegation of the lesbian to the abject, exposing the violent lengths to which homophobes will go to erase the threat of pollution and social destabilization which, in their view, she represents.

The Burnton Widows brings together the Gothic motif of the haunted house with the depiction of the house as the site of murder and crime detection associated with the thriller. The house is exemplified on this occasion by the limestone castle which forms the striking, if incongruous, centrepiece of the American provincial town of Burnton, Oregon. At the start of the novel the castle is uninhabited and the focus of local controversy. The two widows who previously owned it were in a lesbian partnership and the victims of an unsolved murder. As a result, the townspeople of Burnton disagree about the future of the building. One group, led by the local homophobes who loathe the place on account of its lesbian associations, plans to demolish it and develop the site for commercial purposes, while the other, spearheaded by the gay community, aims to preserve it as an object of historical interest. The novel concludes with the triumph of the latter. Summoning assistance from the other gay organizations in the area, they convene a blockade and intervene to prevent the castle's demolition.

The abject connotations of both the castle and its late owners are forcibly impressed upon Nyla when she first arrives in Burnton to take up a post on the local newspaper. Romantically depicting lesbian sisterhood as transcending the bounds of death, McConnell describes the spirits of the two widows communicating with her in a series of disturbingly erotic dreams. They persuade her to track down the identity of their murderer and strive to preserve their former home from demolition. In addition to crossing the boundaries between past and present, life and death, as typifies the abject, the two widows arouse in the locals an ambiguous response of horror and fascination. In investigating the circumstances of their murder, Nyla inadvertently brings to light the intense homophobia which blights the town. As is the case in *Mrs Porter's Letter*, homophobia is discovered to be the 'secret' motivating the crime. The bigotry she encounters in interviewing witnesses and suspects ranges from the 'turn a blind eye' approach adopted by the parents of one of the widows, who refuse to discuss their daughter's lesbianism, to the rampant homophobia manifested by Assistant District Attorney Jim Strunk. Strunk expresses the view that all homosexuals should be annihilated and turns out, predictably, to be the murderer. Positioned between these two extremes is Police Chief Walter Karp who heads the murder enquiry. He disapproves of Nyla's attempt to reopen the case and, when she argues that the murder merits the same attention from the Police as any other crime since the widows were 'members of this community',[20] he disagrees. While admitting that they shopped at the local market and paid taxes like everyone else, he feels that their lesbian orientation relegated them to the role of outsider.

The conversation that takes place between Nyla and Karp, as well as exposing the unwillingness of the police to treat crimes perpetrated against homosexuals seriously, illustrates the contradictions in the relations between gay and heterosexual communities in provincial North America. Despite the fact that the widows lived in Burnton and mixed with the heterosexual citizens, they were nonetheless treated as outsiders. Simultaneously, however, they were regarded as 'the enemy within' and believed to exert a tainting influence on the place. In employing the motif of spectral visitation to explore the way that the memory of the widows and their lesbianism continues to haunt the town after their death, McConnell anticipates certain issues discussed by Fuss and other queer theorists in the 1990s. She investigates the way that, according to Fuss, 'homosexuality is produced inside the dominant discourse of sexual difference as its necessary outside'.[21] She also explores the townspeople's fear of 'the very real possibility and ever-present threat of the collapse of boundaries, an effacing of limits, and a radical confusion of identities' (p. 6).

The widows and their former home, while arousing feelings of disgust and anxiety in certain sections of the local community, also provoke, as is often the case with the abject, a response of fascination. On visiting the castle to investigate the women's murder, the police take a voyeuristic pleasure in exploring the building's nooks and crannies. They express admiration and envy for the opulent furnishings and magnificent view of the sea which, as Karp coarsely remarks, 'those lesbos' enjoyed (p. 83). An intricately carved antique bureau arouses his particular interest. The comment which its appearance elicits from him – 'All these damned little compartments. Damned fascinating!' (p. 78) – epitomizes the pruriently chauvinistic response which he and his colleagues adopt both to the murder mystery and the 'mystery' of lesbian sexuality itself.

Another feature that connects the widows to the concept of the abject is their association with blood. The murder scene is described from a number of different viewpoints but all the witnesses agree on its gory aspect. Blood, as theorists point out, is a conventionally abject substance. As well as carrying connotations of murder and violence, it is related to menstrual pollution and to the splitting open of the body in the act of childbirth.[22]

McConnell's treatment of the lethal consequences of an outbreak of homophobia in provincial society and her representation of the way in which the heterosexual community typecasts the lesbian as abject, though breaking new ground in the year of the novel's publication, is impaired by its lack of subtlety. The characters are represented in moral terms as starkly black or white, and a straightforward equation is assumed to exist between homophobia and other kinds of wrongdoing, such as shady financial dealing and murder. Figures who identify as lesbian, such as the sleuth Nyla and her sidekick Lucy, behave in a manner which is consistently heroic and politically correct, while homophobes, such as Strunk and the sheriff, are depicted as unmitigated villains.

Nonetheless, despite the flaws which the novel displays, *The Burnton Widows* effectively illustrates a key feature of the lesbian Gothic thriller. This is the contradiction that the protagonist embodies. In the role of sleuth Nyla maintains a degree of detachment from the crime and succeeds in tracking down its perpetrator. However, as a lesbian and a subject of supernatural visitation, she displays disturbing connections with the murder victims, the two widows. Assuming the role of lesbian foremothers and surrogate family, they open her eyes to the violent aspects of lesbian history and give her a disturbing insight into the destructive and, on occasion, murderous effects of homophobia. They also function, in certain respects, as her double. As she discovers in the episode when a local hurls a stone through her window, she resembles the spectral couple in being typecast as abject and vulnerable to homophobic assault.

McConnell's two contributions to the Gothic thriller portray the lesbian investigator implicated in the realm of the abject, represented in both novels by death and the corpse. In *Mrs Porter's Letters* Nyla investigates the history and identity of a woman who, she discovers, has been forced by a relative to feign death and, in seeking information about her, visits her counterfeit grave. In *The Burnton Widows* she is haunted by the ghosts of a lesbian couple who were the victims of a particularly gruesome murder and listens to the witnesses' gory accounts of the discovery of their bodies. The investigator in O'Rourke's *Jumping the Cracks*, nicknamed Rats on account of her straggly hair and marginal social position, is even more deeply involved in the abject realm of the corpse. In fact, she spends the major part of the novel haunted by the image of one: the body of a woman she glimpsed one night on the passenger seat of a car parked in the Hackney district of London. The image imprints itself on her memory, prompting her to investigate the circumstances of the crime and to track down the identity of the murderer.

As the metropolitan location of the crime signals, Rats is a very different kind of sleuth from Nyla Wade. With working-class roots and hailing from the city of Hull, she has grown up in an urban environment and has first-hand experience of the violence and hardship of city life. *Jumping the Cracks*, the title which O'Rourke selects for her novel, is by no means a random choice. She utilizes Rats' portrayal to explore the dangers, both material and psychological, that women, and lesbians in particular, can encounter in the city, and to expose the 'cracks' in the fabric of urban society through which, as a result of poverty, sexual exploitation or assault, they can all too easily fall. On moving to London to make a fresh start in life, Rats ekes out a meagre living on social security and occasional spells of casual work. Her isolation and precarious financial position make her an obvious target of victimization – one which Pershing, the slum-landlord in whose housing agency she temporarily works and whom she discovers to have perpetrated the murder, is quick to exploit. He threatens her with violent reprisal if she dares to intervene and divulge his guilty secret.

In addition to being financially deprived and socially insecure, Rats is also a more transgressive protagonist than McConnell's Nyla Wade. She has relatively few friends and, having experienced the readiness of the police to victimize the working class, deliberately refrains from divulging to them the discovery of the corpse. Her independence and solitariness are established in the opening episode of the novel when, on glimpsing the body of the murder victim through the window of the parked car, she rejects the idea of phoning the local constabulary on the grounds that 'All her life, the Police had been on the wrong side, the other side'.[23] The search for justice in which she engages is, in fact, deeply personal. It is motivated more by feelings of anger at the way that, in patriarchal capitalism, the rich and powerful are permitted to dominate the weak, and by subliminal feelings of identification with the corpse which, as the narrative progresses, is increasingly positioned as her double, than by a conventional concern for law and order.

The symbolic correspondence between Rats and the corpse of the murder victim is signalled early on. On first glimpsing it through the car window, she regards its countenance as uncannily 'mirroring back her own shock in its gaping mouth and startled staring eyes' (p. 2). At this early stage of the narrative the corpse chiefly signifies to her the random violence of urban life and the vulnerability of the human body, her own in particular, to physical assault. Its solitariness, the fact that it is female and its inability to communicate the secret of its death, reflect her own isolation and helplessness. They foreground the role of double that O'Rourke assigns to it.

When, on returning to the street the following day, Rats discovers that both the corpse and the car containing it have disappeared, she finds the invisibility which it has suddenly acquired even more disturbing than its former presence. In practical terms, it makes proving its existence difficult, while, on a psychological plane, it mirrors her own invisibility as a closet lesbian. Unemployment is rife in Thatcher's Britain and, when Rats does occasionally manage to find work, she is loath to put the job at risk by 'coming out' to her employers. While painfully aware, as she puts it, of 'holding back, evading certain issues' (p. 17) in conversation, she prefers a working day based on prevarication and half-truths to the poverty and loneliness of life on the dole.

Rats' decision, as far as her relations with employers and the general public are concerned, to keep her sexual identification secret reflects the abject position society assigns to the lesbian, and O'Rourke introduces numerous references to the role of pariah and outcast which people project upon her. And, in addition to foregrounding Rats' abject status, she also emphasizes that of the corpse. She portrays it as epitomizing the detritus and waste of urban life and relates it in Rats' imagination to the numerous other corpses the city ejects which lie 'packaged in plastic bags, labelled with their names, if known, a description if not, to wait in mortuaries and funeral parlours' (p. 8). This reference to 'mortuaries and funeral parlours' forms part of a network of locations associated with death and corporeal decay which furnish the macabre context of the novel's action. They include the River Thames, represented as the last resort of suicides, and the cemetery where Rats is pursued with evil intent by Pershing's henchmen. The latter, with its crumbling mortuary furniture and weed-infested graves, creates an image of culture in the process of slipping back to nature, again revealing connections with the body of the murder victim. The abject position of the corpse is emphasized by the way it is disconcertingly represented as crossing the boundaries between culture and nature, life and death. On glimpsing the slumped figure of the murder victim through the window of the car, Rats initially assumes it to be alive. On looking more closely, however, she perceives it to be on the Other side of the life/death boundary; it is, she grimly and definitively comments, 'no longer a person, but a corpse' (p. 2).

As is usual with the sleuth in the Gothic thriller, Rats is portrayed in terms of contradictions. Whereas the correspondence established between her and the corpse connects her with the abject and with the world of the outcast and the perverse which it signifies, other facets of her characterization relate her, more optimistically, to the Symbolic. Contending with a sense of identification with the murder victim, she experiences a healthy sense of difference. Her encounter with the corpse, though arousing in her feelings of fear and making her doubt her ability to survive, also prompts her to value the fact that she is alive and enjoys a degree of self-determination and agency. This motivates her to break free from the syndrome of inertia and depression into which she has slipped and to make a fresh effort both to find work and to solve the murder mystery. The two aims coincide when she accepts the post of clerk in the housing agency owned by the villain Pershing. As a result, she finds herself in a position to make enquiries about him and to edge closer to discovering the 'secret' at the heart of the crime. In so doing, she puts to good use the roles of observer and 'spy' which the lesbian conventionally occupies. On being unexpectedly dismissed from her post, she suspects that it is her attribute of curiosity which has aroused her employer's ire. Pershing himself, having engineered the death of her pet cat in an attempt to scare her off and put an end to her interference, endorses her suspicions. In an interview aimed to intimidate her, he ironically enquiries, 'How many cats, do you suppose, were killed before curiosity was seen to be the villain?' (p. 102).

Jumping the Cracks resembles McConnell's two novels in that, in addition to introducing a protagonist who combines the contrary roles of crime investigator/Gothic heroine, it concludes on a note of imperfect closure. Rats succeeds in tracing the identity of the murder victim and in locating documents which prove Pershing's guilt and serve to put him behind bars. However, the basic problem of the random violence of city life and its destructive effect on vulnerable members of society such as women and homosexuals which the novel raises remains unsolved. The urban environment remains as brutal and unyielding as ever.

POSTMODERN MYSTERIES

The publication of Wings's *Divine Victim* and Schulman's *After Delores* in the late 1980s and the 1990s heralded a new sophisticated stage in the development of the lesbian Gothic thriller. The narratives the two writers create, though differing in style and location, both utilize the motif of spectral visitation to address the problems which the lesbian subject experiences in coping with the memory of a broken relationship. The anonymous narrators on whose subjectivities they centre are both haunted by erotic memories of an ex-lover and, in consequence, emerge as psychologically entrapped in fantasy images of the past. The postmodern dimension of the two novels is reflected in the treatment of character and narrative, as well as in strategies of parody and intertextual allusion.

In contrast to McConnell and O'Rourke, who characterize their investigator protagonists relatively simply, Wings and Schulman introduce narrators whose subjectivities are fractured and who live, to a significant degree, in the delusive world of memory and fantasy. Reacting against earlier works of lesbian crime fiction, they go out of their way to undermine the politically correct image of the sleuth and the rational approach she adopts towards the crime investigation. Wings blurs the distinction that conventionally exists between the investigator and the perpetrator of the crime by unexpectedly portraying the sleuth herself involved in a murder. Schulman creates a sleuth whose perceptions, far from being trustworthy, are obscured and confused by grief at her lover's infidelity and the dependence on drink to which it is driving her. Both investigators emerge, in this respect, as unreliable narrators. The versions of events which they give the reader, as a result of either omission or elaboration, are unsound. The account that Wings's narrator constructs is, in fact, accurate as far as it goes. However, in describing her turbulent relationship with her Swedish lover Ilona Jorgensen, she postpones revealing until the final chapter a key fact about it: namely, that she herself was responsible for Ilona's death. This piece of information significantly alters our view of her; it indicates that she is not merely the wronged victim of Ilona's capricious behaviour which, up to now, she has made herself out to be, but, on the contrary, was the agent of her demise. Schulman's narrator also emerges as unreliable, though she is not deliberately so. Her feelings of distress and anger at her lover Delores' infidelity, along with her taste for melodramatic sexual scenarios, lead her to mistake the identity of the murderer and to interpret the circumstances of the crime as more complicated than in actual fact they are.

The novels of Wings and Schulman differ from those of McConnell and O'Rourke not only in the characterization of the sleuth but also in their narrative complexity. The Gothic thriller as a genre is notably rich in the production of narrative lines, with the investigator, the suspects and the witnesses all creating conflicting versions of events and spinning rival yarns. Wings's and Schulman's two texts are particularly fertile in this respect.

Narratives reproducing different genres and discourses and reflecting conflicting viewpoints interact and clash, creating a web of intermeshing storylines – Gothic, detective, romantic, fantastic, erotic and queer. Discussing the distinguishing features of postmodern fiction, Hutcheon comments on the interest many writers display in 'the linking of "fictitious" to "mendacious" stories'.[24] Wings and, to an even greater degree, Schulman foreground just such a link between fiction and mendacity. This feature of their work prompts the reader, while enjoying the ambiguities of storyline and characterization, to ponder the narrow boundary that exists between invention and lying.

As is illustrated by her novels focusing on the sleuth Emma Victor,[25] which create a lesbian version of the Chandleresque thriller, Wings excels in the art of parody and pastiche. In relinquishing the format of the hard-boiled American crime novel and taking as her model du Maurier's *Rebecca*, she applies her skills of parody to a text of a very different kind. *Rebecca* is a Gothic romance which, in the later stages, with the discovery of Maxim de Winter's murder of his glamorous but morally decadent first wife, introduces strategies of intrigue and detection associated with the thriller. The contrast that the novel inscribes between the bourgeois model of femininity exemplified by Maxim's second wife and the seductively transgressive image of Rebecca, combined with the lesbian subtext hinted at in the references to the latter's illicit love affairs and in the passionate devotion she inspired in her maid Mrs Danvers, has understandably provoked discussion.[26] It raised a number of intriguing questions. Is the second Mrs de Winter, who accompanies Maxim to Manderley as his new wife and performs the role of narrator, sexually attracted to Rebecca or does she merely envy her beauty and sophistication? What precisely are the 'unspeakable'[27] vices in which Rebecca indulged during her surreptitious visits to London? And, as Wings herself asks in the essay in which she discusses the writing of *Divine Victim* and refers to du Maurier's own emotionally fraught lesbian involvements, 'Was *Rebecca* an inner drama related to du Maurier herself? Was killing Rebecca symbolically killing the lesbian impulse?'[28] By teasing out and developing the lesbian subtext in du Maurier's novel, Wings contributes to the debate which it has provoked. She also creates a fast-moving Gothic thriller which, set in contemporary North America, addresses with wit and panache issues of interest to a lesbian/queer readership.

In commenting on the writing of *Divine Victim*, Wings lists the features of du Maurier's novel that particularly caught her eye and refers to the way that, in creating, as she terms it, 'a twentieth-century Gothic for queers',[29] she transmuted and reworked them. She explains that, like du Maurier, she chose to centre her novel on 'a nameless narrator who is additionally a world wanderer' (p. 31). Du Maurier's heroine, who earns a living by accompanying the rich Mrs Van Hopper on her travels and subsequently becomes Maxim's second wife, is transformed in *Divine Victim* into an untenured academic who travels the globe in search of employment. Like du Maurier's heroine, her relationship with her present partner is haunted and destabilized by the image of a female figure from the past. As Wings comments, 'Her new girlfriend Marya, like Maxim, is boring. The sex isn't exciting the way it was with Ilona' (p. 31).

The parodic relationship existing between *Divine Victim* and *Rebecca* is signalled in the opening pages of the former in the episode in which the unnamed narrator arrives, in a manner resembling the second Mrs De Winter's arrival at Manderley, at the isolated mansion in rural Montana which her partner Marya has inherited from a great-aunt. Not only was the great-aunt fortuitously named 'Rebecca Cascia' but also the narrator, on first setting eyes on what she jokingly terms this 'old gothic horror house'[30] and sensing its uncanny atmosphere, feels moved to quote the famous opening lines of du Maurier's novel: 'Last night I dreamt I went to Manderley again ...' (p. 7). The two houses, though differing in appearance and location, display pronounced similarities. Both are associated with the harshness of the elements: Manderley with the sea and the house in Wings's novel with the bitter Montana winter. Both, in addition, are haunted by the memory of female figures from the past. Whereas Manderley is pervaded by the memory of Maxim's first wife Rebecca and the erotic attraction which she exuded, the house in *Divine Victim* resonates with the echoes of two deceased women: Rebecca Cascia the former owner, whose life as a renegade nun the narrator attempts to investigate, and Ilona Jorgensen, the Swedish art historian with whom, while visiting Italy, the narrator had a tempestuous affair. Both women, the reader perceives, are re-creations of du Maurier's Rebecca and reflect, in different ways, aspects of her transgressive sexuality. Rebecca Cascia, the excommunicated nun who fled from the convent on account of the scandal she aroused by engaging in a lesbian affair, reflects Rebecca's recklessness and her association with ecclesiastical institutions. Commenting on the writing of *Divine Victim*, Wings reveals that it was the description of Rebecca's lingerie in Hitchcock's famous film as 'made by the nuns in the convent of St Clare'[31] which inspired her, as she humorously puts it, to 'create roles for the underwear-producing nuns ... and give them a few steamy relationships of their own'! (pp. 31–2). In associating convent life with lesbian love, Wings brings up to date a popular fictional topos. As is illustrated by a series of novels ranging from Denis Diderot's *La Religieuse* (1760) to Dorothy Strachey's *Olivia* (1949), the same-sex environment of the convent or the girls' boarding school has traditionally furnished a suitable location for female erotic involvements, one which writers have eagerly exploited.[32]

While the sacred associations of Rebecca (or, rather, her underwear) are developed in the portrayal of the renegade nun Rebecca Cascia, the profane are elaborated in the character of Ilona Jorgensen, the narrator's ex-lover. According to Wings, Ilona 'has the ego of a Camille Paglia but she is a feminist and a lot more beautiful'.[33] Ruthlessly ambitious and incredibly sexy, Ilona stirs up trouble wherever she goes. Both women enact, in different ways, the titular role of 'Divine Victim'. Rebecca and her sister novices are expected, on taking their vows, 'to become something other, something holy, something divine. Victims. Divine victims',[34] while Ilona is divinely beautiful and, as we discover in the novel's conclusion, the victim of a murder. Both also carry connotations of the abject. The scandalous circumstances in which Rebecca left the convent, confessing to a lesbian attachment and fleeing in the dead of night with stolen valuables concealed under her cloak, result in her transgressing the border between the sacred and the profane and make her name taboo in ecclesiastical circles. Ilona's outbursts of temper and violent behaviour destabilize the boundary between sanity and madness. The role of murder victim which Wings assigns to her, combined with her connection to the carcass of a dead cat which, while camping in Italy, she insists on carrying around in a shoe box, relate her in addition to that most abject of objects, the corpse.

By making both Rebecca Cascia and Ilona Jorgensen substitutes for du Maurier's Rebecca, Wings interweaves reference to the patriarchal family unit with an alternative lesbian 'family' formation. In investigating the history of Rebecca Cascia, while reliving in memory her emotionally stormy relationship with Ilona, the narrator embarks on an intricate journey back into the past which interrelates two different time schemes. She recovers, in the process, the history of two very different 'foremothers'. The one carries sacred associations, the other profane.

Another character in du Maurier's novel who, Wings acknowledges, inspired her talent for parody, is Rebecca's devoted handmaid Mrs Danvers. 'Danny' is transformed in Divine Victim into Helen Danroy, the rural dyke who attempts to prevent the narrator from investigating Rebecca Cascia's past. Wings utilizes Danroy to articulate the theme of lesbian passion at which, in her portrayal of Mrs Danvers, du Maurier merely hints. In one of the playfully over-the-top episodes with which Divine Victim abounds she represents Danroy donning the disguise of a nun in order to administer poison to the narrator. When the latter, in order to foil her murderous scheme, ties her to a bedstead in a local motel, Danroy is temporarily transmuted into a parodic image of lesbian S&M – although her bondage, as the narrator humorously acknowledges, is 'non-consensual'! (p. 187).

As is generally the case in the Gothic thriller, Divine Victim concludes on a note of ambiguity. The narrator, though foiling Danroy's attempt to murder her, fails to prevent the priceless heirloom concealed in Rebecca Cascia's Montana residence from being destroyed. And, on a personal level, she is unable to liberate herself from the memory of Ilona and the baleful influence she continues to exert from beyond the grave.

Wings addresses Divine Victim to a youthful and intelligent lesbian readership whose members, as well as being familiar with the conventions of the Gothic romance, are capable of recognizing the references to lesbian and queer culture which underpin the numerous squibs of humour she lets fly. Lesbian S&M, the queer Sisters of Perpetual Indulgence who dress as nuns and the readiness of urban lesbians to patronize their country cousins are some of the topics on which she touches. However, though written primarily for entertainment, *Divine Victim* also introduces issues of a serious kind. Wings emulates du Maurier in structuring her novel on two contrasting images of femininity and challenging restrictive stereotypes of womanhood. Whereas du Maurier problematizes the respectable 1940s model of bourgeois femininity by juxtaposing it with the glamorously transgressive image of Rebecca, Wings, in her portrayal of Ilona Jorgensen, subverts the politically correct image of the lesbian promoted by the 1970s lesbian feminist movement. Ilona emerges as quarrelsome, egocentric and domineering. She has casual sex in toilets, behaves promiscuously with members of both sexes, engages in slanging matches with feminist colleagues and comes close to strangling her partner in a fit of rage. Cast in the role of the lesbian from hell, she is a parodic version of the image which, as the film *Basic Instinct* illustrates, continues to haunt popular horror film and fiction – the lesbian as epitome of the 'monstrous-feminine'. By recreating the image in humorous terms, Wings successfully exorcizes its power.

Differing from Wings's novel in tone and style, though similarly postmodern in its approach to subjectivity and culture, is Schulman's *After Delores*. Schulman's narrator resembles Wings's in the fact that she is unnamed and haunted by the memory of a former lover. However, her characterization in other respects is very different. A member of the casual labour force that services New York City, she works as a waitress in a diner and, as she herself sullenly admits, is downtrodden and underprivileged. She is consumed with bitterness at her lover Delores's infidelity and suffers from bouts of depression. As the narrative progresses she drifts into alcoholism and finds increasing difficulty in decoding the fractured, decentred world of American urban life. She represents an extreme example of the contradictions of agent/victim which the protagonist of the Gothic thriller conventionally embodies. Her efforts to investigate and avenge the murder of the disco dancer Marion Walker, whom she nicknames Punkette, are undermined by emotional outbursts and errors of judgment which are at odds with the attributes of perception and self-control we expect from the figure of the sleuth. Not only is she, like the majority of lesbian investigators, an amateur, but she becomes involved in the search for Punkette's murderer by accident rather than design. Her decision to track down Punkette's killer and avenge her death, like her behaviour in general, is motivated by passion rather than reason. The pursuit of the murderer in which she relentlessly engages compensates emotionally for the vengeance which she longs to wreak on the faithless Delores. It enables her to express, in displaced form, the anger and sense of injustice she feels at her desertion.

The narrator's obsessional involvement with past events, though limiting her abilities as a crime investigator, makes her an obvious candidate for an encounter with the uncanny – and the opening lines of the novel portray her in the act of trying to avoid or, at any rate, postpone such an event. As she laconically remarks, as if recording an everyday occurrence, 'I walked out in the snow trying to get away from Delores's ghost. It was sitting back in the apartment waiting for me' (p. 1). Her efforts to elude the uncanny are, however, unsuccessful since, like other Gothic heroines before her, she discovers that, in turning her back on the spectral presence, she is, ironically, moving towards it. On leaving her apartment to escape the ghost of Delores, she runs headlong into the realm of Gothic fantasy. Schulman updates and urbanizes this realm, making it applicable to present-day lesbian life and transforming it to accommodate urban locations such as the disco hall, the park and the subway. It takes the form of a labyrinthine domain of doubling, encounters between the self and Other and sexual and theatrical role-play. The familiar is defamiliarized and people and events turn out to be the reverse of what they initially appear.

The first scene of this uncanny kind which the narrator encounters in her promenade through the wintry New York streets is a gay fancy-dress party taking place in a local basement. Here, in a surreal setting where, as she comments, 'The winter night that had been walls turned into men and women dancing together and by themselves ...' (p. 1), she encounters the larger-than-life figure of Priscilla Presley. Priscilla, as suits the role of Elvis's wife which she is enacting for the evening, is dressed in the 1960s gear of black wig and mini-skirted wedding dress. However, as becomes apparent when she starts attacking one of the girls on the dance floor and calling her abusive names, her behaviour mirrors the narrator's fixation with revenge. Priscilla too has been jilted in love and, as the narrator gleefully perceives, is 'doing a dance called getting even' (p. 4). The gun which she carries, a tiny, pearl-handled model described as 'deadly sleek and feminine' (p. 10), is a prop appropriated from the film noir and accentuates the violence of her act. The narrator is enthralled by Priscilla's performance of avenging Fury; it demonstrates in her eyes that, 'if you waited for the right moment you could eventually get revenge' (p. 4).

Priscilla's sudden appearance in the surreal arena of the disco is, in fact, the first of the series of displacements and substitutions that proliferate throughout the novel. They signal to the reader that the narrator's encounters with the various characters she meets, while existing on a realist plane and open to literal interpretation, simultaneously represent a journey of exploration into her own disturbed psyche where she has to confront her own personal fears and desires. Another character who plays a similar role in her life is Punkette, the disco dancer and murder victim. In referring to her lover Charlotte and Charlotte's partner Beatriz, Punkette introduces yet another set of substitutions which lead the narrator still deeper into the Gothic world.

After the murder of Punkette, Charlotte and Beatriz play an increasingly important part in the narrator's life, both in actual terms and on a fantasy plane. The couple epitomizes for her a sophisticated world of culture and art from which she feels excluded. She is fascinated by the air of duplicity and masquerade pervading them. They work in alternative theatre and their passion for role-play, reflected in their personal life as well as in their performance on stage, represents a seductive though dangerous world of illusion and deceit where the difference between fact and fiction is blurred. Their propensity for lying and pretence, illustrated by the conflicting accounts they give of even the most mundane events, illustrates the relation between mendacity and storytelling which, as Hutcheon comments, is a frequent feature of postmodern fiction.[35] Their habitual lying, instead of alienating the narrator, serves to bind her more closely to them. It feeds her craving for sensationalistic scenarios, ones spiced with an element of S&M. As she smugly remarks, congratulating herself on the masochistic attachment she forms with the couple, 'Their lies enabled them to keep a passionate relationship. I was one of them now. I was so evil I was in love with them' (p. 126).

The narrator's feelings of attraction towards Charlotte and Beatriz are apparent the first time she sees them performing on stage together. In fact, she becomes so engrossed in the scene of lesbian self-humiliation which Charlotte is enacting that she initially mistakes her performance for real life; as she admits, ' It was only when she finished that I remembered it wasn't real. I felt like a spy in a private conversation, and when the conversation was over, I had a stake in it' (p. 36).

The role of spy, which the narrator applies to herself here, is mentioned again on a later occasion, when it is transferred from the public world of the theatre to the intimate, domestic setting of the couple's apartment. Peering through the peephole in the front door, she surreptitiously watches the two women perform a love scene – and this time, it *is* for real. She describes how,

> The light was out in the hallway, so I stood, like a thief in the night, like a traitor committing espionage. I looked in and they were naked. Charlotte sitting strong and beautiful on a kitchen chair with her arms round Beatriz's tiny waist. They were sweating and so terrific ... (p. 126)

Schulman's portrayal of the narrator spying on the couple while they are making love introduces the theme of voyeurism which, as we have seen from novels focusing on spectral visitation such as Zanger's *Gardenias Where There Are None* and Martinac's *Out of Time*, marks the initial stage of the subject's entry into the world of Gothic fantasy. The episode also represents a version of the primal fantasy of origins in which the child secretly watches her parents engage in sex, a scene which, as mentioned above, Martinac also introduces. This helps to explain the intensity of the passion that Schulman's narrator invests in the relationship she forms with Charlotte and Beatriz. Though appearing, from a commonsense point of view, irrational and excessive, the relationship reflects the search for an alternative 'family' in which, as her expressions of loneliness and *déréliction*[36] indicate, she is subliminally engaged. It represents a perverse version of the motif of 'queer family' which, as we have seen, is a common feature of lesbian Gothic.

The narrator's entry into the world of Gothic fantasy, with its proliferation of mirror images, displacements and substitutions, is accompanied by the introduction of imagery evoking horror and death. She continues to feel haunted by 'the phantom devil Delores' (p. 80) and, in an episode which brings together images of physical violence, the grotesque body and woman as menstrual monster, dreams that she is wearing a white corset which is filling with blood. When, in the dream, she sees Delores approaching, she attempts to hide the corset under a chair, but fails to conceal it successfully. On waking, she purchases a picture postcard representing the Statue of Liberty. In a fit of savage irony she mails the card to Delores, with a message announcing that she longs to smash her face.

As this episode illustrates, in recasting the format of the lesbian thriller Schulman transforms the sleuth from a politically correct figure with a potential for heroism to an emotionally disturbed queer with a propensity for violence who only feels relaxed with a drink in her hand. In addition to updating the thriller to incorporate features of contemporary American urban life and the darker aspects of lesbian subjectivity and sexuality, she also, in accord with the postmodern focus on intertextuality, introduces parodic allusions to nineteenth-century *fin-de-siècle* images of lesbianism. Appropriating the decadent image of the lesbian popularized by Baudelaire and Renée Vivien, and the association of her with perverse versions of religious imagery and ecclesiastical locations in Barnes's *Nightwood*, the narrator fills her sitting room with thirty novena candles. Having transformed the room into a replica of a mausoleum, she assumes a deathlike pose and lies prostrate on the couch in 'the warm glow'. However, instead of allowing the reader to take her pose seriously, she undercuts it in typically postmodern manner. She selfconsciously draws attention to its narcissistic element of performativity by flippantly admitting to 'feeling like a funeral, with me stretched out, open casket' (p. 81).

As is typical of Schulman's unorthodox thriller, the discovery of the murderer's identity, with which it concludes, depends not on skill but chance – and reverses the expectations of both reader and sleuth narrator. The latter discovers to her surprise that Charlotte and Beatriz, whom initially she regarded as suspects, are innocent, and that the murderer is, in fact, male. Having teased us into thinking that the crime took place 'between women',[37] Schulman unexpectedly reveals, at the last moment, that it did not. Similarly anticlimactic is the fact that the murderer, rather than playing a central role in the narrative, is revealed, on the contrary, to be a figure who is peripheral and insignificant. This, as well as disappointing our expectations of a psychological struggle between the sleuth and the perpetrator of the crime, makes the murder and its investigation appear somehow random and pointless.

However, the conclusion that Schulman imposes on her postmodern murder mystery, though disappointing from a conventional point of view, is, in terms of the interests of lesbian Gothic and the novel's emphasis on the emotional intensity of lesbian desire, strikingly apt. As well as being convincing from a sociological perspective (the majority of urban crimes of violence are committed by men), it agrees with the novel's key theme, the transforming power of erotic fantasy. Led astray by her feelings of attraction for Charlotte and Beatriz, and by her addiction to the melodramatic S&M scenarios they create both on stage and in their personal life, the narrator mentally transforms the murder mystery into a lesbian romance, ignoring, to her cost, the mundane nature of many acts of urban violence.

As is characteristic of the Gothic thriller, Schulman's novel avoids closure and concludes on a note of uncertainty. The narrator's increasing immersion in the world of Gothic fantasy has the effect of severely diminishing her agency, making her vulnerable to forces (passions, people, events) over which she has little or no control. Although she succeeds, by luck rather than judgement, in avenging Punkette's murder and achieving a form of justice, this brings her little sense of fulfilment. On the contrary, it leaves her feeling lonely and depressed. The act of avenging Punkette's death turns out to be something of an anticlimax; it fails to exorcize the ghost of Delores or to liberate the narrator from her feelings of infatuation with her. As she wryly comments in the novel's concluding lines, alerting attention to the circular trajectory of entrapment which she has traced since she was first portrayed on the opening page, leaving her apartment on a snowy winter's night to escape the presence of Delores's ghost, 'None of it meant anything to me. There was only one thing I really missed. I missed Delores' (p. 158).

The Gothic thriller is an appropriate topic with which to conclude this study of lesbian Gothic fiction since it illustrates the way in which, in novels and stories of this kind, Gothic interests and motifs, rather than remaining discrete, interact with other generic conventions, influencing them intellectually and stylistically. In addition, examples of the Gothic thriller bring together many of the themes and ideas that inform lesbian Gothic fiction in general. The motif of spectral visitation, which thriller writers such as McConnell and Schulman utilize either literally or as a metaphor for the operations of fantasy and memory, links their novels to the fiction of Martinac, Brown, Winterson and Donoghue discussed in Chapter 3. The focus they place on the typecasting of the lesbian as abject and the outcast role which society assigns to her also relates them to the transgressive recasting of the image of the witch discussed in Chapter 2 and the vampire in Chapter 4.

However, the Gothic thriller, striking though its ability to encapsulate key aspects of lesbian Gothic in general certainly is, is not the only fictional category that merits attention in the concluding section of this study. It represents merely one strand in a tapestry which, as we have seen, is complex and multifaceted. In her essay discussing the writing of *Divine Victim*, Wings ponders the question, what a work of queer Gothic might represent as fear and terror.[38] Having studied a number of lesbian/queer texts, we are now in a position to furnish an answer – or, at any rate, to move towards doing so. The emotions of fear and terror assume in lesbian Gothic not one form but several, manifesting themselves in numerous different ways. They can reflect apprehensions and anxieties concerning death, whether in relation to childbirth and the physical and psychological maladies arising from it, as depicted by Hanrahan in *The Albatross Muff*; as a result of acts of homophobic violence, as in Allard's *Légende* and McConnell's *The Burnton Widows*; or motivated by the AIDS crisis, as is the case in Schulman's *Rat Bohemia*. Alternatively they can reflect the individual's feelings of sexual guilt or confusions about her gender identity, as in Zanger's *Gardenias Where There Are None*; or they can mirror a sense of anomie and *déréliction*, as experienced by the narrators of Brown's *The Haunted House*, Donoghue's *Hood* and Schulman's *After Delores*.

Two other standard Gothic themes besides fear and terror which play an important part in lesbian versions of the genre are sexuality and subjectivity. Examples include the focus on oral sex and S&M in the vampire stories of Forrest and Califia, Martinac's and McConnell's illustrations of the excess which lesbian desire signifies in phallocentric culture and its destabilizing effect on the individual and the group, and the representation of the production of lesbian/queer subjectivity in the novels of Brown and Schulman. Another topic with erotic connotations that writers frequently address is the interaction between the roles of mother and lover and the enfolding of the one into the other which, as theorists and writers point out, lesbian partnerships and sexual encounters tend to reflect. Tennant's *The Bad Sister*, Gomez' *The Gilda Stories* and Califia's 'The Vampire' furnish pertinent illustrations. They relate the topic, explicitly or by implication, to the queer movement's problematization of the patriarchal family unit and its biological ties, and its readiness to experiment with alternative groups and relationships.

As well as transforming the themes associated with Gothic, writers of lesbian Gothic also manipulate the stylistic features of the genre and the character stereotypes which it has produced. By inverting or parodying the monstrous images of woman/lesbian which Gothic texts generate, they exorcize their destructive effect and take a step towards resignifying the boundaries of the abject, the realm to which society has traditionally relegated the lesbian. The comic versions of the vampire narrative created by Livia and Scott, the postmodern recasting of the image of the witch in the fiction of Galford and Donoghue, and Wings's parodic portrayal of the glamorous but disruptive Ilona Jorgensen as 'the lesbian from hell' furnish lively examples. The stylized roles and scenarios with which Gothic fiction abounds provide writers with a vehicle to explore the construction of role and identity and to foreground its performative dimension. The subversive effect of the parodic performance of the roles and scripts which society assigns to women and gays, articulated in the Irigarayan concept of mimesis and in the Butleresque theory of 'gender and performativity', achieves fictional representation in a number of novels and stories.

Another feature of Gothic that writers exploit and transform is the connections which it displays with historical fiction. Hanrahan, Allard and Zanger utilize this facet of the genre to recreate episodes from the lesbian past and to explore lesbian 'myths of origin'. Martinac, Livia and Galford, adopting a more sophisticated poststructuralist approach, compare and contrast earlier models of lesbian identity and female relationships with present-day constructs. Writing self-reflexively, they interrogate the lesbian subject's fascination with investigating and recreating episodes from lesbian history and draw attention to the dangers of idealizing and misreading the past to which it can give rise. The historical affiliations of the genre also furnish writers with a means to comment on issues relevant to present-day lesbian culture and politics. Topics that they address include radical feminist ideals of sisterhood, exemplified in Hanrahan's *The Albatross Muff* and Tennant's *The Bad Sister*; the cultural feminist emphasis on female creativity and woman's relationship with the natural world, treated seriously by Allard in *Légende* and parodically by Galford in *The Fires of Bride*; and the queer movement's emphasis on alternative familial formations and a range of transgressive sexualities in Winterson's *Sexing the Cherry*, Gomez' *The Gilda Stories* and Schulman's *Rat Bohemia*.

Lesbian Gothic fiction has developed considerably in the past twenty-five years, evolving from the radical feminist representations of the witch in the fiction of the 1970s and the early 1980s to encompass an extensive array of motifs, styles and ideological viewpoints. Responding sensitively to shifts in lesbian/feminist politics and culture, it shows itself, like its mainstream counterpart, to be a highly versatile mode, capable of introducing new ideas and perspectives as occasion demands. One of the most striking modifications it has undergone in recent years is the increasingly self-conscious and critical approach which writers adopt to genre and convention. Texts produced in the 1970s and the early 1980s, such as Hanrahan's *The Albatross Muff*, Allard's *Légende* and McConnell's *The Burnton Widows*, while challenging and transforming the misogynistic/homophobic attitudes that popular versions of Gothic encode, make little attempt to interrogate other aspects of the genre. They plunge the reader into an emotionally powerful narrative which, while demanding that she suspend disbelief as regards the uncanny events recounted, also allows her to enjoy the conventional pleasures of character identification. This strategy, since it creates no distance between reader and text, permits little room for irony or critique but unquestioningly endorses orthodox concepts of character and reader response.

In contrast, texts published in the late 1980s and the 1990s, such as Galford's *The Fires of Bride*, Winterson's *The Passion* and Wings's *Divine Victim*, influenced by postmodern and queer perspectives, approach Gothic conventions with a greater degree of radicalism. As well as challenging the prejudices which the genre encodes, they advertise the artifice and ideological limitations of the scenarios and stereotypes it produces. By treating its motifs parodically, they foreground their role as a vehicle for discussing issues of sexual politics. Instead of representing character and subjectivity in terms of depth, texts of this kind signal to the reader the fact that they are constructs, operating in terms of performativity. And by juxtaposing a range of transgressive sexualities – lesbian, queer, butch and femme – with Gothic stereotypes, they prompt the reader to compare sexual constructs with literary ones. They also interrogate the limitations and problematic aspects of the genre itself. Donoghue's *Hood* critiques the clichés of the popular ghost story and Schulman's *Rat Bohemia* exposes the melodramatic excesses of horror fiction and film. Developments of this kind illustrate the vitality of lesbian Gothic and the capacity it reveals for growth and change. It will be interesting to see the further shifts and modifications it reflects in future years.

NOTES

1. Sarah Schulman, *After Delores* (Sheba Feminist Publishers, 1980), p. 1. Further page references are to this edition and are in the text.

2. Studies of the lesbian thriller include Sally Munt, *Murder by the Book? Feminism and the Crime Novel* (Routledge, 1994), pp. 120–46; and Paulina Palmer, *Contemporary Lesbian Writing*, pp. 63–77.

3. Topical and/or controversial issues which the lesbian thriller treats include the lesbian club scene (Forrest, *Murder at the Nightwood Bar*, Naiad, 1987), S&M relations (Barbara Wilson, *The Dog-Collar Murders*, Seal Press, 1989), trans-sexualism (Wilson, *Gaudi Afternoon*, Seal Press, 1990), and New Age communes (Wings, *She Came in a Flash*, Women's Press, 1988). For discussion of this aspect of the thriller see Paulina Palmer, 'The Lesbian Thriller: Crimes, Clues, and Contradictions', in Gabriele Griffin (ed.), *Outwrite: Lesbianism and Popular Culture* (Pluto, 1993), pp. 86–105.

4. Day, *In the Circles of Fear*, pp. 50–1.

5. Maureen Reddy, *Sisters in Crime: Feminism and the Crime Novel* (Continuum, 1988), p. 9.

6. For reference to the contradictions which the lesbian sleuth embodies see Palmer, *Contemporary Lesbian Writing*, pp. 63–76.

7. See Day, *In the Circles of Fear*, pp. 62–9.

8. Walter Benjamin, *Charles Baudelaire: A Lyric Poet in the Era of High Capitalism* (New Left Books, 1973), pp. 40–4.

9. Dana Brand, 'From the *Flâneur* to the Detective: Interpreting the City of Poe', in Tony Bennett (ed.), *Popular Fiction: Technology, Ideology, Production, Reading* (Routledge, 1990), pp. 220–37.

10. Munt, 'The Lesbian *Flâneur*', in *Mapping Desire*, pp. 114–25.

11. See Sedgwick, *The Coherence of Gothic Conventions*, pp. 9–31, 37–47.

12. Geraldine Pederson-Krag, 'Detective Stories and the Primal Scene', in Glen W. Most and William W. Stowe (eds), *The Poetics of Murder: Detective Fiction and Literary Theory* (Harcourt Brace Jovanovich, 1983), pp. 13–20.

13. Sedgwick, *Epistemology of the Closet* (Harvester, 1990), pp. 67–77.

14. See Forrest, *Amateur City* (Naiad, 1984); and Wilson, *Murder in the Collective* (Seal Press, 1984).

15. Munt, *Murder by the Book?*, p. 129.

16. See Fuss, *Inside/Out*, pp. 1–10; and essays by Tim Davis and Tracey Skelton in David Bell and Gill Valentine, *Mapping Desire*, pp. 264–303.

17. Vicki P. McConnell, *Mrs Porter's Letter* (Naiad Press, 1982), p. 27. Further page references are to this edition and are in the text.

18. Kristeva, *Powers of Horror*, p. 4.

19. Kristeva, *Powers of Horror*, pp. 3–4; Creed, *The Monstrous-Feminine*, p. 10.

20. McConnell, *The Burnton Widows* (Naiad Press, 1984), p. 179. Further page references are to this edition and are in the text.

21. Fuss, *Inside/Out*, p. 5.

22. See Kristeva, *Powers of Horror*, pp. 59–66.

23. Rebecca O'Rourke, *Jumping the Cracks* (Virago, 1987), p. 2.

24. Hutcheon, *The Poetics of Postmodernism*, p. 108.

25. *She Came Too Late* (Women's Press, 1986) and *She Came in a Flash* (Women's Press, 1988).

26. See Alison Light, '"Returning to Manderley": Romance Fiction, Female Sexuality and Class', *Feminist Review*, 16 (1984), 7–25. Male non-feminist writers also reveal the influence of *Rebecca*. King creates an individualistic, if unconvincing, version of du Maurier's Mrs Danvers in *Bag of Bones*. As is to be expected, he reveals no interest in the novel's lesbian subtext!

27. Daphne du Maurier, *Rebecca* (Gollancz, 1935), p. 323.

28. Wings, 'Rebecca Redux', p. 13.

29. *Ibid.*

30. Wings, *Divine Victim* (The Women's Press, 1992), p. 8. Further page references are to this edition and are in the text.

31. Wings, 'Rebecca Redux', p. 16.

32. For reference to this tradition see Faderman, *Surpassing the Love of Men*, pp. 45, 93, 116–7.

33. Wings, 'Rebecca Redux', p. 31.

34. Wings, *Divine Victim*, p. 146.

35. Hutcheon, *A Poetics of Postmodernism*, p. 108.

36. For reference to the theory of *déréliction* see Chapter 3, note 32.

37. See Castle's discussion of lesbian narrative in *The Apparitional Lesbian*, pp. 67–86.

38. Wings, 'Rebecca Redux', p. 13.

Bibliography

NOVELS AND STORIES

Note: Dates of first publication appear in square brackets after the title.

Allard, Jeannine, *Légende* (Boston: Alyson Publications, 1984).

Atwood, Margaret, *Lady Oracle* (Toronto: McClelland and Stewart, 1976).

Austen, Jane, *Northanger Abbey* [1816] (Harmondsworth: Penguin, 1972).

Baldick, Chris, *The Oxford Book of Gothic Tales* (Oxford: Oxford University Press, 1993).

Barnes, Djuna, *Nightwood* (London: Faber and Faber, 1936).

Baudelaire, Charles, *Les Fleurs du Mal* [1857], trans. by Richard Howard (Brighton: Harvester, 1992).

Brontë, Charlotte, *Jane Eyre* [1847] (Harmondsworth: Penguin, 1966).

——, *Villette* [1853] (Harmondsworth: Penguin, 1979).

Brontë, Emily, *Wuthering Heights* [1847] (Harmondsworth: Penguin, 1968).

Brown, Rebecca, *The Haunted House* (London: Picador, 1987).

Byron, George Gordon, Lord, 'Fragment of a Novel', in Alan Ryan (ed.), *The Penguin Book of Ghost Stories* (Harmondsworth: Penguin, 1988).

Califia, Pat, 'The Vampire', in *Macho Sluts* (Los Angeles: Alyson Publications, 1988).

Carter, Angela, *The Bloody Chamber and Other Stories* (London: Gollancz, 1972).

Collins, Wilkie, *The Woman in White* (Harmondsworth: Penguin, 1985).

Dane, Clemence (Winifred Ashton), *The Regiment of Women* (London: Virago, 1995).

de la Mare, Walter, *The Riddle and Other Stories* (London: Selwyn and Blount, 1923).

Donoghue, Emma, *Hood* (Harmondsworth: Hamish Hamilton, 1995).

——, *Kissing the Witch: Old Tales in a New Skin* (New York: Joanna Cotler Books, 1997).

Doyle, Sir Arthur Conan, *The Hound of the Baskervilles* [1902] (Harmondsworth: Penguin, 1981).

Forrest, Katherine V., *Amateur City* (Tallahassee: Naiad, 1984; London: Pandora, 1987).

——, *Murder at the Nightwood* Bar (Tallahassee: Naiad, 1987; London: Pandora, 1987).

——, 'O Captain, My Captain', in Pam Keesey (ed.), *Daughters of Darkness: Lesbian Vampire Stories* (Pittsburgh: Cleis Press, 1993).

Frayling, Christopher, *Vampyres: Lord Byron to Count Dracula* (London: Faber and Faber, 1991).

Galford, Ellen, *The Fires of Bride* (London: Women's Press, 1986).

Garber, Eric, *Embracing the Dark* (Boston, Alyson, 1991).

Gilman, Charlotte Perkins, *The Yellow Wallpaper* [1892] (London: Virago, 1981).

Gomez, Jewelle, *The Gilda Stories* (London: Sheba Feminist Publishers, 1991).

——, 'White Flowers', in Sheba Feminist Publishers (ed.), *Serious Pleasure* (London: Sheba, 1989).

Gray, Alasdair, *Something Leather* (London: Jonathan Cape, 1990).

Hall, Radclyffe, *The Well of Loneliness* [1928] (London: Virago, 1982).

Hanrahan, Barbara, *The Albatross Muff* (London: Women's Press, 1978).

Herbert, James, *The Survivor* (London: New English Library, 1976).

Hill, Susan Elizabeth, *The Woman in Black* (London: Mandarin, 1992).

Hoffmann, Ernest Theodor Amadeus, 'The Sandman', in *Tales of Hoffmann* [1816], selected and trans. by R.J. Hollingdale (Harmondsworth: Penguin, 1982).

Hogg, James, *The Private Memoirs and Confessions of a Justified Sinner* [1824] (Oxford: Oxford University Press, 1981).

Jackson, Shirley, *The Haunting of Hill House* [1960] (London: Robinson, 1987).

James, Henry, *The Turn of the Screw and Other Stories* [1898] (Harmondsworth: Penguin, 1969).

James, M.R., *Casting the Runes and Other Ghost Stories* [1931] (Oxford: World's Classics, 1987).

Keesey, Pam (ed.), *Daughters of Darkness: Lesbian Vampire Stories* (Pittsburgh: Cleis, 1993).

Keesey, Pam (ed.), *Dark Angels: Lesbian Vampire Stories* (Pittsburgh: Cleis, 1995).

King, Stephen, *Bag of Bones* (London: Hodder and Stoughton, 1998).

——, *Pet Sematary* (London: Hodder and Stoughton, 1983).

——, *The Shining* (New York: Doubleday, 1977).

La Tourette, Aileen and Maitland, Sarah, 'The Wedding Stories', in *Weddings and Funerals* (London: Brilliance Books, 1984).

Lawrence, D.H., *The Rainbow* (Harmondsworth: Penguin, 1949).

Le Fanu, J. Sheridan, 'Carmilla' [1872], in Pam Keesey (ed.), *Daughters of Darkness: Lesbian Vampire Stories* (Pittsburgh: Cleis Press, 1993).

Lessing, Doris, *The Summer Before the Dark* (London: Cape, 1973).

Livia, Anna, *Minimax* (Portland: Eighth Mountain Press, 1991).

Lovecraft, H.P., *The Lurker at the Threshold* [1945] (London: Gollancz, 1968).

Mars-Jones, Adam and White, Edmund, *The Darker Proof: Stories from a Crisis* (London: Faber, 1987).

Martinac, Paula, *Out of Time* (Seattle: Seal Press, 1990).

Maturin, Charles Robert, *Melmoth the Wanderer* [1820] (Oxford: World's Classics, 1989).

McConnell, Vicki P., *Mrs Porter's Letter* (Tallahassee: Naiad, 1982).

——, *The Burnton Widows* (Tallahassee: Naiad, 1984).

Millett, Kate, *Sita* (New York: Farrar, Strauss and Giroux, 1977).

O'Rourke, Rebecca, *Jumping the Cracks* (London: Virago, 1987).

Poe, Edgar Allan, 'The Fall of the House of Usher' [1839], in *Tales of Mystery and Imagination* (London: Minerva Press, 1971).

Polidori, John, ' The Vampyre', in Alan Ryan (ed.), *The Penguin Book of Vampire Stories* (Harmondsworth: Penguin, 1988).

Radcliffe, Anne, *The Mysteries of Udolpho* [1794] (Oxford: Oxford University Press, 1966).

Reynolds, Margaret (ed.), *The Penguin Book of Lesbian Short Stories* (Harmondsworth: Penguin, 1993).

Rice, Anne, *Interview with the Vampire* (London: Futura, 1977).

——, *The Vampire Lestat* (London: Futura, 1986).

Riley, Elizabeth, *All That False Instruction* (London: Angus and Robertson, 1975).

Roberts, Michèle, *The Visitation* (London: Women's Press, 1983).

Russ, Joanna, *The Female Man* (New York: Bantam, 1975).

Rymer, James Malcolm, 'Varney the Vampire, or the Feast of Blood', in Alan Ryan (ed.), *The Penguin Book of Vampire Stories* (Harmondsworth: Penguin, 1988).

Saul, John, *Nathaniel* (London: Corgi, 1984).

Schulman, Sarah, *After Delores* (New York: E.P. Dutton, 1988; London: Sheba Feminist Publishers, 1988).

——, *Rat Bohemia* (New York: E.P. Dutton, 1996; London: Plume, 1996).

Scott, Jody, *I, Vampire* (New York: Ace Science Fiction Books, 1984; London: Women's Press, 1986).

Shelley, Mary, *Frankenstein* [1818] (Oxford: Oxford University Press, 1994).

Stevenson, Robert Louis, *The Strange Case of Dr. Jekyll and Mr. Hyde and Other Stories* [1886] (Harmondsworth: Penguin, 1979).

Stoker, Bram, *Dracula* [1897] (Oxford: Oxford University Press, 1988).

Swinburne, Charles Algernon, *Selected Poems*, ed. Humphrey Hare (London: William Heinemann, 1950).

Tennant, Emma, *The Bad Sister* (London: Gollancz, 1978; Picador, 1979).

——, *Two Women of London: The Strange Case of Ms Jekyll and Mrs Hyde* (London: Faber, 1988).

Warner, Sylvia Townsend, *Lolly Willowes* [1926] (London: Women's Press, 1978).

——, *Summer Will Show* [1936] (London: Virago, 1988).

Wilson, Barbara, *Murder in the Collective* (Seattle: Seal Press, 1984; London: Women's Press, 1984).

Wings, Mary, *Divine Victim* (London: Women's Press, 1992).

Wings, Mary, *She Came Too Late* (London: Women's Press, 1986).

Winterson, Jeanette, *Sexing the Cherry* (London: Bloomsbury, 1989; Vintage, 1990).

——, *The Passion* (London: Bloomsbury, 1987; Harmondsworth: Penguin, 1988).

White, T.H., *The Sword in the Stone* (London: Collins, 1964).

Wittig, Monique, *The Lesbian Body*, trans. by David LeVay (New York: Avon, 1975).

Wittig, Monique and Zeig, Sande, *Lesbian Peoples: Materials for a Dictionary* (London: Virago, 1980).

Zanger, Molleen, *Gardenias Where There Are None* (Tallahassee: Naiad, 1994).

THEORETICAL AND CRITICAL WORKS

Bakhtin, Mikhail, *Rabelais and His World*, trans. by Hélène Iswolsky (Bloomington: Indiana University Press, 1984).

Bell, David and Valentine, Gill (eds), *Mapping Desire: Geographies of Sexualities* (London: Routledge, 1995).

Benjamin, Jessica, 'Master and Slave: The Fantasy of Erotic Domination', in Anne Snitow, Christine Stansell and Sharon Thompson (eds), *Desire: The Politics of Sexuality* (London: Virago, 1984), pp. 292–311.

Benjamin, Walter, *Charles Baudelaire: A Lyric Poet in the Era of High Capitalism* (London: New Left Books, 1973).

Brand, Dana, 'From the *Flâneur* to the Detective: Interpreting the City of Poe', in Tony Bennett (ed.), *Popular Fiction: Technology, Ideology, Production Reading* (London: Routledge, 1990), pp. 220–37.

Bridgwood, Christine, 'Family Romances: The Contemporary Popular Family Saga', in Jean Radford (ed.), *The Progress of Romance: The Politics of Popular Fiction* (London: Routledge and Kegan Paul, 1986), pp. 167–93.

Bunch, Charlotte, 'Not for Lesbians Only', in Charlotte Bunch and Gloria Steinem (eds), *Building Feminist Theory: Essays from Quest* (New York: Longman, 1981), pp. 67–73.

Butler, Judith, *Bodies That Matter: On the Discursive Limits of Sex* (London: Routledge, 1993).

——, *Gender Trouble: Feminism and the Subversion of Identity* (London: Routledge, 1990).

Califia, Pat, 'Feminism and Sadomasochism', *Heresies: Sex Issue* (1981), 26–45.

Carr, Helen (ed.), *From My Guy to Sci Fi: Genre and Women's Writing in the Postmodern World* (London: Pandora, 1989).

Case, Sue-Ellen, 'Toward a Butch-Femme Aesthetic', in Lynda Hart (ed.), *Making a Spectacle: Feminist Essays on Contemporary Women's Theatre* (Ann Arbor, MI: University of Michigan Press, 1989), pp. 282–97.

——, 'Tracking the Vampire', *Differences: A Journal of Feminist Cultural Studies* (1991), 3:2, 1–20.

Castle, Terry, *The Apparitional Lesbian: Female Homosexuality and Modern Culture* (New York: Columbia University Press, 1993).

Cixous, Hélène, 'Fiction and Its Phantoms: A Reading of Freud's *Das Unheimliche* (The "Uncanny")', *New Literary History: A Journal of Theory and Interpretation*, 7:3 (Spring 1973), 525–48.

Clark, Danae, 'Commodity Lesbianism', in Henry Abelove, Michèle Aina Barale and David M. Halperin (eds), *The Lesbian and Gay Studies Reader* (London: Routledge, 1993), pp. 186–201.

Clément, Catherine, 'The Guilty One', in Catherine Clément and Hélène Cixous, *The Newly Born Woman*, trans. by Betsy Wing (Manchester: Manchester University Press, 1987), pp. 3–59.

Cranny-Francis, Anne, *Feminist Fiction: Feminist Uses of Generic Fiction* (Cambridge: Polity Press, 1990).

Creed, Barbara, 'Lesbian Bodies: Tribades, Tomboys and Tarts', in Elizabeth Grosz and Elspeth Probyn (eds), *Sexy Bodies: The Strange Carnalities of Feminism* (London: Routledge, 1995), pp. 86–103.

——, *The Monstrous-Feminine: Film, Feminism and Psychoanalysis* (London: Routledge, 1993).

Daly, Mary, *Gyn/Ecology: The Metaethics of Radical Feminism* (London: Women's Press, 1979).

Day, William Patrick, *In the Circles of Fear and Desire: A Study of Gothic Fantasy* (Chicago: University of Chicago Press, 1985).

De Lauretis, Teresa, 'Sexual Indifference and Lesbian Representation', in Henry Abelove, Michèle Aina Barale and David M. Halperin (eds), *The Lesbian and Gay Studies Reader* (London: Routledge, 1993), pp. 141–58.

——, 'Eccentric Subjects: Feminist Theory and Historical Consciousness', *Feminist Studies*, 16:1 (1990), 115–50.

Dikstra, Bram, *Idols of Perversity: Fantasies of Feminine Evil in Fin-de-Siècle Culture* (Oxford: Oxford University Press, 1986).

Doane, Janice, and Hodges, Devon, 'Undoing Feminism: From the Pre-oedipal to Postfeminism in Anne Rice's *Vampire Chronicles*', *American Literary History*, 2:3 (1990), 422–42.

Dollimore, Jonathan, 'Sex and Death', *Textual Practice*, 9:1 (1995), 27–53.

Donoghue, Emma, *Passions Between Women: British Lesbian Culture 1668–1801* (London: Scarlet Press, 1993).

Duncker, Patricia, *Sisters and Strangers: An Introduction to Contemporary Feminist Fiction* (Oxford: Blackwell, 1992).

Dyer, Richard, 'Children of the Night: Vampirism as Homosexuality, Homosexuality as Vampirism', in Susannah Radstone (ed.), *Sweet Dreams: Sexuality, Gender and Popular Fiction* (London: Lawrence and Wishart, 1988), pp. 47–72.

Ellis, Kate Ferguson, *The Contested Castle: Gothic Novels and the Subversion of Domestic Ideology* (Urbana: University of Illinois Press, 1989).

Faderman, Lillian, *Odd Girls and Twilight Lovers: A History of Lesbian Life in Twentieth-Century America* (Harmondsworth: Penguin, 1992).

——, *Surpassing the Love of Men: Romantic Friendship and Love between Women from the Renaissance to the Present* (London: Women's Press, 1985).

Farwell, Marilyn R., *Heterosexual Plots and Lesbian Narratives* (New York: New York University Press, 1990).

Ferguson, Ann, 'Patriarchy, Sexual Identity, and the Sexual Revolution', in Nannerl O'Keohane, Michèle Rosaldo and Barbara C. Gelpi (eds), *Feminist Theory: A Critique of Ideology* (Brighton: Harvester, 1982), pp. 147–76.

Fleenor, Juliann E. (ed.), *The Female Gothic* (Montreal: Eden Press, 1983).

Fletcher, John, 'Poetry, Gender and Primal Fantasy', in Victor Burgin, James Donald and Cora Kaplan (eds), *Formations of Fantasy* (London: Methuen, 1986), pp. 109–41.

Forster, Margaret, *Daphne du Maurier* (London: Chatto and Windus, 1993).

Freud, Sigmund, *The Complete Psychological Works*, ed. and trans. by James Strachey in collaboration with Anna Freud (London: Hogarth Press, 1956–66).

Fuss, Diana, *Inside/Out: Lesbian Theory, Gay Theory* (London: Routledge, 1991).

Gallop, Jane, *Feminism and Psychoanalysis: The Daughter's Seduction* (London: Macmillan, 1982).

Gardiner, Judith Kegan, 'Mind Mother: Psychoanalysis and Feminism', in Gayle Greene and Coppélia Kahn (eds), *Making a Difference: Feminist Literary Criticisms* (London: Methuen, 1994), pp. 113–43.

Gelder, Ken, *Reading the Vampire* (London: Routledge, 1994).

Griffin, Gabriele, *Heavenly Love? Lesbian Images in Twentieth-Century Women's Writing* (Manchester: Manchester University Press, 1993).

Grosz, Elizabeth, *Jacques Lacan: A Feminist Introduction* (London: Routledge, 1990).

Grosz, Elizabeth and Probyn, Elspeth (eds), *Sexy Bodies: The Strange Carnalities of Feminism* (London: Routledge, 1995).

Gubar, Susan, 'Sapphistries', *Signs*, 10:1 (1984), 43–53.

Hanscombe, Gillian H. and Forster, Jackie, *Rocking the Cradle – Lesbian Mothers: A Challenge in Family Living* (London: Peter Owen, 1981).

Hart, Lynda, *Fatal Women: Lesbian Sexuality and the Mark of Aggression* (London: Routledge, 1994).

Healey, Emma, *Lesbian Sex Wars* (London: Virago, 1996).

Holmlund, Christine, 'The Lesbian, the Mother and the Heterosexual Lover: Irigaray's Recodings of Difference', *Feminist Studies*, 17:2 (1991), 283–308.

Howells, Coral Ann, 'The Pleasures of the Woman's Text: Ann Radcliffe's Subtle Transgressions in *The Mysteries of Udolpho* and *The Italian*', in Kenneth W. Graham (ed.), *Gothic Fictions: Prohibition/Transgression* (New York: AMA Press, 1989), pp. 151–62.

Hutcheon, Linda, *A Poetics of Postmodernism: History, Theory, Fiction* (London: Routledge, 1988).

Irigaray, Luce, *The Irigaray Reader*, ed. Margaret Whitford (Oxford: Blackwell, 1991).

——, *This Sex Which Is Not One*, trans. by Catherine Porter with Carolyn Burke (Ithaca, NY: Cornell University Press, 1985).

Jackson, Rosemary, *Fantasy: The Literature of Subversion* (London: Methuen, 1981).

Johnson, Barbara, 'My Monster/My Self', *Diacritics*, 12 (Summer 1992), 2–10.

Jones, Jonathan, 'He Created the Horror Movie, and Then His Life Became One', *Guardian*, Review Section, 5 September 1998, p. 18.

Kahane, Claire, 'The Gothic Mirror', in Shirley Nelson Garner, Madelon Sprengnether and Claire Kahane (eds), *The (M)other Tongue* (Ithaca, NY: Cornell University Press, 1985), pp. 334–51.

Knight, Stephen, ' " A Hard Cheerfulness": An Introduction to Raymond Chandler', in Brian Docherty (ed.), *American Crime Fiction* (Basingstoke: Macmillan, 1988), pp. 71–87.

Kristeva, Julia, *Powers of Horror: An Essay on Abjection*, trans. by Leon S. Roudiez (Hemel Hempstead: Harvester Wheatsheaf, 1991).

——, *Strangers to Ourselves*, trans. by Leon S. Roudiez (Hemel Hempstead: Harvester Wheatsheaf, 1991).

Light, Alison, ' "Returning to Manderley": Romance Fiction, Female Sexuality and Class', *Feminist Review*, 16 (1994), 7–25.

Madoff, Mark S., 'Inside, Outside, and the Gothic Locked-Room Mystery', in Kenneth W. Graham (ed.), *Gothic Fictions: Prohibition/Transgression* (New York: AMS Press, 1989), pp. 49–62.

Modleski, Tania, *Loving with a Vengeance: Mass-Produced Fantasies for Women* (New York: Methuen, 1984).

——, *Feminism without Women: Culture and Criticism in a 'Postfeminist' Age* (London: Routledge, 1991).

Moore, Lisa, 'Teledildonics: Virtual Lesbians in the Fiction of Jeanette Winterson', in Elizabeth Grosz and Elspeth Probyn (eds), *Sexy Bodies: The Strange Carnalities of Feminism* (London: Routledge, 1995), pp. 104–27.

Munt, Sally, *Murder by the Book? Feminism and the Crime Novel* (London: Routledge, 1994).

——, 'The Lesbian *Flâneur*', in David Bell and Gill Valentine (eds), *Mapping Desire* (London: Routledge, 1995), pp. 114–25.

Nestle, Joan, *A Restricted Country* (Ithaca, NY: Firebrand Books, 1987).

Nichols, Nina da Vinci, 'Place and Eros in Radcliffe, Lewis, and Brontë', in Juliann E. Fleenor (ed.), *The Female Gothic* (Montreal: Eden Press, 1983), pp. 187–206.

Palmer, Paulina, *Contemporary Lesbian Writing: Dreams, Desire, Difference* (Buckingham: Open University Press, 1993).

——, 'The Lesbian Thriller: Crimes, Clues and Contradictions', in Gabriele Griffin (ed.), *Outwrite: Lesbianism and Popular Culture* (London: Pluto, 1993), pp. 86–105.

——, '*The Passion*: Storytelling, Fantasy, Desire', in Helena Grice and Tim Woods (eds), *'I'm Telling You Stories': Jeanette Winterson and the Politics of Reading* (London: Routledge, 1998), pp. 103–16.

Pederson-Krag, Geraldine, 'Detective Stories and the Primal Scene', in Gerald W. Most and William W. Stowe (eds), *The Poetics of Murder* (New York: Harcourt Brace, Jovanovich, 1983), pp. 13–20.

Punter, David, *The Literature of Terror: A History of Gothic Fiction from 1765 to the Present Day* (London: Longman, 1980).

Reddy, Maureen, *Sisters in Crime: Feminism and the Crime Novel* (New York: Continuum, 1988).

Rich, Adrienne, 'Compulsory Heterosexuality and Lesbian Existence', in *Blood, Bread and Poetry: Selected Prose 1979–1985* (London: Virago, 1980), pp. 23–75.

Ringe, Donald A., *American Gothic: Imagination and Reason in Nineteenth-Century Fiction* (Lexington: University Press of Kentucky, 1982).

Russo, Mary, *The Female Grotesque: Risk, Excess and Modernity* (London: Routledge, 1994).

Ryan, Joanna, 'Psychoanalysis and Women Loving Women', in Sue Cartledge and Joanna Ryan (eds), *Sex and Love: New Thoughts on Old Contradictions* (London: Women's Press, 1983), pp. 196–209.

SAMOIS, *Coming to Power: Writing and Graphics on Lesbian S&M* (Boston: Alyson Publications, 1982).

Sedgwick, Eve Kosofsky, *The Coherence of Gothic Conventions* (London: Methuen, 1980).

——, *Epistemology of the Closet* (Hemel Hempstead: Harvester Wheatsheaf, 1991).

——, 'Queer and Now', in *Tendencies* (London: Routledge, 1994), pp. 1–20.

Stanley, Julia Penelope, 'Uninhabited Angels: Metaphors for Love', *Margins*, 23 (1975), 6–16.

Terry, Jennifer, 'Theorizing Deviant Historiography', *Differences: A Journal of Feminist Cultural Studies*, 3:2 (1991), 55–73.

Veeder, William, 'Children of the Night: Stevenson and Patriarchy', in William Veeder (ed.), *Dr. Jekyll and Mr. Hyde after One Hundred Years* (Chicago: University of Chicago Press, 1988), pp. 107–60.

Vicinus, Martha, 'They Wonder to Which Sex I Belong: The Historical Roots of the Modern Lesbian Identity', in Dennis Altman, Carole Vance, Martha Vicinus and Jeffrey Weeks (eds), *Homosexuality, Which Homosexuality?* (London: GMP, 1989), pp. 171–98.

Vincent, Sybil Korff, 'The Mirror and the Cameo: Margaret Atwood's Comic/ Gothic Novel *Lady Oracle*', in Juliann E. Fleenor (ed.), *The Female Gothic* (Montreal: Eden Press, 1983), pp. 153–63.

Waugh, Patricia, *Feminine Fictions: Revisiting the Postmodern* (London: Routledge, 1989).

Weiss, Andrea, *Vampires and Violets: Lesbians in the Cinema* (London: Jonathan Cape, 1992).

White, Patricia, 'Female Spectator, Lesbian Specter: *The Haunting*', in Diana Fuss (ed.), *Inside/Out: Lesbian Theories, Gay Theories* (London: Routledge, 1991), pp. 142–72.

Whitford, Margaret, *Luce Irigaray: Philosophy in the Feminine* (London: Routledge, 1991).

Williams, Linda Ruth, *Critical Desire: Psychoanalysis and the Literary Subject* (London: Edward Arnold, 1995).

Wilson, Scott, 'Passion at the End of History', in Helena Grice and Tim Woods (eds), *'I'm Telling You Stories': Jeanette Winterson and the Politics of Reading* (Amsterdam / Atlanta: Rodopi, 1998), pp. 61–74.

Wings, Mary, 'Rebecca Redux: Tears on a Lesbian Pillow', in Liz Gibbs (ed.), *Daring to Dissent: Lesbian Culture from Margin to Mainstream* (London: Cassell, 1994), pp. 10–32.

Wittig, Monique, *The Straight Mind and Other Essays* (Hemel Hempstead: Harvester Wheatsheaf, 1992).

Zimmerman, Bonnie, 'Daughters of Darkness: The Lesbian Vampire on Film', in Barry Keith Grant (ed.), *Planks of Reason: Essays on the Horror Film* (Metuchen, NY: Scarecrow Press, 1984), pp. 153–63.

——, 'Lesbians Like This and That: Some Notes on Lesbian Literary Criticism for the Nineties', in Sally Munt (ed.), *New Lesbian Criticism: Literary and Cultural Readings* (Hemel Hempstead: Harvester, 1992), pp. 1–15.

——, *The Safe Sea of Women: Lesbian Fiction 1969–1989* (London: Onlywomen Press, 1992).

Index